Art Dealer's

Field Guide

How To Profit In Art Buying And Selling Valuable Paintings

Ron Davis

Capital Letters Publishing • Jacksonville, Florida

Art Dealer's
Field Guide
How to Profit in Art
Buying and Selling Valuable Paintings

Ron Davis

Corrections requested: We'd like to know about any errors you find in reading this book, both typographical and in content. If you use other Web sites or different buying and selling practices, let us know so that we can include them in future editions.

Special discounts on bulk quantities of this book are available to corporations, professional associations, and other organizations. For details, contact the publisher at the below address.

Published by:
Capital Letters Press
4276 Verona Avenue
Jacksonville, FL 32210
Orders/E-mail: Rondavis77@aol.com

Unattributed quotations are by Ron Davis

Second Printing 2009
Includes Index
ISBN, Print ed. 0-9755031-0-3
Library of Congress Control Number: 200409971
Cover Credit: Royal Picture Gallery Mauritshuis The Hague

Printed in the U.S.A.

Contents

Preface—Note to the Reader

The purpose of this book is to open your eyes, mind, and spirit to the world of art. While increasing your knowledge of art, ultimately the goal of this book is to prepare you to buy and sell paintings for a profit.

This is an exciting time to work in the business of art. Experiencing triumphs and challenges, you will learn how to discover, negotiate, purchase, promote, and sell valuable artworks. As an art dealer, you'll play an important role in bringing distinguished paintings to market. Sharing profit and knowledge, you'll work with gallery directors, museum curators, art historians, researchers, auction houses, collectors, investors, and other art dealers.

Initially, the subtitle of this book was: *Make a Deal. Don't be Shy.* However, wise friends prevailed, and the subtitle was changed to *How to Profit in Art: Buying and Selling Valuable Paintings.* Nevertheless, the underlying principle of "make a deal, don't be shy" prevails, and this book instructs and encourages you to do just that. You'll find joy, success, and reward when you *play to win*, not just so that you don't lose. Don't be so overly cautious that you fail to take a risk; just make sure it's a "calculated risk," not a reckless one. If you've found a painting that you like, in good to excellent condition, in a School of art that is appreciating, fairly priced, you've done your research and due diligence, and it's affordable, *buy it*! Enjoy your prize for its beauty and financially for its profit appreciation for years to come.

A single book cannot include everything you should know about buying and selling art. Ask questions, experiment, and take calculated risks; never a reckless one. Find an art dealer who can assist you. Learn about the trade at every opportunity you can. Let this book be your trusted mentor.

Ron Davis, Jacksonville, Florida

Acknowledgments

I have not attempted to cite in the text all the authorities and sources consulted in the preparation of this field guide. I have tried to cite authors and publications wherever I have made direct quotes. Any omission in this regard is an oversight, and I will gladly include such mentioning in future editions.

I owe a special gratitude to Preston Haskell and Dr. Arnie Landsman for reading portions of the manuscript, and for making valuable suggestions. Thanks also are due to Frank Green and Ted Weeks for providing excellent editorial assistance, Les Johnson for unraveling computer glitches in which I often found myself entangled, and Steve Lavell for patiently working with me on the cover design.

Finally, I would like to thank the many art dealers, gallery directors, antique store owners, auction house specialists, and art experts with whom I have worked over the last twenty-five years. It has been a pleasure doing business with you. I thank you for buying my paintings and selling me yours.

And lastly, I thank my family and friends, always. May God bless you all with health, prosperity, and continued success.

This book is dedicated to Caroline,
whose love, joy, and laughter
make all things possible.

Warning—Disclaimer

This book is designed to provide information on art, including buying and selling art at auctions, galleries, and from private sources. It is sold with the understanding that the publisher and author are not engaged in rendering legal, accounting, or other professional services. If legal or other expert assistance is required, the services of a competent professional should be sought.

It is not the purpose of this field guide to cover all the information that is otherwise available to art collectors, investors, and dealers, but instead to complement, amplify, and supplement other texts. You are urged to read all available material, learn as much as you can about buying and selling art, and tailor the information in this book to your individual needs.

Buying and selling art is not a get-rich quick scheme. Anyone who decides to buy and sell art must expect to invest a lot of time and effort in it; not to mention considerable money, when you're ready to make that leap and commitment. For many people, buying and selling art is more lucrative than other investments, and many have built a solid, growing, and rewarding business in art.

Every effort has been made to make this field guide as complete and accurate as possible. However, there *may be mistakes*, both typographical and in content. Therefore, this text should be used only as a general guide and not as the ultimate source for buying and selling art.

The purpose of this field guide is to educate and entertain. The author and Capital Letters Publishing shall have neither liability nor responsibility to any person or entity with respect to any loss or damage caused, or alleged to have been caused, directly or indirectly, by information contained in this book.

If you do not wish to be bound by the above, you may return this book to the publisher for a refund.

1

Buying and Selling Art: An Overview

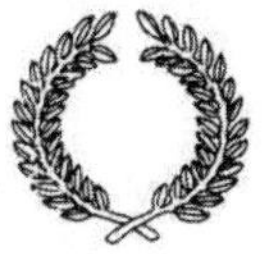

Among the most exquisite achievements of mankind, art, especially old paintings, can enrich your life, beautify the home or office, and gain impressive value while just hanging on the wall.

This book examines art, especially valuable paintings. Not a coffee-table art book, but a book with information that will be priceless for those who apply the principles to be learned here.

It will take years off your journey in becoming a successful art collector, investor, or dealer. Shortening the learning curve and turning your art apprenticeship into a profitable enterprise, this book will save you time and money. It will help you avoid costly mistakes while revealing how to create opportunities in art where none existed previously for you.

Written for the new collector and investor, this book will be an invaluable reference guide for even the experienced dealer. You will find contact telephone numbers, Web sites, and trade information. Learn here the mind-set and game plan of the art collector, investor, and dealer, because each has a different motivation, buying and selling strategy, and outcome objective.

We will focus on the art dealer of old paintings. He's the professional who earns his living buying and selling art. We'll examine his techniques, strategies, and business practices. Because the dealer buys, sells, and negotiates art transactions every day, he has more art know-how—more insider techniques up his sleeve, as it were—than either the collector or the investor. The collector and the investor need to learn what the dealer knows, acquiring the skills of the art dealer. This book aims to equip you with the parallel skills and abilities as those of the art dealer, so that you can buy and sell art for a profit.

"Antique paintings" as termed in this book refers to all "valuable old art." Most examples will come from periods between 1850 and 1910, but can extend as far back as the 16th century.

The best, however, of Modern and Post-Modern paintings from the early 20th century through 1960 sustains active market appeal and great value. Traditionally Modern Art is regarded as beginning with Cubism initiated with Pablo Picasso's landmark oil painting of 1907, "*Les Demoiselles d'Avignon.*"

THE ART DEALER

A "dealer" bargains and negotiates the buying and selling of art. But there are two kinds of art dealers: one who exhibits and sells paintings in a gallery, the retail art dealer; the other, the private art dealer who buys and sells paintings behind closed doors, does what you can do after learning and practicing what this book instructs.

You can learn the trade of the gallery dealer by working in a New York City art gallery, perhaps even on famed 57th Street by apprenticing there. Rarely, if ever will you have a chance to apprentice with a private art dealer. The private dealer prefers to keep secret his successful business techniques, including how to find and buy valuable paintings, and where to sell them. This book will help you to develop your skills as a private art dealer, where privacy and non-disclosure are a premium and where art deals are rarely discussed in public. The emphasis on the private art dealer in this book is not to discredit the gallery art dealer, but to emphasize the difference between the gallery dealer and the private dealer.

GALLERY DEALER

A gallery dealer specializes either in antique paintings (before 1910), Modern, or Contemporary art. If the gallery represents 19th century art, it might specialize in French Impressionism, Belle Epoch, or Barbizon paintings, or in paintings by Academic artists. Other galleries might specialize in British paintings by Pre-Raphaelite or Victorian artists, American Impressionism, or Hudson River School artists.

As a private dealer you need to develop working relationships with art galleries not only in your local area, but also across the country, even internationally (via telephone and e-mail, of course). Since you will be selling and consigning artworks to galleries, you must cultivate mutually beneficial relationships with the retail trade. Gallery business will contribute significantly to your gross income as a private art dealer.

MODERN AND CONTEMPORAY ART DEALERS

Dealing in modern and contemporary art is altogether different from working with older paintings. The Modern art dealer has an eye for innovation and break-through art, which can signal a new wave or a transition in art.

The Modern art dealer is always looking for an "undiscovered artist," like the next Picasso, Monet, or Van Gogh. Conversely, the private art dealer of old paintings is always looking for a well-discovered artist, like a Picasso, Monet, or Van Gogh, so that he can buy or broker the sale of a painting by a famous artist. The Modern art dealer tries to find an unknown artist of genius, while the private art dealer tries to find a *known* artist of genius, someone with proven commercial success. The Contemporary art dealer has to rely on art critics and favorable write-ups in newspapers and magazines to help establish the value of new art, while the art dealer of antique paintings relies on auction records and price guides to determine the value of old art. The Modern art dealer considers what might be, while the art dealer of antique paintings considers what already is, and has proven to be distinguished and lastingly popular.

The legendary art dealers of the nineteen-forties, fifties, and sixties, in New York City, such as Betty Parsons, Martha Jackson, Sydney Janis, Andre Emmerich, Joan Washburn, and Leo Castelli were trail blazers all. They helped bring to the world great works of art by the likes of Jackson Pollock, Hans Hoffman, Willem de Kooning, Franz Kline, Mark Rothko, Frank Stella, Andy Warhol, Robert Rauschenberg, Jasper Johns, Jacob Lawrence, and Romare Bearden, to name a few. The world owes these pioneers a great debt.

But Moderns and Abstract Expressionists were few, their production limited compared to hundreds of thousands of European artists and millions of their paintings created between the 15th and 19th centuries. Nevertheless, 20th century art can be every bit as valuable as antique paintings. Just before this book went to print, Picasso's "*Garcon a le Pipe*" ("Boy with a Pipe") sold at Sotheby's New York for $104,168,000, a record price for any painting. Not a bad investment for Mr. and Mrs. Whitney, who reportedly paid $30,000 for the masterpiece in 1950.

PRIVATE ART DEAERS

Private art dealers, on the other hand, are generalists, and they adopt an auction-house mentality as their credo:

> If it's worthy art by a recognized artist with established auction records, regardless of the School or period, the work has a market. If there's money to be made, the painting ought to be bought and sold.

Gallery dealers, however, are not enamored with private art dealers, often considering them the bane of their existence. Why is this? It's because private dealers compete with gallery dealers for the same paintings and the same customers. Wealthy patrons who buy expensive paintings have traditionally supported galleries. When a patron tires of his painting, usually he can return it to the gallery for resale, then buy another, more expensive painting. This resale business—the renewing of a painting's availability—produces a stream of revenue for gallery dealers who understandably don't like giving up market share to private dealers.

So when a private dealer snags a painting out of an important art collection and arranges a private sale for the painting, the gallery is cut out of the picture. Art galleries also complain when a dealer buys and sells a painting privately because the artwork is never shown publicly; equally important, the documentation trail—the provenance (a painting's history of owners), is sometimes broken. Galleries also have high overhead costs in setting up exhibitions, supporting and promoting new artists, and paying exorbitant prices for retail space in cities like London, Paris, and New York.

While some gallery dealers resent private art dealers, most have had to work with them because they need the artworks brought to market. So even though you may work off the kitchen table at home with a PC, **you still have plenty of opportunities to compete with major galleries for the same wealthy customers and for the same artworks**. Reading this book, you will learn how to compete.

In recent times, gallery dealers and private dealers have tried to adopt each other's signature traits:

galleries are becoming flexible, agile, and responsive while private dealers are establishing Web sites, hosting shows and exhibitions.

EXCEEDING THE PARETO RULE

The Pareto Rule states that 80 percent of your profits come from 20 percent of your products. The goal of this book is to ensure that 100 percent of your profits come from 100 percent of your art transactions. No losers should exist among the paintings you buy after applying diligently lessons gained here. You can make money on every art transaction, from every painting purchased. Buying and selling art does not have to be risky, like buying and selling stocks. With stocks, no matter what the broker tells you, and no matter how much you research you do, occasionally you wind up with a loser, having to sell at a loss. With art, your portfolio can and should be filled only with winners. In this book, discover where to find paintings to buy—the winners of course—and how to buy them. Ultimately, learn where and when to sell your art investments and for how much.

But before writing a check to take home an expensive painting, first develop an "eye" for art, what we call critical visual instincts. Equally important, is the need to acquire a substantial art knowledgebase. In short, train yourself. This book serves to be your hands-on guide and mentor. Keep a copy of it in your car or shoulder bag. Refer to it before buying or selling a valuable painting, before bidding at auction, and before entering into any art transaction. Be prepared: exciting art opportunities are in your future!

FOR LOVE OR MONEY

Do you buy art for love or money? "Never buy art to make money," says the pseudo-aristocrat. He'll pontificate, "Aesthetics are the only reason to buy art." Hogwash! Don't let any blue-blooded would-be nobleman intimidate you, or imply you have to be a Yale Art History graduate or a Rhodes Scholar to work in the field of art. Sure, it helps to have an M.A. in Art History and the love of art; you'll certainly be a better art dealer or investor. But many valid reasons exist for buying and owning a work of art. Profit is chief among them.

A certain successful art dealer doesn't have a particularly "good eye" for art nor even have a traditional love for art. But having practical knowledge about art, he successfully buys and sells old paintings through applying the techniques and strategies you will learn in this book. By not having a "natural" eye for art, this dealer sometimes misses a winner. But for those masterpieces missed, he equalizes by "kicking up" some of the best art deals in the business. Relentless in the pursuit of art, this dealer knows what to do when he finds a deserving painting. Perhaps limitation hurts him a little, but it doesn't stop him. Nor should any limitation you might encounter stop you. If you really want to work in the field of art, be aware of any possible limitation, compensate for it while building your own success.

25/25/50 RULE

The 25/25/50 Rule seems to apply in every situation whether you're an engineer, teacher, or an art dealer. This rule says that 25% of success will come from your *knowledge*, 25% from your *skills*, and 50% of success will come from your *relationships.* Remember well this rule, because it will apply to your success in the art world—and in life as well.

25% OF YOUR SUCCESS WILL COME FROM YOUR KNOWLEDGE

Chapter 2, "Valuing Art," offers you a knowledgebase on how to value art. It explains why some paintings are more valuable than others, which ones to look for, and which ones to walk away from. Chapter 3, "Becoming a Connoisseur," lays out the path of study to follow in order to acquire art knowledge sufficient to identify a quality example in a School of art, say, a Barbizon, Pre-Raphaelite, or Hudson River School painting from across a room. Drawing near to that painting, learn to recognize if the work is an original by a master or a mere copy by a proficient admirer. You will need to acquire an eye through experience so keen that intuitively you will bypass a painting upon realizing that the signature is not original but "floating" (added on not by the artist [it "bounces" under black light]), and therefore can't be right. After knowing the technique or brush strokes are not from the artist's hand, you will reject a particular painting. Examine forensic data to determine if the age of a canvas belies the date the artist painted. Perhaps you will notice that the varnish is deliberately hiding something. Therefore examine the painting under ultra violet or "black light" to confirm and identify your suspicion. Deeper art knowledge will give you an advantage over the competition, and will help you see opportunities in art that others will overlook. (See Chapter 5, "Technical Examination.")

If you grew up in a family where art did not adorn the walls of the home, or art was not admired, discussed, or passed down from generation to generation, then you, like most people need to acquire an appreciation for art through extensive exposure and study. Choose a total immersion in art, by working with a mentor who will teach you sound knowledge and techniques of the art business. With diligence, this book will become your treasured guide and mentor.

25% OF YOUR SUCCESS WILL COME FROM YOUR SKILLS

Chapter 1 discusses the "why" about art. Chapters 2 through 10 answer the questions "how," "what," and "where" to find outstanding art, significantly contributing to your skill-development in buying and selling paintings. Whole chapters are dedicated to valuing, researching, appraising, buying, and selling quality art. You will learn when to ask a gallery to place a 24-hour hold on a painting, how to raise money to buy a work, when to bring in a partner, and how to structure an art sale or purchase. This book will instruct how to write a consignment agreement, a bill of sale, and how to transfer a painting's title free of encumbrances, of course, after you've been paid in full. It will specify the kind of galleries to consign paintings to, auction rooms to buy from, and which to sell through. Your skill level will increase through experience; as your confidence grows, art opportunities will open up magically. Starting to attract business, you will have even higher-value paintings offered to you for sale. Finding investment art will no longer be a challenge. Making enough time and raising the necessary money to buy what you like will be more demanding. Even these problems, however, have solutions, as you will learn.

50% OF YOUR SUCCESS WILL COME FROM YOUR RELATIONSHIPS

Clearly, success in art as in life will come from the relationships you develop. Fully 50% of your success as an art dealer relates to this single fact. Think of the professional relationships needed to develop as you begin to work with art galleries, museums, auction rooms, conservators, collectors, investors, and other art dealers. Some of these people will become friends while most will be customers and colleagues with whom you will do substantial business over time. How you look, talk, and conduct yourself, will bear upon your effectiveness as an art dealer, and ultimately upon personal and professional success. Shoddiness and dishonesty in the art world cannot be tolerated. Colleagues and customers must know you to be trustworthy, of admirable character and integrity; they must believe that your word is beyond reproach. You must be perceived as knowledgeable, professional, and helpful at all times. To the degree that we all self-promote, you must project a public awareness as being a serious buyer of fine art, willing to pay substantial money for quality paintings.

SELF-ASSESSMENT

Assess your knowledge and skill level in the field of art and basic art history, particularly in your specialty areas. Try to gain understanding in the areas where you are weak. Study, ask questions, and commit to a learning track that will raise your level of competency. To negotiate a winning art transaction, you must gain knowledge and skill in buying and selling art. Research diligently, then make a calculated decision based on facts and evidence. A "calculated risk" in the art business is always superior to an emotional one.

THE THREE CLASSIFICATIONS OF ART

Paintings available for purchase will fall into three categories: Decorative Art (under $2,500), Collectible Art (up to $5,000) and Investment Art (examples valued over $5,000). These are relative classifications. Christie's and Sotheby's might classify "investment art" as the minimum value at which a painting is allowed to be included in the main salon for auction, which today is $20,000 to $25,000. Regardless at which level you begin, the goal eventually is to buy investment-grade art, as described below. (Christie's and Sotheby's also have secondary salons for lower-end artworks: Christie's East, and Sotheby's Arcade.)

DECORATIVE ART

Decorative art is known as "furnishing pictures," and typically is used for decorating purposes according to a person's taste. This class of art usually is thematic, selected in various categories such as a "nautical," "country," or a "sporting" look. The desired effect can be achieved by hanging a decorative painting in a den or living room.

Generally speaking, little intrinsic value exists in decorative art. Many examples of decorative art are mass-produced, such as assembly-line paintings from Taiwan, which can cost less than $100. But *distinctive* decorative art can be expensive, especially if it's antique. If you desire a hunting scene, for example, a nineteenth century British original foxhunt painting, even unsigned, can cost you several thousand dollars or more. Generally though, decorative art by unsigned or unlisted artists is of little value, unsuitable as investments.

COLLECTIBLE ART

Collectible art suggests that someone else also collects the same artworks. Therefore, a market already exists for your painting, albeit small. Collectible art can either be signed or unsigned. If a listed artist painted the artwork, the auction value will be modest, but usually more than unsigned works. For purposes of this book, collectible art is valued between $1,000 and $5,000. The artist might have local recognition, perhaps even a following within a state or region. But no national or international demand for the artist's work exists because the quality of work generally is mediocre or specifically regional in character.

Demand in relation to scarcity drives or governs prices. The greater the quality of artistic expression and workmanship, the greater the demand will be for the artist's work which creates scarcity and drives up prices. (See Chapter 2, "Valuing Art.") Collectible art would not be accepted in major auction rooms, such as Christie's or Sotheby's, but might be accepted in smaller auction houses. Often collectible art is consigned to local antique stores or country auction rooms. The reverse scenario, however, can be lucrative. Keep a vigilant watch for a valuable work of art that finds its way into a local antique store or country auction.

Collectible art does not have to be by a listed artist or even a signed piece. Unsigned paintings in very good to excellent condition, of distinctive quality in the manner of a famous artist, can fetch over $5,000 at auction, and be considered investment art.

Art dealers frequently began by buying collectible art, hoping it was investment quality, but in fact wasn't. They had to learn discerning true quality; so must you. Start out buying collectible art if you lack experience or financing. But move on to purchasing investment art as soon as you're ready and able. Avoid an apprenticeship where you buy too many decorative or collectible artworks: they're difficult to sell. For example, if you buy 100 paintings at $200 each, you could have $20,000 invested in garage-sale merchandise. Avoid that. Try to limit your "training paintings" to 10 or fewer. Be sure to document the outcome of each painting you buy. Do keep a record!

INVESTMENT ART

High caliber, well-listed artists generally create investment quality paintings. Sought by collectors, investors, and dealers, investment art appeals to potential buyers beyond the state or local region, meeting national and international demand. Investment art always increases in value. Therefore, it can easily be resold for profit. If investment art is ever lost, the finder, essentially holds a bearer instrument—the equivalent of cash. This is why investment art usually is insured. A national radio station reported a Picasso artwork was lost, *accidentally* left on a New York City subway. Can you imagine? The radio station asked the finder of the artwork to call the police. *Hello.* Leaving a painting by Picasso on a New York City train is like leaving a bag containing a million dollars cash on a park bench. Forget it! (See Chapter 8, "Due Diligence," and be aware of the role the FBI and INTERPOL play in lost and stolen art.)

THE THREE BUYERS OF ART

The collector, investor, and dealer form the principal buyers of investment art. Each has a different motivation towards buying and selling strategies, and outcome objectives. Study the mindset and game plan of each. Decide which role *you* want to play in the field of art.

COLLECTOR

The art collector should have the purest motivation. He buys art for its own inherent sake. Purchasing only art he likes, it should fit his acquisition plan, while matching his interest or focus. A collector generally has no exit strategy when he buys an artwork. He has no predetermined plan to sell or trade a painting. Often, a collector might keep a work of art all his life, willing his collection to his children or a museum as a charitable gift.

The collector has a love for art but not a compelling schedule to buy it. Possibly he purchases only one painting a year. No financial performance objectives affect what art a collector buys. Like the investor and dealer, the collector needs to avoid being taken advantage of, trying to buy art that only increases in value. The collector also must be concerned with a painting's authenticity, subject, size, condition, and yes, its price.

Art is a labor of love for the collector. He studies the artists, School, or other areas of appeal, and ultimately a collector can become a recognized expert. A collector might specialize in Hudson River School paintings, more specifically in Mohawk Valley scenes, or even more particularly in Woodstock artists. A collector with such regional interest might have to seek the help of Upstate New York dealers to assist in finding suitable paintings to buy. If a collector has very expensive taste, and he wants to acquire first-tier Hudson River School artworks, say, by Thomas Cole, Frederick Church, or Thomas Moran, he might need the help of a high-end New York City art gallery to help him find suitable paintings to buy, such as Questroyal Fine Art, www.Questroyalfineart.com. He also might need to engage an art consultant (see Chapter 4, "Investing in Art").

INVESTOR

The art investor definitely develops a financial plan to achieve his goal of making a profit on every painting he buys. The word "investment" implies a return on our money, generally a 25% ROI. Therefore, the investor will only buy paintings that will sell for a higher price than he paid. To achieve this goal, he must buy paintings strategically, according to strict buying criteria, following extensive research to eliminate risks associated with buying art.

The investor has a long-term view, which includes selling a painting at some future date, say, five to seven years out. If the investor builds a retirement portfolio in art, beginning in the seventh year he can start retiring one painting annually. This will ensure financial security and comfort in later years. He also can use this investment money to pay for a child's education, or buy a summer home. (See Chapter 4, "Investing in Art.")

DEALER

The art dealer's business is buying and selling paintings, and brokering art transactions. Like any business owner, the dealer is on the telephone every day talking with customers and suppliers: collectors, investors, galleries, auction rooms, and other dealers. The dealer stays in contact with sources of distinguished art, talks with anyone who has a painting worth buying, even if the owner does not want to sell it. He doesn't forget a painting once seen, always remembering a contact once made. He never lets an opportunity go by where he can buy, sell, or broker compelling artwork. The dealer knows which valuable art is scarce so he's willing to travel to wherever desirable art is, whether across town, across the country, or around the world. When an exceptional painting comes to market, the dealer pursues it relentlessly. Knowing he can buy a truly great painting he can name his own price, regardless of the artist's previous auction records.

The art dealer knows that success depends upon his credibility, reputation, and knowledge of art. Giving no appearance of dishonest practice, he maintains high ethical standards in all business transactions. Many dealers obtain certification from art appraisal associations, and some seek membership in the Art Dealers Association of America. By being trustworthy, most art dealers are prepared to walk away from dishonest, illegal, or shady art deals, regardless of how much money can be made.

Successful art dealers often seek ways to give back to the community, by advising a nonprofit foundation, mentoring a young collector, and/or giving free consulting service to a local historical society. Such generosity can only help his business and reputation.

THREE REASONS TO BUY AND SELL ART

1. MONEY

Dealing in art gives you a unique opportunity to make money doing something you love at your own pace, according to your own goals.

- **Increase Your Income:** Once you understand how to buy and sell art, you can enter into art transactions at will, casually on weekends or once a month—wherever and whenever. You might like driving through New England, or going to country auctions; these are great opportunities to find paintings, testing yourself on what you've learned about buying art. Set modest goals as a weekend art dealer, and grow into augmenting your income by $10,000 or $15,000 or more a year.

- **Increase Your Retirement Money:** Supplement your retirement income with $25,000 a year by following the investment strategies in Chapter 4, "Investing in Art."

- **Earn a Living:** As a professional art dealer you can set higher financial goals, say $50,000 a year or more, to support your family or way of life. In this book you'll find all the techniques and strategies needed to earn a living buying and selling valuable paintings.

  In each of the above three examples, tax advantages, travel write-offs, and business incentives for buying and selling art can benefit you in the most beneficial way at the most advantageous times.

2. **ADVENTURE**
   For many art collectors and dealers, the *hunt*, not the find, gives them greatest reward. Buying and selling art can be surprisingly exciting and fulfilling. (See Appendix 1, "Making the Art Deal.")

3. **CULTURE AND AESTHETICS**
   Imagine: you, alone, or with your family, live within bare, plain walls without art, or possibly displaying just a few posters. *Now* imagine: beautifully lighted, outstanding original antique oil paintings and watercolors, exquisitely framed, grace each wall, stimulating your senses and enriching your spirituality.

PUTTING THE ART DEAL TOGETHER

Appendix 1, "Making the Art Deal," lets you see how an art transaction is put together, thereby showing you how to create opportunities in art where none existed. This case example uses sophisticated strategies, which probably is not where you'll begin, but it might open doors to your thinking about future art business that you can put together.

2

Valuing Art

According to INTERPOL, between $4 billion and $6 billion worth of art is stolen every year. To cope with the global problem of art theft, the FBI has set up a special office in Washington, D.C., which maintains a computer database of more than 100,000 files of stolen art.

WHY IS ART SO VALUABLE?

Fine art, like any commodity, is valuable because of its scarcity, thereby appealing strongly to buyers. Some people who deem scarcity as prize-worthy, are willing to pay an exorbitant price for the last anything on earth that someone else wants, needs, or admires. You might have heard the news: they stopped making 19th century art more than one hundred years ago. Imagine what the last made Studerbaker car would be worth today, if found in mint condition. It's like waterfront property: it isn't made any more, which is why it costs 10 times more than rural farmland.

To gain an understanding of the construction of value for any rare commodity, we only have to look back a few hundred years to Adam Smith's treatise in his 1776 book, *The Wealth of Nations*. It's a bit 18th century in style, but if you grasp what Smith is talking about, you'll understand why art is so valuable.

> *The market price of every particular commodity is regulated by the proportion between the quantity which is actually brought to market, and the demand of those who are willing to pay the natural price of the commodity.*
>
> *When the quantity of any commodity which is brought to market falls short of the effectual demand, all those who are willing to pay the whole value cannot be supplied with the quantity which they want. Rather than want it all together, some of them will be willing to give more. A competition will immediately begin among them, and the market price will rise more or less above the natural price, according as either the greatness of the deficiency or the wealth and wanton luxury of the competitors. Among competitors of equal wealth and luxury the same deficiency will generally occasion a more or less eager competition, according as the commodity happens to be of importance to them. Hence the exorbitant price of the necessaries of life during the blockade of a town or in a famine.*
>
> **—Adam Smith,** *The Wealth of Nations* (1776)

Guess what? The effectual demand for art today far exceeds the supply of art being brought to market. So the price for quality art will rise naturally according as either the greatness of the deficiency or the wealth and wanton luxury of the competitors.

DEFICIENCY IN THE SUPPLY OF ART

The deficiency in the supply of outstanding art is great indeed, and will only grow more deficient as time passes. For example, finding today an authentic Renaissance painting around town for sale is extremely rare or highly suspicious. Even paintings from the 17th century of requisite quality and condition are rather scarce. Examples from the 18th century, however, are more common, and are sometimes shown in galleries, while 19th century paintings, of course, are still abundantly available. But distinguished 19th century examples are becoming less available in the marketplace. The *"best"* 19th century art is rare, difficult to gain access to, and available only at a steep price. Let's look at where art seems to disappear to, and why it continues to increase in value.

MUSEUMS

There is more money in the world than great artworks, resulting in a competition between museums and wealthy collectors to acquire the world's great works of art. Museums, however, are not always the successful bidder for a great painting. For example, Canadian billionaire Kenneth Thomson outspent the J. Paul Getty Museum for Peter Paul Rubens's "Massacre of the Innocent." The winning bid was $76.7 million. In the case of Andy Warhol's "Sixteen Jackies," the Smithsonian Institute's Hirshhorn Museum outbid a major collector and bought the silkscreen canvas of Jacquelyn Kennedy Onassis for $1.7 million.

Collectors generally take home one painting at a time. Museums, on the other hand, sometimes acquire whole collections, often causing market prices to readjust, usually upward, following a major acquisition.

Museums and historical societies around the country are poised waiting for a wealthy patron of the arts to die so an important art collection can pass from an estate to a museum. Trustees and curators of museums all over the world continually pursue art collections. It's their job, not unlike an art dealer who pursues an important work of art once he discovers it. Your job is to discover where important art is located, which is available for sale, and pursue such art with the intent to buy or represent its purchase. (See Chapter 9, "Buying Art.")

When an entire art collection is bequeathed to a museum, the market price for privately owned paintings by the same artist, or School of art, generally will increases in value. When a museum receives an art collection, a sizable portion of an artist's work, or School of art, is permanently removed from the marketplace. Once the supply of a commodity diminishes, and scarcity achieved, people are willing to pay exorbitant prices for art that becomes scarcer, rare, or possibly even one of a kind. Such art can be near priceless.

Great patrons sometimes leave, if not their entire art collections, huge sums of money for the acquisition of art. Such a patron was J. Paul Getty. The Getty Museum in California is a formidable buyer of world-class art. Its curators and trustees are continually searching for art to buy from art sources all over the world. As museums buy and acquire whole collections, the future supply of that art to the marketplace greatly diminishes. Consequently, similar objects of art remaining in private hands increase in value proportionate to the deficiency created by public acquisitions.

To further deplete the marketplace of world-class art, wealthy patrons can buy masterpieces, then circumvent the IRS under the Rules of Charitable Giving by promising to bequeath the artwork to a museum after the patron's death. This tax scheme provides a bit of immortality and posthumous recognition for the donor, who pays no taxes while still enjoying the art during his lifetime.

WEALTH AND WANTON LUXURY

Adam Smith's second explanation for the rise in price in any commodity is the *"wealth and wanton luxury of competitors."* This aspect of *wealth and wanton luxury* comes into play more so now than in any other time in history. Today there are an estimated five million *millionaires* in the United States. Many are worth hundreds of millions; some even billions of dollars. Few collect baseball cards and comic books as investments, but most of them collect art.

"New money" currently is buying art just as "old money" used to, when it was new money early in the post-industrial age. Huge art collections were amassed at the end of the nineteenth century and early twentieth century by America's banking and industrial giants. The likes of Morgan, Frick, Mellon, Ford, Lehman, and Rockefeller, all bought 18th century British Art *en masse*, in order to crown themselves with nobility. They filled their East Coast mansions with portraits by Gainsborough, Reynolds, Romney, and with landscapes by Constable, Crome, and Wilson.

The wealth and wanton luxury of today's art buyer is just as competitive as it was a century ago. The only difference is that the paintings today are being shipped to *dotcom* addresses, instead of to East Coast mansions. The wealth and luxury of today's collectors and investors, and those who buy art for social recognition, continue to diminish the supply of art in the marketplace, thereby forcing the price of quality art ever upward.

Once artworks by first-tier artists—the masters of the 16th through the 19th centuries, are off the market—bought up by collectors or housed in museums, then examples by lesser artists move up a notch, assuming a new ranking in a redefined market. Consequently, the artworks of lesser artists begin to rise in value because they're now the only show in town. Next, a competition begins to rise for the best of the second-tier works of art. And so it goes.

Since 19th century art can never again be created, one might think its supply and availability would diminish continually, gone forever one day. Bought up. But that won't happen. There will *always* be willing buyers and willing sellers of art to create a marketplace, establishing fair-market value for a painting. People come upon hard times, need to sell a family heirloom, and a possible masterpiece suddenly appears back on the market. Sometimes a masterpiece appears mysteriously on the curb with the garbage, or sold at a garage sale. The marketplace continues to evolve, while collectors and investors will always look for quality paintings to buy.

WHAT IS WORTHY ART?

Worthy art has to be viewed in terms of *quality*. John Keats best described quality when he wrote "A thing of beauty is a joy forever: Its loveliness increases; and it will never pass into nothingness." And so it is with good art.

QUALITY IN ART HAS ABSOLUTE STANDARDS

Fine art has "quality." Such quality can best be seen in paintings hanging in museums. High quality art has predetermined standards, which have been determined by scholars, curators, historians, connoisseurs, dealers, and the marketplace, and by the demands of collectors and investors. This quality would be easiest for you to see if someone—a curator—walked you through a museum and exclaimed, "There! That's what I'm talking about. That's a masterpiece! That's quality." And if she pointed out the elements of quality in a masterpiece, you would have a benchmark with which to compare other artworks. Eventually, however, you must get to the point where you can *feel art at a gut level*, and know instinctually what is outstanding art. This only happens after you've looked at and studied thousands of paintings. (See Chapter 3, "Becoming a Connoisseur.")

HALLMARKS OF GOOD ART

Exceptional art has a *master's touch*. It's a gift. Few artists possess or develop such extraordinary skill and talent. Hence, the expression, "a stroke of genius," could well refer to the brushwork and technique of a great artist. Such artists, for example, can load a brush with paint, then with a single stroke, or perhaps with a turn of the wrist, paint an element of composition so strong or sensitive as to evoke a stirring emotional response from the viewer.

Embodied in all fine painting is the masterful handling of *anatomy, perspective, composition, color* and *contrast.* Distinctive art draws your eye to the picture's focal point and commands attention, growing on you as it reveals increasing meaning to you. Such strokes of genius are found, for example, in the mystic smile of Leonardo Da Vinci's "Mona Lisa," in the battle cry of Eugene Delacroix's "Liberty Leading the People," or on the frightened faces of the peasants about to be executed in Francisco Goya's "The Third of May."

There are four elements of art that master artists convey consistently and exceedingly well.

ANATOMY

Anatomy in truly professional art must be authentic and convincing, whether expressed realistically, expressionistically, or impressionistically. Moreover, whatever activity depicted, be it peasants working in a field by Jean Francois Millet, a young woman pouring milk from a pitcher by Jan Vermeer, or in "Christ's Descent from the Cross" by Peter Paul Rubens, they all look humanly believable, sometimes even heartbreakingly real. Flesh in exceptional art is honest, whether loose and sagging as Lucian Freud paints, or taut and muscular as Michelangelo painted.

PERSPECTIVE

The skillful handling of perspective adds depth to a flat surface, making angles, planes, and lines architecturally correct. Nothing is more conspicuous than a wrong slope on a roof of a house painted by an unschooled artist. To view architecture and perspective at its best, one must study the architectural settings and dramatic vantage points of Andrea Mantegna (1430 – 1506), and the interior scenes of the northern Renaissance master, Albrecht Durer. (See Saint Jerome [1514] engraving, as an example.)

COMPOSITION

Composition tells a story through strategic arrangement of its parts: none better conveyed than by Winslow Homer in his rescue-at-sea pictures, where one can feel vicariously the impending danger of crashing waves. Superior artists evoke moods, such as hope for the shipwrecked survivors in Theodore Gericault's "The Raft of the Medusa." Objects painted by a master always balance the composition, utilizing space and appropriate proportions deliberately. Great works of art are powerful, often unforgettable. They draw you inexorably into the picture. In the case of "The Raft of the Medusa," Gericault's composition evoked compassion for the downtrodden, launching in 1819 the School of French Romanticism.

COLOR AND CONTRAST

Color is to art what salt is to bread: the flavor in the finished product. Dark colors can evoke moods of fear and sorrow, while light colors raise joy and gladness. Color also complements composition and perspective: objects far away are painted in lighter tones and with less intensity in order to achieve distance. Skies are deeper blue near the zenith, diminishing to lighter blues at the horizon. Color in the hands of a master can anchor a painting to its surroundings, the way a simple dab of light blue paint in the middle of a dark green tree can give the illusion of the sky beyond, and distance. The effective use of shadows can add weight and dimension to objects, making them look real and believable. Jan Vermeer's "The Kitchen Maid" is an example of color use at its best.

QUALITY

Quality determines the value of a painting, elevating some artworks as more valuable than others. Looking at thousands of paintings over time, you will learn to identify exceptional quality in art, whether expressed in the Academic School, Realistic School, or even the Modern School. A quality painting will magnetize your attention, forcing you to stare at it, returning to it again and again until you yearn to own it. No doubt, you have stumbled upon a quality work of art. An important artist probably painted it. Quality artwork stands out. It has been said, "Don't try to discover a great work of art, but let a great work of art discover you."

HOW TO DETERMINE IF ART IS VALUABLE

Now that you understand *why* art is valuable, and how scarcity and market conditions can drive up the price of art, let's try to answer the most important question in art: "how to determine which art is valuable, and which is not." In other words, which art you should buy, and which you should walk away from.

Many factors affect the value of art, but chief among them are these seven: (1) artist's name, (2) quality and workmanship, (3) subject matter, (4) condition, (5) size of painting, (6) authenticity, and (7) provenance. Let's examine how each of these elements affects the price of art.

ARTIST NAME

An artist's name has *everything* to do with a painting's value, and when you begin your research, the artist's name will be the first thing you will check. (See Chapters 6, "Research and Appraisal.") But before we look up an artist's name, let's first examine some commercial factors that determine how an artist gets his name listed in a price index guide, and what he must do to be considered a "well-listed" artist?

> *A painting has no intrinsic worth. It is a luxury commodity for which a market is deliberately created and maintained by financially interested parties.*
>
> —**Robert Wraigth**, *The Art Game Again! (1974)*

Most valuable art club. Serious collectors and investors *are* the "financially interested parties" who create and maintain the art market. This group of elite collectors and investors sets the standards for what is "valuable art," by virtue of the art they covet and collect. Consequently, they also determine which artists get into the most valuable art club.

Every artist who produces quality artwork during a prolific career becomes a target for collectors and connoisseurs. Thus a market is created for these artworks, *ipso facto*. It's like an invitation for a hostile corporate takeover: when an acquiring company (the art buyer) sees undervalued quality (unknown artist) that hasn't yet been discovered in the marketplace (unlisted artist), it tries to buy up and control all the available stock (artworks). Because an artist's work is finite and limited, the financially interested parties will compete for the artist's best works (the scarce few). Therefore the price for that artwork will increase, sometimes dramatically, especially as supply diminishes. Ultimately there well may be a "waiting list" for an artist's work—a queue, so to speak, which happens when collectors ask dealers to notify them when a certain artist's work becomes available. Then you have the makings of a bidding war. Whenever two or more collectors want the next available painting by the same artist, the price for that artist's work suddenly goes up. Every time an artist's work is sold the sale price is recorded if the sale was transacted at a large public auction. In this manner, an artist becomes "listed."

So buy paintings only by listed artists who are sought after by collectors and investors, thereby guaranteeing you a buyer when you decide to sell. For this to happen, both the artist and his artworks must be available for discovery.

Prodigious work. The dictionary describes "prodigious" as *wonderful; amazing; enormous; huge.* The word "prodigious" is derived from the word "prodigy," which means "child of genius." This describes precisely a world-class artist: a genius who paints wonderful and amazing works of art, in abundant quantities during a lifetime.

Winslow Homer was such an artist who produced a prodigious amount of artwork during his lifetime—over 700 watercolors alone. In his day, Homer's artworks were considered currency—as good as gold, so to speak. Another excellent artist, who was in England, such as Henry Mark Anthony (1817-1886), one of the British Pre-Raphaelites, was anything but prolific, and he did not help himself become discovered. In fact, he became a virtual recluse. Consequently, Anthony never achieved commercial success. Yet the eminent art critic of his day, William Michael Rossetti (1829-1919), declared Anthony, "the most outstanding landscape painter in England." Likewise the diaries of Ford Madox Brown are full of praise for Anthony—"Like Constable, only better." So how could, arguably, the best landscape painter in 19th century England wind up a virtual nobody?

The answer is an artist needs to be more than just a genius to be admitted into the "most valuable art" club. He needs to be *prodigious*, and be available for discovery. Within the context of his period, he needs to be part of a movement, or School of art that he either started or followed. While Anthony's peers (The Pre-Raphaelite Brotherhood) were painting in studios around London, and regularly exhibiting at the Royal Academy, Anthony was mostly out in the woods painting *plein-air* pictures, and little concerned about his own career or finances.

No artist paints alone. At one time or another every listed artist painted with other artists, or studied under a master, or was influenced by a School or period of art. Find out how the artist of your painting was connected with other artists. Whom did he paint with, what School of art did he study in, and what influences shaped his artistic perspective? At what time frame in a movement was your artist painting? Were his works exhibited, perhaps at the Royal Academy in London, at the Salon in Paris, or at the National Academy of Design in New York?

Did he win prizes or awards? Then try to determine the stature of your artist within the movement or School of art. Was he the breakthrough artist who started the movement or was he a follower? Did he paint contemporaneously with one of the leaders, or was he painting only in the *manner* of the master, many years later? Was he a genius, or one of the pack of copiers?

Works of art painted in the early stages of a movement, generally speaking, are worth more than examples executed at the end of an art period. And of course, those painted by the *originators* of a movement—the masters, like Monet (Impressionism), Picasso (Cubism), Dali (Surrealism)—breakthrough artists all, are exceedingly valuable. You need to learn how to classify and rank artists according to their stature within a School of art. (See Chapter 3, "Becoming a Connoisseur.")

Listed artist. When an artist's name is "listed," it means the artist's work has previously sold at recognized auctions, and has established auction records. In other words, the artist's name is *listed* in published price guides. A painting by an "unlisted" artist, on the other hand, can never be sold as investment art. It can only be sold as decorative work, as a "furnishing picture." In Chapter 6, "Research and Appraisal," you will learn how to research and appraise listed artists. A painting with no signature, however, might still be sold as investment art, *providing,* the painting is of exceptional quality, and can be authenticated by an expert who can attribute it to a School or artist worthy of investment.

"Decide to collect the generals or the sergeants," said art connoisseur, the late Emile Wolf. You need to learn how to classify and rank artists. While all listed artists are considered "professional," not all professional artists are worth collecting. Below are sample price rankings of American artists, as though in U.S. Army officer grades, from four-star general to sergeant.

Sample Price Rankings of American Artists				
	Rank	**Artist Caliber**	**Price Range**	**Example Artists**
PROFESSIONAL ARTISTS	1	★★★★ General	Over $1 Million	Mary Cassatt John S. Sargent
	2	★★★ General	$500,000 - $1,000,000	Frederick Church Thomas Moran
	3	★★ General	$250,000 - $500,000	John F. Kensett Jasper Cropsey
	4	★ General	$100,000 - $250,000	Wm. T. Richards Asher B. Durand
	5	Colonels	$50,000 - $100,000	W. Whittredge Willard L. Metcalf
	6	Lt. Colonels	$25,000 - $50,000	Leon Kroll Samuel Coleman
	7	Majors	$10,000 - $25,000	Jane Peterson H. Bolton Jones
	8	Captains	$5,000 - $10,000	Emile Gruppe Edmond D. Lewis
	9	1st Lieutenants	$2,000 - $5,000	Richard H. Lever S. Hyde Harris
	10	2n Lieutenants	$500 - $2,500	Newbold H. Trotter Chas. Paul Gruppe
	0	Non-Professional Unlisted Artists	The Sergeants of Art No Price Records	Weekend Painter Local Artists

The above artists are roughly classified by price rankings; however, any artist can move up or down a rank based on the quality of a single painting. An exceptional painting by an artist that typically sells for $50,000 (5th Rank), might actually fetch a world-class record at auction, say, $200,000 (4th Rank), because the quality of the work is so superior. Conversely, another painting by the same artist might fetch only $5,000 (9th Rank) at auction because the quality of that work was inferior and substandard, perhaps damaged.

So before saluting an artist by buying his painting, make sure whether you're standing in front of a "general" or a "sergeant." You might first have to gain experience buying the art of 2nd and 1st Lieutenants before moving up to the rank of Captain, and that's OK. But as soon as you can, become a "Major" player in the art business (7th Rank). That's where the big money starts.

> Buy paintings only by listed artists, of a caliber you can afford, whose works are so good and prolific that the works themselves can be used as currency. The artwork should be valued as a bearer instrument, and there must be a demand for the artist in an appreciating School or market. It also is important that the artist's work was exhibited, shown at major salons during his lifetime. When the provenance shows a distinguished past, paintings become even more desirable. These conditions will help increase the value of your painting.

QUALITY AND WORKMANSHIP

Fine art sells well, and easily. Bad art does not. Artists with high auction records paint exceedingly well; therefore commanding premium prices. Look for the hallmarks of excellence—the superb handling of paint texture and brush in the rendering of anatomy, architecture, composition, and color and contrast. These elements, in the highest quality, are the consummate standards that produced the great works of art the world admires. Study the masters to see why their works are so extraordinary, which also is why they became famous, and why their creations are so valuable.

Second and third-tier artists also painted beautifully by practicing their craft diligently. By example, when an art box from the High Renaissance Period in Rome, which was discovered in the 1900s, was opened, a note inside read, "Draw Antonio! Draw Antonio! Draw!" The note was signed Michelangelo. The great master, Michelangelo, was admonishing his pupil, Antonio, to practice, practice, practice! There is no other way to get to Carnegie Hall, or to become a great artist, except by practice.

Is your painting the artist's best work. With practice came a prodigious body of work, the best of which was used as currency, traded, and sold. Art dealers today continue to use the same currency. "Practice," however, resulted in a lot of sketches, unfinished pictures, and studies used toward the completed canvases. In his Newsletter: *Comments on the Art Market,* Howard Rehs says, "Only the final canvas will fetch the record price" (www.rehsgalleries.com), so make sure you're not buying an unfinished picture, a sketch, or a mere study that was painted by a well-known artist, unless exceptional in quality and condition, and a documented study for a major masterpiece. The price of an artist's work varies depending upon provenance, condition, quality, and other factors discussed below.

As an example, a small painting by Renoir once passed at auction for $45,000, because the workmanship was hurriedly executed, a rushed, painted picture like a sketch. The painting's authenticity was not in question; it was simply one more example of so many mediocre quality paintings Renoir failed to repaint or destroy. He painted over 6,000 works of art in his lifetime. In his later years, he had to have his paintbrushes *strapped* to his hand in order to paint. Even great artists sometimes produced inferior work, so make sure the picture you buy represents the artist's best period. Examples painted in an artist's early career are usually tight and detailed while those painted in an artist's mid-career are generally flowing and energetic. Paintings from an artist's late years are usually loose and emotional, sometimes even messy.

Buy what you like. Buy what you like is still sound advice, especially since you have to live with it. Regardless of the artist's name, if the work is poor quality, you will have a difficult time selling the artwork. You might not get back what you paid for it. Beware of infatuations that can blind you to basic flaws in a work.

While the collector can afford to buy art that pleases him alone, the investor and dealer must buy art that also pleases other people. So choose subject matters that appeal also to other collectors and investors. All poor quality work, and some subject matter, is difficult to sell. You don't want to get stuck with a picture you can't sell or have to sell at a loss.

SUBJECT MATTER

Subject matter can make or break a work of art; so **determine how you plan to sell your painting before you buy it.** Some subjects are more valuable than others. (See below, "Which Subjects are Best.")

Artist's *oeuvre*. *"Oeuvre"* is a French word meaning *the main work of an artist.* It is the collective work for which an artist is best known. An artist's central-theme paintings sell for higher prices than pictures the artist might have experimented with or when he painted a peculiar scene or subject. Collectors are willing to pay top dollar for the finest works of what an artist is best known for, and generally avoid substitutes. For example, Mary Cassatt (1844-1926) is renowned for her paintings of mothers with babies. These portrait pictures are highly sought after, and more valuable than Mary Cassatt's floral still lifes. An oil painting by Thomas Moran (1837-1926), depicting an allegorical scene of mythical India where he once painted, might be worth $500,000. But an equally large painting of the Grand Teton Mountains, for which Moran is best known, might be worth $5 million. William M. Hart (1823-1894) was a middle-range Hudson River School artist, but a painting by Hart dated 1852 would signal a Scottish scene, because Hart painted in Scotland at that time. Hart's Scottish pictures depict foreign not United States scenes; they are worth much less than his Hudson River School landscapes, for which he is better known. Always buy paintings within an artist's strongest, most characteristic areas of his *oeuvre.* U.S. scenes by an American artist generally cost more than foreign ones unless he is an expatriate artist.

Farmhouse portraits. Many 19th century America settlers had portraits of themselves painted by schooled itinerant artists who roamed the countryside painting portraits for a living. Most of these portraits were bust-size pictures of successful local farmers, whose expressions were typically solemn and unhappy. Regardless of how masterly a portrait might have been painted, most people don't want such a picture of someone else's grandfather hanging on their living room wall. Farmhouse portraits, generally speaking, have interest to and value for the family of the deceased subject. Most portraits become heirlooms remaining with their families of origin. If such a painting makes it to market, pass it up. An exception might be a portrait painted by a well-known artist, like Norman Rockwell; then a certain value can be assigned to the work.

Primitive and naïve portraits. Portraits painted by *unschooled* artists, such as Ammi Phillips (1787-1865), are said to be primitive and naïve. Unschooled artists had ample materials, time, and inspiration to paint, but lacked academic training to paint well. The most noted *unschooled* artist perhaps is Anna Mary Robertson (Grandma) Moses (1860-1961), whose artwork can fetch over $100,000 at auction. Primitive and naïve art are sometimes classified as "Folk Art," and the best of this genre can be very expensive. Naïve paintings typically lacked a ground layer of gesso, and few had finished varnishes; consequently, most naïve paintings are fragile and damage easily.

Farmhouse portraits often show up in country auctions, fetching up to $500. However, an exceptional primitive or naïve portrait, because of its unique historical perspective, could bring $50,000 at auction. There's a difference. The Folk Art Museum in New York City is an excellent resource for this period art. Visit their Web site at www.folkartmuseum.org, or call 212-265-1040.

Professional portrait artists. Professional portrait artists also are not much appreciated in today's marketplace. Herbert Abrams (1921 –), as an example, is a portrait artist of considerable stature. His works include portraits of Presidents Carter and Bush and Barbara Bush, to name a few notables. The White House might have paid $30,000 for each President's portrait, which would not be unreasonable considering the historical importance of the commission. But these were "commissioned portraits," their prices set by private agreement and not determined by supply and demand or marketplace conditions. When looking at the auction records for Herbert Abrams, *only two records exist.* One painting sold for a meager $342 in 2001, the other sold for only $162 in 1997, both landscapes. These are paltry prices for such a distinguished artist. The marketplace has never been kind to portrait artists, but the marketplace does reflect what people are looking for. Portraits by professional artists are not very high on a collector's buying list. Don't make them high on yours, unless by established general artists such as Raphael Soyer and Andrew and James Wyeth.

0

Historical portraits. Historic portraits, however, can be very valuable, especially as legacies of the men and women who shaped America during its early years. These portraits show families or individuals who controlled the wealth and power of a great nation—Presidents, generals, statesmen, industrial leaders—American nobility all. While itinerant artists moved about the country painting farmhouse portraits, historic portraits were painted in established studios in New York and Philadelphia. The very best of these portrait artists were trained in 18th century British portraiture, influenced by the likes of Gainsborough, Reynolds, and Raeburn.

America's aristocracy was painted by such artists as James Northcote (1746 – 1831), Benjamin West (1738 – 1820), Gilbert Stuart (1755 – 1828), Thomas Sully (1783 – 1872), and Rembrandt Peale (1778 – 1860) to name a few. All of these are noted portrait artists. Their works are highly sought by collectors, investors, and museums.

Portraiture combined with composition. Portraiture combined with composition describes 18th century British portrait art, and the masters of that School were the likes of Gainsborough, Hoppner, Romney, and Raeburn. Not only did they combine composition with portraiture, but they used background props to enhance the picture's meaning. In these pictures we see interior settings, furniture, chandeliers, window treatments, or light streaming in upon a subject. Portrait artists such as John Singer Sargent, Gustave Courbet, and Daniel Ridgway Knight, often used *outdoor compositions* to complement their portraits of 19th century men and women. Portraiture of this stature is extremely valuable.

American religious paintings. American religious paintings, as a genre, are very hard to sell. They have a similar effect on people as farmhouse portraits: not many people want a picture of a crucifix hanging on their living room wall. Again, the exception might be a religious subject painted by a well-known artist.

European religious paintings. European religious paintings, however, can be very valuable, especially prior to 1800, and are quite different from American religious pictures. The Catholic Church commissioned artworks in Europe for many centuries, therefore paintings of the 15th, 16th, and 17th centuries were dominated by religious themes. Prior to 1700, most Old Masters (except from Holland) painted religious pictures, and these artworks remaining are extremely valuable, and desired highly by collectors, investors, and museums. The majority of these remain in European museums and churches, but some are in America, and a few still wait discovery.

Illustrative and W.P.A. Art. Illustrative and W.P.A. art certainly is easier to sell than farmhouse portraits or religious pictures. But as a genre, it still has limitations. Illustrative artists perhaps are the unsung heroes of 20th century art. Many illustrators created exceptionally high quality works of art. But collectors and investors never took illustrative artwork seriously, perhaps because it was on the cover of so many popular magazines and comic books for decades.

The 1930s was a lost generation, commercially speaking, for American artists. But in Mexico, a new art movement took place at the same time, based on Italian fresco art. The artworks of Mexican muralists Diego Rivera and Jose Clemente Orozco (who painted historically important frescos in Dartmouth College's library) inspired American artists and politicians alike. In 1935, President Franklin D. Roosevelt's *New Deal* gave birth to the Federal Arts Project. To help provide economic relief during the Great Depression, the Federal Arts Project (F.A.P.), a division of The Works Progress Administration (W.P.A.), put an estimated 5,000 artists to work, who produced a staggering 350,000 works of art in eight years (1935 – 1943), comprised of murals, easel paintings, and fine prints. Many W.P.A. artists produced truly great works of art during this period, but were paid only stipends for their work.

During the 1940s and 1950s the marketplace was flooded with illustrative artworks. But illustrators never achieved the commercial success of the Modernists who preceded them, or the *avant-garde* status of the Abstract Expressionists who followed them. Today, however, a growing market and rising demand for illustrative and W.P.A. art has emerged with dealers that specialize in this genre. But few illustrators made it to the top ranks; N. C. Wyeth, Norman Rockwell, and Frederick Remington (who preceded the Great Depression) are the exceptions.

An excellent Web site to check for this period of art is www.wpamurals.com. It links other W.P.A. sites and art information in general, including Art Conservation, Art Definitions, Curriculum Sites, and W.P.A. Artist Biographies. It also has State listings, so you can click on your state, and print out a list of W.P.A. artists who painted where you live. This can make identifying W.P.A. artists considerably easier.

Which subjects are best? Which subjects are best to buy is a question frequently asked by new collectors. There *are* preferences to be sure, and serious collectors are willing to pay higher prices for better subjects. Commercial acceptability is an important consideration. For example, pictures of women are generally more valuable than pictures of men; and young girls are more desirable than young boys. And looks count, so be sure the face is pretty. An unsmiling or homely face for a picture's central character can kill a painting's chance of achieving a good price at auction. An owner might lose thousands of dollars because of a carelessly painted, unattractive face in a picture. And a masculine face on a woman dressed in fine satin clothes has little chance of realizing a fair price at auction. The deft handling of paint and brush, combined with genius, makes all the difference. Collectors are willing to pay top dollar for exceptional paintings by highly listed artists.

All things being equal, landscapes are more valuable that seascapes. And open landscapes with rivers or lakes sell better than interior forest pictures. Life-pictures sell better than death scenes: morbid subjects are hard to live with and difficult to sell. Flowers and fruit make better still lifes than inanimate objects, and day is preferred to night in any picture. Domestic animals have more appeal than wild animals, and dead animals will kill any art sale. Cows are hard to sell, but kittens and horses do well.

Big is better than small, up to 60 inches wide and tall. Horizontal is always more desired than vertical pictures. More is better than less—with fruit, flowers, and fish, etc. Thick is always better than thin where the application of paint is concerned; impasto is better than a washed or dry-brushed technique. Bright lustrous colors outshine soft tonal shades.

Try to buy paintings that have happy and cheerful subjects. Children playing sport or recreation form a generally safe buying guide for subject matter. Kittens pawing a ball of string, goldfish swimming in a bowl, or children chasing fireflies on a summer evening are all wonderful subjects, and many important artists have painted such genre scenes.

Historical subjects. Historical subjects are of interest to many collectors, who are willing to pay top dollar for historical art. The British artist, Thomas Baines (1822 – 1875), for example, accompanied Stanley and Livingston on their expeditions in Africa. Had Baines not painted African pictures, the world would never know what Stanley and Livingston encountered on their journey. Remember, until the end of the 19th century, "art," not cameras, was the visual medium of pictorial journalism. Art told the story of world events. Thanks to such artists as Edwin Lord Weeks (American), Fabio Fabbi (Italian), and David Roberts (British)—Orientalists who painted in the Middle East—the world is able to see the forbidden treasures of Arab culture and civilization of a century ago.

Old paintings that identify towns, landmarks, battle scenes, and architecture, or show the names of ships, streets, and buildings can add value to a work of art. A painting of Atlantic City, New Jersey, for example, by minor artist Newbold Trotter (1827 – 1898) could have historical value. There are collectors who would like to know what Atlantic City looked like in 1885, and would be willing to pay, say, $10,000 for this Trotter painting, even though Trotter's work typically sells only for $2,000. Historical perspectives can add value to a work of art.

CONDITION! CONDITION! CONDITION!

Condition is to art, what "location" is to real estate. Yes, condition is *extremely* important when considering a painting's value. Regardless of the subject matter, or the artist's name, or how low the price is, if the painting's condition is seriously flawed, be most cautious. You might not want to buy such a painting. Remember that even after paying a lot for fine conservation, your conserved artwork will never have the value of a comparable example that is undamaged, in excellent or original condition.

Do not become emotionally tied to a painting; and do not ignore a valid condition report that says your painting has serious condition problems—or you buy at your own possibly high risk.

Condition report. You cannot be shy about a painting's condition. Ask questions! Ask someone in an antique store or auction room if you can take a painting off a wall to look at it closely. If they say no, suspect something is wrong with it and move on. Never buy a painting you cannot examine, front and back, unless you have some other reliable source for providing you a competent condition report. Better auction rooms will give you a condition report on a painting you are interested in bidding on, if you request it. Therefore, do request it. If the condition report indicates damage to be considerable, extensive, or located in crucial places, be wise to reject. If you like it so much, you just *have* to have it, then bargain hard for a discount.

Eventually you will be buying paintings at out-of-state auctions by phone bids. Never rely on a digital image to determine a painting's condition. Because of not having seen the paintings physically, you must request a condition report. Request that the condition report be sent in writing by fax or e-mail. So if there is a variance in the condition of the painting you receive and what was reported in the fax, you have reason to request your money back, if the variance is significant. (See Chapter 9, "Buying Art," for a discussion on buying paintings at out-of-state auctions.) Below are example Condition Reports from Christie's Auction House.

Disclaimer. Christie's prefaces its condition reports with the following disclaimer, which you should read:

> *Further to your recent inquiry, we are pleased to provide you the condition report(s) you requested. This report has been prepared by Christie's specialists and is no substitute for physical examination by you or your advisors. Christie's*

specialists are not trained restorers and the report set forth below is not a comprehensive condition report prepared by a professional conservator. While we make certain observations on the work which we trust are helpful, we recommend you consult your own restorer for a more complete report. Prospective purchasers should bear in mind that this report will not disclose any imperfections that may only be revealed during the course of subsequent restoration. Buyers are reminded that Christie's warranties with respect to property are limited as set forth in our Conditions of Sale and do not extend to condition.

Lot 198 **Arthur Parton (1842 – 1914)**

Cows by the Water

Condition: *This work is not lined and appears dirty. The canvas has come undone from the stretcher along the upper left edges, with areas of paint loss along all four edges. There is an inverted 'U' shaped tear approximately ¼" x ½" inch in the upper right quadrant in the sky, with a corresponding patch on the reverse. There is a repaired puncture in the lower right corner with a corresponding patch on the reverse. There appears to be surface cracking throughout, with areas of paint loss scattered throughout the work. There appear to be small spots of inpaint and crackfill scattered in areas of the work.*

The above report indicates serious condition problems with this painting. The painting needs to be lined with a new support canvas (major restoration), and cleaned, requiring significant infilling and inpainting throughout. You will pay $1,000 or more for a professional restorer to make this painting right. Arthur Parton is a minor American painter; even in good condition this painting might be worth only $3,000.

Consequently, don't buy this painting. (Unless, however, you wanted to donate this painting in restored condition to the Historical Society in Hudson, New York, where Arthur Parton was born, or you had some other personal reason for wanting to restore a damaged painting by Arthur Parton.) This is not a desirable painting to buy.

Lot 273 Circle of Edmund Osthaus (1858 - 1928)

A Setter at Point

Condition: *This picture is unlined and the support is stable. The paint surface appears to be in good original condition and there are no paint losses or abrasions visible to the naked eye. Under ultraviolet light, there are several small areas of retouching visible; these are confined to the upper center of the picture. This conservation was carried out sensitively. The varnish is even and the picture is ready to hang.*

This is a proper, sound condition report. The painting also had no reserve at Christie's Summer House Sale (identified by a "red dot" in the printed catalogue), and the hammer price was only $1,000, which was a reasonable buy if you wanted a 19th century sporting picture. (See Chapter 5, "Technical Examination," for a detailed discussion on condition.)

Condition preferences. Damage to a painting will seriously affect its value. As the oil in oil paint slowly dries during many scores of years, breakdown and deterioration are inevitable, and inherent in the Second Principle of Thermal Dynamics, which also applies to paintings. Since puncture holes and tears in a canvas, however, are caused by human carelessness, care must be taken to avoid such sloppy treatment. Paintings also become damaged because of natural aging and chemical and environmental factors.

An untouched damaged painting (not restored) is always more valuable than a damaged painting poorly restored. If a painting is poorly restored, you have the original damage, plus the new damage caused by the amateur restorer. If a painting shows poor restoration, you must consider this a red flag discouraging its purchase, except, perhaps, at a deep discount, providing it can be restored again.

Collectors first want to buy paintings that are in "near excellent" or "excellent" and "original condition" (not restored); second, valuable paintings that are damaged but not yet restored; and third, valuable paintings that have been restored well. Collectors will not want to buy damaged paintings that were poorly restored. Serious collectors prefer to use their own restorers for conservation work. Should you need a painting conservator or "paper conservator," consult the nearest major art museum's curator or director for references. (Also check www.aic.stanford.edu.)

You might not detect poor restoration work beneath a painting's surface until years later. But you can always spot improper inpainting, particularly in the areas of the hands and face, especially when examining it very carefully in direct sunlight and/or under ultra-violet light.

CASE EXAMPLE: Poor Inpainting

An English dealer came to the United States to examine and buy several paintings, but when he saw the badly painted touch-up work in the hands and face of the central woman subject in one painting, he passed on an otherwise beautiful Victorian picture. His comment, "The price doesn't scare me," he said (which was $15,000). "In fact, I'd be willing to pay more if the condition were good." This painting probably would have fetched $50,000 in London if it were never damaged, or had been restored by a superior conservator. Mediocre restorers can never match a master's touch when significant inpainting is applied to the hands and face. Serious collectors will reject restoration work that is shoddy. Always exercise caution when thinking about buying damaged paintings. Determine, if you can, when and how the damage occurred.

Restoration. Major conservation work, however, is sometimes needed on valuable and important paintings, and a competent restorer can perform miracles on a badly damaged painting. For example, a badly torn and tattered canvas painted by Lilly Martin Spencer (1822 – 1902) recently sold for $10,000, which seemed an outrageously high price for nothing more than shredded canvas. But after restoration, the picture sold at auction for $65,000. Even if the restoration work cost $5,000, the painting netted $50,000 profit to a wise dealer.

Craquelure, which is one of the most common forms of damage to occur in paintings, generally comes from drying and aging, over time. Craquelure can be more than just an acceptable nuisance to see. The value of a painting can be diminished if the craquelure is seriously exaggerated or obviously irregular due to abusive stress. The manifestation of cracks can take many forms, each having a different effect on the canvas. Cracks are classified according to the patterns they form, such as: net spiral cracks, grid cracks, wedge cracks, spoke cracks, garland cracks, corn-ear cracks, and alligator cracks. Concentric or spiraling craquelure results from a pointed object pressing against the back of the canvas. (For pictorial examples of craquelure, see *The Restoration of Paintings* (Konemann 1998) by Knut Nicolaus.

Humidity and excessive hot and cold temperatures can seriously affect the soundness of a painting. Also, moving a painting can disturb the bond between the paint and the canvas primer. If the undercoat is thin, for example, there is more potential for cracking, and if thick, it is less likely to crack. If the gesso undercoat on wood panels was sanded smooth before applying paint, it is more likely for cracks to occur, as a smooth gesso surface can permit "sliding," where the layers of paint can shift or slide over the support. All this, of course, was set in motion hundreds of years before you bought your old painting by the materials and practices used at the time. (See Chapter 5, "Technical Examination," for a detailed discussion on environmental effects on paintings.)

Conservation vs. Restoration. The terms *conservation* and *restoration* are sometimes used interchangeably, but there is a difference. Conservation is aimed at *preservation*, which is like changing the oil in your car to give your engine a better chance for a longer life. Passive conservation measures, such as where and how you hang your artwork, and room temperature, can preserve the health of your painting. Restoration, on the other hand, is more like doing a major overhaul to your engine, for the purpose of restoring the engine to its original condition. Restoration is heftier work; the person performing either job is rightly called a "restorer." In more sophisticated circles, however, you'll meet conservators. (See Chapter 5, "Technical Examination," for conservation tips.)

SIZE

Paintings come in all sizes. All things being equal, big is better than small, providing that workmanship, subject matter, and condition in the big painting are as fine or better than in the small painting. Serious collectors almost always want to buy full-size paintings. When evaluating prices in auction record books, make sure you are comparing the size painting previously sold at auction with the size painting you are currently appraising. Don't compare an auction price record of a 5" X 9" painting which sold for, say, $10,000, with a 24" X 36"painting you are considering buying. The 24" X 36" painting should be worth much more than the 5" X 9" painting, other factors being equal. While there is no official guide for classifying paintings by size, here are some examples, ± 25%: Small Size: 5" X 9". Medium Size: 16" X 24". Full Size: 24" X 36".

While big is better than small; too big is not advisable either. Paintings with one side longer than 72 inches, is considered too large for most collectors. Apart from museums and institutional collections, few have wall space suitable for a six-foot long painting; and oversized paintings are awkward to handle and costly to transport. The most saleable size painting is 24" X 36" But a 5" X 9" painting by an excellent artist might be the only size painting available to you by that artist, in which case, if the price is right, and other factors are favorable, you have to buy it. A 5" X 9" painting in excellent condition could be worth more than a 24" X 36" painting in poor condition by the same artist.

AUTHENTICITY

A painting's true value can only be determined by the strength of its authenticity. Knowing if the painting you intend to buy is *"real,"* or not, is obviously essential. You certainly can't afford buying or selling even one artwork that isn't "real." But where do you start? you might ask. Remember the expression, "If it looks like a duck, walks like a duck, and quacks like a duck, it must be a duck." Well, to a large degree, this applies to paintings, giving you a valuable first test. If you have a painting, for example, that looks like a Winslow Homer (1836 – 1910), feels like a Winslow Homer, and has the makings of a Winslow Homer, it might indeed be a painting by Winslow Homer. Take it to an expert; his or her authentication will be well worth the fee. Conversely, if someone is trying to sell you a painting, for example, by William Merritt Chase (1849 – 1916), but the painting does not *look* like a Chase, does not *feel* like a Chase, and has none of the *makings* of a Chase, be very cautious. It's probably not a Chase painting. Make sure you study scores of clear, sharp accurately colored reproductions, including enlargements of Chase's brushwork. Even better, examine actual paintings by Chase.

Always seek expert advice before making a major acquisition. An excellent place to start is with the curatorial staff at a museum specializing in the artist or School of art you intend to buy.

PROVENACE

Provenance is the pedigree that proves a painting has been owned by certain individuals or families. All certificates, conservation records, bills of sale, auction records, etc., associated with a work of art become part of its provenance. The provenance is extremely important to the successful sale of a painting. A painting, for example, by Franz Kline (1910 – 1960) could be very valuable indeed, especially one from his abstract period. But proving a work really is by Franz Kline can be difficult if it's unsigned. If you have written documentation, however, (bill of sale, letter from the artist, etc.) showing the painting passed directly from the artist to Mr. So-and-So, then to So-and-So's daughter, then to the present owner, you have an established trail proving your painting's authenticity. Likewise, if more than one expert has examined your painting, even from previous owners a century ago, and each expert attributed the work to a single artist, and these findings are listed in *catalogues raisonnés*, you have a rock-solid case for your painting's attribution. (See Chapter 8, "Provenance, Due-Diligence, Forgeries, and *Catalogues Raisonnés*.)

3

Becoming a Connoisseur

A connoisseur is a person who has *expert knowledge* and *keen discrimination,* especially in the fine arts. Well, doesn't that describe you precisely? If it doesn't, then you'll need to pay attention to the instructions in this chapter. Becoming a connoisseur in the field of art can change your life.

Acquiring expertise is not a passing fancy. Once you become an "expert," and continue diligent learning, you're one for life! You won't forget what you are, and you never have to pay for what you already know. Circumstances in life can change. You can even fall on hard times, but your *expertise* can never be taken from you. In a moment of good fortune, for example, you can stumble upon a work of art that might be worth thousands of dollars, which you might be able to buy with the last five dollars in your pocket. So "expertise" can lift you out of poverty if you know how to use it. The winnings in poker go not to the one with the best hand, but to the one who knows how to best play his cards. So do the best paintings.

GET UNDERSTANDING

The *Book of Proverbs* tells us, "In all that you get, get understanding" (4:5). But how do we get understanding that leads to expertise and connoisseurship? How do we learn how to "look," and how to "understand" with an eye? The truth is, we achieve understanding through the pursuit of knowledge, through perseverance and hard work. *We earn it.*

Learning about art is a lifelong pursuit. Potentially you will be looking at 500 years of art as you pick and deal, everything from Renaissance to Modern art. There's a treasure out there waiting to be discovered, and you won't want to miss it. You'll have to study art—all 500 years, generally, and specifically in one or two periods or specialties.

What separates a museum curator from an antique shop picker is scholarship. The curator continually studies, reading the art magazines and journals recommended in this chapter. Curators also gain knowledge and expertise by working in collaboration with art historians and connoisseurs; you also must align yourself with dealers and experts from whom you can learn. You must develop learning experiences that will lead to scholarship and expertise. This chapter will be your study guide. The suggested learning tracks below will lead you to knowledge and know-how sufficient for you to start making money in art.

How you apply the following information to your life, and turn it into operational knowledge will determine whether you dabble in mediocrity, or move up the ladder of excellence to heights of connoisseurship. Application of the information in this chapter will separate amateurs from professionals. The choice is yours. Only you can decide how hard you want to work to raise your level of competence in the field of art.

ART EDUCATION

The world needs experts. To become an expert in any field requires three things: (1) commitment and dedication, (2) intense study and deep exposure to the specialty you've chosen, and (3) professional guidance and mentoring.

EXPERTISE

Expertise usually begins with a fascination or curiosity for something, in this case, *art.* You've bought this book, so you must have an inclination that art is important to you. You may well have an "eye" for art, and/or develop such discernment. When you study a sunset you probably wait, lingering to catch the "green flash" at the moment the sun slips behind the horizon. If you see art and nature in all its colors and shapes, then the Master painted just for you.

Anything that comes natural is a gift. People with a natural "eye" for art are drawn to learning about their passion. Moreover, they are willing to invest in their education to the point of becoming an expert. Developing to be an expert is like preparing for your Ph.D., so make sure the time you spend studying art is profitably spent. After all, you want to become a *connoisseur*, not a used furniture dealer.

DEGREE PROGRAM vs. EXPERIENTIAL LEARNING

Several avenues exist which you can take to achieve connoisseurship in the field of art, including a formal M.A. degree program at Christie's in New York, Paris, London, or Melbourne. The M.A. degree program at Christie's will cost you about $30,000 for tuition alone, and take 16 months to complete. This program also requires foreign language study, field trips, and other expensive accoutrements. Figure spending $50,000 for your art education (without room and board). Sotheby's also has an excellent, and equally expensive art curriculum, including a Ph.D. program.

Or, you can read this book, design your own curriculum, invest that same $50,000 in art, and determine to become a millionaire by the time you retire, say in 10 to 20 years. If you take the same time to acquire your experiential education as the M.A. degree program, and apply the principles in this book, you can be at the threshold of connoisseurship in 16 months, or at least ready to deal in art for profit and pleasure. If you aspire for a position in academia, however, or hold a corporate art position, you'll need credentials. Therefore, earn your M.A. degree from a distinguished college or university with a renowned department of Art History, Art Marketing and Administration, or Art Museum Studies.

But if you want to delve into art part-time, and start picking up side money, adding, say $20,000 to $25,000 a year to your income, follow the instructions in this book. You can earn substantial money employing the techniques and procedures of an art dealer while working another job or in retirement.

THE STUDY PROGRAM

The study program outlined in this chapter suggests eight hours of study a week: two hours with a mentor or friend, reviewing and discussing art (see "Tea-Session Art" below), and six hours a week researching art at museums, galleries, auction rooms, and conservation studios. These most enjoyable eight hours can be spent all on a Saturday, or as your schedule permits, either alone or with a learning partner. This still leaves you evenings for study, and the entire workweek for your regular job.

CORE LEARNING TRACKS

The learning tracks listed below suggest a study program for you to follow. Do not be alarmed at the breadth of the material you have to learn. You have 16 months—or as much time as you need—to acquire this education. Understanding art concepts and market values will flow naturally from chapter to chapter as you read. The core curriculum is outlined below with detailed discussions following, so you can see now what is important. In this way you will know what to look out for and concentrate on when you explore art museums, galleries, and auction houses. Add other study tracks to suit your interests or specialty. Take as much time as you need to become a connoisseur. Learning about art is lifelong. Expertise enriches your life. “Happy is the man who finds wisdom, and the man who gains understanding” (Prov. 3:13).

CORE CURRICULUM	
LEARNING TRACK	**STUDY GOALS**
Study the timelines for 600 years of Western Art: periods from the Renaissance to 1960. Cover Early, High, and Northern Renaissance; Mannerists; Baroque (Italian, Flemish, French, Spanish, and Dutch); Rococo; Neoclassicism & Romanticism; The British School; French Romanticism; Pre-Raphaelites; French Realism; Barbizon; The Impressionists; 19th century American Art; Post-Impressionism; 20th Century Modern Art; Expressionism; Cubism; Abstract Art; Surrealism; and Abstract Expressionism.	Know Period timelines, and the reason for departure from previous School. Know the political or social context for each Period. Know the style of painting, materials, and techniques used in each Period. Take a college course in “Survey of Art History.” Sister Wendy Beckett’s book, *The Story of Paintings* is an excellent resource guide for this exploration. (See Appendix 4, Timeline for 600 Years of Art.)
Be able to place a painting in its historical context, and in the correct Period or School of art.	At a glance, be able to identify an artwork by its School or Period.
Know the works and names of 3 top-tier artists from each School of art from the Renaissance to 1800.	Renaissance (Early, High, Northern); Baroque; Rococo; Neoclassicism; and the British School.
Know the work of 5 top-tier artists from each School of art from 1800 to 1950.	French Romanticism; Pre-Raphael; French Realism; Impressionist; 19th C. American Art; Post-Impression; and 20th

CORE CURRICULUM	
LEARNING TRACK	**STUDY GOALS**
	century Moderns through 1950.
Identify the School of art that is or will become your Specialty.	Example: Hudson River School, California Impressionism, Dutch Baroque, French Realism, Moderns, W.P..A. Illustration Art
Know price range of 5 top-tier artists in that School. Know price range of 5 second-tier artists in that School. Know price range of 5 third-tier artists in that School.	Study price guides, auction results, biographies. See Chapters 6 & 7. (Know works and price range of 15 artists in your specialty/School.)
Be able to recognize 5 signatures from that School.	Study Monograms & Signatures (www.signaturehelp.com).
Know which regional museums and galleries exhibit works of art from your School or specialty.	Search Internet for museums and galleries for your artists/School (www.amn.org).
Know the names and phone numbers of 3 high-end dealers who buy and sell art from your specialty/School.	Google for specialty dealers near you; research fine art magazines; check galleries, local references.
Know a recognized expert for your specialty/School.	Internet search; check with galleries and museum curators.
Identify 3 significant regional auction rooms within 300 miles.	Google (sales over $5 million per year). Also See Appendix 6.
Identify 3 country auction houses within 100 miles.	See Yellow Pages, local references.
Know how to use price guides and research books	See Chapters 6, libraries, and museums.
Understand the basics of art conservation.	See Chapter 5.
Know the basics of art research techniques.	See Chapter 6 & 7.
Know the basics of art appraisal techniques.	See Chapter 6 & 7.
Know Internet research techniques.	See Chapter 7.

CORE CURRICULUM	
LEARNING TRACK	**STUDY GOALS**
Know names and phone numbers of 2 art conservators.	Check local museums; the Am. Inst. of Conservation: 202-452-9545, at www.aic.stanford.edu.
Know a professional picture framer.	See Yellow Pages and local references.
Know a Museum Curator.	Check local museums.
Know an art historian.	Check local museums and universities; Google.
Know an art researcher.	Check libraries and universities.
Obtain a Resale Tax ID Number.	Check your State Dept. of Revenue.
Identify a mentor. Build positive relationships. Gain expertise.	Be part of the fine art community. Do research, ask questions, study, participate.

TOTAL IMMERSION

Whether your developing expertise began with a fascination or a notion is incidental to developing your passion. To become an expert you must *saturate* yourself in every aspect of the art.

STUDYING

Studying with a partner or small group is recommended, but not essential. Making field trips and taking art vacations with a friend is always more enjoyable than exploring the catacombs alone. Partners also can be accountable to one another, test one another, and help one another establish goals or timelines for completing learning tracks. A knowledgeable peer group also is beneficial for critiquing, evaluating, and appraising each other's acquisitions. Friends and small groups are especially conducive for forming Art Investment Clubs. See Chapter 4, "Investing In Art."

MEMORY

You will need to figure out a way to remember different Schools of art, and specific artists' work. Here's why: When a high quality, unsigned painting (of course, authentic and in near excellent or excellent condition) sells at auction for a ridiculously low price, it's because neither the seller nor the auction house truly know who the artist is. But you know or think you know. You recognize the work. It has all the hallmarks of Jean Francois Millet (1814 – 1875): the style, technique, age of canvas, brush strokes, muted colors, even the subject—peasants working in a field at sunset. The 44" X 33" canvas is the same size canvas on which Millet often painted, and the stretcher bears French identification marks. The painting has never been lined, it's in original condition, and the varnish looks to be from the period. Exquisite, it has the Master's touch.

Before the auction you double-check, you do a search at www.Artnet.com and study Millet's works. You confirm your informed intuition: everything about this painting looks Millet! The only thing missing is Millet's signature, and that might appear after the painting is cleaned. You're ready to bid, and you show up at the auction with confidence.

Even with very good unsigned paintings at auction, most speculators back off before the bidding reaches $5,000. But since you're prepared to go that much and higher for this painting, you'll bid aggressively right from the beginning. Bidding fiercely, you prevail.

Bid only with conviction if your memory is sure that a painting is by a certain artist whom you've researched. Otherwise, you'd be wise to back off, and probably before the bidding reaches $5,000.

On the same evening, you have an opportunity to buy another painting at auction, one that has an "indistinguishable" signature. This period French landscape has an estimate of only $2,000, because no one can make out the artist's name. The signature only has two letters that are legible, which are "o" and "t," at the end of the name. But because you know and remember the work of Camille Corot (1796-1875), which is exactly like the painting being auctioned, you need only see the last two letters in the name, "o" and "t," to make the connection. So you bid fiercely for this painting, and this night you take home a Millet and a Corot. These are fabulous artists, and these are fabulous and extreme examples. Such intuitive successes have indeed occurred in the past and will in the future. It's as easy as remembering an artist's work.

> The most successful art dealers not only have a fantastic "eye" for art, they also have an incredible memory for art, which is what you'll have to develop to be an exceptional art dealer and/or investment collector.

Case Example: Mistaken Identity

An astute art dealer made a live telephone bid to an out-of-state auction. The painting he was interested in bidding on was classified as a European landscape: "*Shepherd with Sheep and Cows on a Country Lane.*" It had an indistinct signature, and was in a period gilded frame. Studying the digital image posted on the Web site, the dealer was quite sure he recognized the School of art, and possibly also the artist.

The night of the auction, the dealer heard the auctioneer call out, "Who will start the bidding at $500 for this lovely 19th century landscape? The signature is indistinct. It looks like T... Roy ... something. Can't make it out. Anyway, it's a beautiful landscape. All right," he said, "Who will start the bidding at $500?"

The hammer came down one minute later, and the phone handler told the dealer, "You just bought the painting for $800, sir." "*I did?*" replied the dealer. He was stunned. Flabbergasted. By now he knew who the artist was when the auctioneer tried to pronounce the indistinct signature: "*T ... Roy ... something.*"

What the dealer had seen in the digital image was a Barbizon School painting. He knew that, because he had studied the Barbizon School, including its major artists. So when he heard the auctioneer separate the "T" from the "Roy," as in "T ... Roy ... something," he knew that the artist was none other than Constant Troyon (1810-1865). He also knew that Constant Troyon painted landscapes with sheep and cows. Before the auction he researched Barbizon School artists and confirmed that Constant Troyon indeed painted such landscapes, exactly as in the painting being auctioned. Now this dealer was certain. And he was right.

For $800, this dealer bought an exceptional painting by Constant Troyon, a leader in the Barbizon movement. Troyon's works hang in the Hermitage, the Louvre, and in the Metropolitan Museum of Art in New York.

USING COGNITIVE PSYCHOLOGY IN ART

Reinforce your learning experiences with memory techniques found in cognitive psychology. This will help your long-term memory index dates, facts, art prices, and painting styles. Apply these memory-building techniques during and after visits to museums, galleries, or live auctions.

- **PRACTICE** is key to strengthening memory.
  "Practice increases the strength of learning exponentially. Double the practice at least squares the strength of the learned information in memory; triple the practice increases the strength by a factor of nine." *Forshay, Training Materials that Work,* Jossey-Bass (2003)

  We learn primarily through repetition. Practice is examining hundreds of paintings to learn about condition. Try to understand and remember the different kinds of damage caused by water, excessive heat and cold, mold and fungus, punctures and tears, and flaking paint. Examining the back of a painting (when the back is original), whether canvas, wood, academy, or canvas board, is often as revealing as the front. Only after you've examined hundreds of paintings can you fully rely on your judgment.

You also could practice by researching 10 artists from the School you've chosen as your specialty. Try to remember their names, dates, price ranges, painting styles, signatures, *oeuvre*; even the frames they used. Rehearse facts and figures. Create 3" X 5" cards with an artist's name on one side and relevant facts on the reverse side (dates, movement, peers, price range, etc.), and practice with a partner. After completing a study track, try to recall what you've learned. Return to a museum or gallery to study a painting again and again, until you understand with your "eye" all the properties in a painting.

Only you can decide how much practice you want to invest in your art education.

- **FEEDBACK.** If you've found a mentor, ask how you're doing applying new knowledge, or what problems you're having. Ask for honest feedback from a partner or peer group. If you haven't yet identified a mentor, search one out.

- **SUMMARIZE.** Strengthen new knowledge by summarizing dates and facts. Draw timeline-sketches summarizing what you've learned.

- **TEST** what you've learned by using new knowledge in different situations. Write a paper. Tell someone in your group about an art movement, School, or artist. Teach what you know. You truly learn a subject when you have to teach it.

- **APPLICATION.** Apply what you've learned by testing yourself in the field, or in a mockup. Set up several paintings, then go before each one and try to evaluate a painting in less than one minute. Practice until you can make an accurate assessment in one minute, which should include an opinion about:

  1. Quality of workmanship (1-5, 5 being world class).
  2. Age: evaluate canvas, nails, stretcher, patina, etc.
  3. Condition (1-5, 5 being original, excellent condition).
  4. School or period of art.
  5. Subject: pleasing, saleable, or undesirable.
  6. Signature and date, signs of authenticity
  7. Frame; hand carved; maker's mark; style-appropriate.
  8. Value classification: Decorative, Collectible, Investment.

  You'll want to develop speed in assessing paintings. If you spot an exceptional painting in an antique store, take it off the wall and hold on to it. Keep the painting in your hand as you walk around; it's yours until you put it back on the wall. Many a hesitant buyer made one more pass around an antique mall, only to return where a painting once hung to find it gone. Look! The man at the counter with his checkbook out is taking your painting home.

- **YCDI.** "You can do it." Expect that you'll be successful in art, and declare that nothing will keep you from achieving your goals.

- **WIIFM.** Remind yourself, "What's in it for me." It's OK to make money with art. Many people do, and so can you. Don't give up.

COMMITMENT AND DEDICATION

Commitment and dedication turn fascination into a passion, ultimately compelling you to become an expert. Some people remember the capitals of all fifty states; others, albeit die-hard fans, remember the names of the baseball players on the 1956 Brooklyn Dodgers (World Series Champions). You figure. There's no end to what people can and will remember. Remembering the names of artists, the School or movement in which they painted, and the price range they sell for can and will become increasingly easy for you to recall. What you remember can make you an expert.

> The human memory becomes phenomenal when commitment and dedication are the gasoline that fuels interest.

MUSEUMS

Museums preserve and showcase splendid art. To become expert, we must see and examine great examples in order to acquire knowledge sufficient to be considered an "expert." The masterpieces you will see in museums are the benchmarks against which you will measure the quality of other paintings found in galleries and auction rooms.

Many museums also offer access to their research libraries. You might find rare art books, journals, and catalogues not available elsewhere. A museum's curatorial staff also can provide you expert advice about artists, paintings, and frames. A museum will not, however, appraise your painting, as that potentially could lead to conflicts of interest and legal problems. But a museum person generally will offer an unofficial opinion concerning condition, quality, and rarity. If you make an appointment in advance, curators will often arrange for you to view art not then on exhibit but in storage.

Museums are obviously potential buyers of art, as you will learn in Chapter 10, "Selling Art." You would be wise to nurture good relationships with museum staff. Make the acquaintance personally or informally of the director, curator, registrar, and research librarian. And don't forget the bookstore manager. A museum also can connect you with conservators, appraisers, and other experts in the field, as well as with other museums around the country. These connections can benefit your art business immensely. (See Chapter 7 for a discussion on "The Curator.")

DISCOVERING WHAT YOU LIKE

If you don't already know the period or School of art you wish to collect, spend time roaming around a museum like the Metropolitan Museum of Art in New York City. There, in different wings and sections of the museum you'll find rooms just for Italian, Flemish, British, and American paintings. You'll find artworks to look at covering most periods of art, from the Middle Ages to the present. At some national museums you'll see paintings by the world's most famous artists: Leonardo Da Vinci, Michelangelo, Raphael, Rubens, Rembrandt, Vermeer, Poussin, and Velazquez. Depending upon how quiet you are, you can spend an entire day studying art in a museum. So take advantage of one of Western Civilization's great institutions, the art museum.

YOUNG COLLECTORS CLUBS

Young Collectors Clubs are being started at museums around the country. At these gatherings you'll find young professionals with a penchant for art. There is ample opportunity for you to learn and socialize. Depending upon which club you join, you could find free lectures, luncheons with specialists, gallery tours, discussions with experts, art workshops, and trips to other museums and private collections. There also are travel opportunities with curators, social events, private studio visits, seminars on how to buy art at auctions, city walking tours, and even black-tie exhibition openings. Some events are free, most require registration, and some are for members only. Check with the museum or art center in your city for social and educational events that you can participate in. Here are some general contact numbers.

Young Collectors Clubs	
Christie's, New York "Young Collector's Program" 212-636-2000 www.christies.com	**The Cleveland Museum of Art** "Young Friends Program 216-707-2268 www.clemusart.com
Fine Arts Museum of San Francisco "Art Point" 415-750-7648 www.thinker.org	**High Museum of Art, Atlanta** "Young Careers" 404-733-4428 www.high.org
Institute of Contemporary Art, Boston "The New Group" 617-927-6612 www.ica.org	**Los Angeles Museum of Art** "Muse Program" 323-857-6000 www.lacma.org
Museum of Modern Art, New York "Junior Associates Program" 212-708-9400 www.momoa.org	**Museum of Fine Arts, Boston** "The Museum Council" 617-369-3268 www.mfa.org
National Gallery of Art, Washington, D.C. "The Circle" 202-842-6865 www.nga.gov	**Sotheby's, New York** "New Collectors Program" 212-606-7375 www.sothebys.com

EXPERTISE

Expertise comes at a price. Furthermore, it must bear the test of cross-examination. Expertise implies that you have acquired substantial knowledge in the field of art, and in your specialty. Secondly, you must be able to demonstrate persuasively that you're able to identify a painting in the School of art in which you profess to be an expert. Expertise requires the ability to attribute a work of art to a specific artist, or his *studio*, his *circle*, or next in rank would be to identify the painting as by a *follower* of the artist, *manner* of the artist, or *after* the artist (see "Explanation of Cataloguing Practice" on page 199). But it is difficult to become an expert in a field that you have not yet identified as your specialty. This is where your art study program will help. After examining scores, then eventually hundreds of paintings, you will find your specialty as you spend time studying art.

CHOOSING YOUR SPECIALTY

Choosing a School of art in which to specialize should reflect your personal preference and not hot market trends, current fads, or financial projections. Foremost priority is to decide what you want to collect, then what you want to invest in. Following the instincts of your heart and intuition will lead you to authentic learning, thereby enabling you to acquire expertise faster than if you pursued only a quick return on your investment.

PERIODS OF ART

You might like certain periods of art for the social, political, or historical themes, or for the costumes or customs of the day. Collecting period art could include, for example, Seventeenth Century Dutch paintings. There are artworks still available by second and third-tier artists of this Period. With any period art, it generally is **better to buy the best quality work of second or third-tier artist than to buy poor quality work of top-tier artists.**

Trying to collect very early Dutch Masters, however, is almost a waste of time, and truly risky because works by the likes of Robert Campin, Jan van Eyck, or Rogier van der Weyden, are all but gone from the marketplace. If you found a genuine Dutch Master work of merit and in very good to excellent condition, you probably would not be able to afford it.

Other periods of art are, however, suitable for collecting and potentially sound investments. Consider Baroque and Eighteenth Century Italian Art, Eighteenth Century British Art, and lesser Impressionist Art. The major Impressionists are priced beyond most collectors. Finding a major Impressionist work in the marketplace at a reasonable price would be extraordinary luck or of dubious attribution, authenticity, and/or condition.

FOLLOW YOUR INSTINCTS

What happens if you particularly like Baroque art? That's OK. Enjoy it. Study it. Saturate yourself in Baroque art. It'll be more difficult to find than Impressionist art, or outstanding American art, but if Baroque examples are what you really like, that's where your learning curve will be sharpest.

You might have to spend your summers in Europe, according to your preference for Italian, Spanish, French, or Dutch Baroque art. You'll find Baroque art in American museums, and to a lesser extent in American art galleries. Baroque art is still available, especially in Europe. Hunting it down will be a key part of your education. Meeting European experts and visiting galleries where Old Master paintings still hang are great ways to spend your vacation.

SCHOOLS OF ART

If you want to narrow the field, you could collect certain subjects, such as marine art, hunting pictures, still lifes, portraiture, or urban scenes. You could also collect work by a single artist, by investing, for example, only in paintings by Herman Herzog, Emile Carlsen, or James Butterworth. But as you will learn in Chapter 4,

"Investing in Art," it's generally risky to put all your eggs in one basket. Diversity in art, as in stocks, is prudent and most profitable in the long run.

A School of art to consider might be Regionalism, where artists gathered and painted in certain locations. Most American Schools of art grew out of "art colonies," where like-minded artists gathered to paint outdoors under bright sunlight (*en plein-air*). The common thread that ran through most art colonies was camaraderie, beautiful scenery (landscapes, coastlines, and rolling hills), and inexpensive support systems for lodging, food, and art supplies.

CALIFORNIA IMPRESSIONISM

California Impressionists formed art colonies along the Pacific coastline, in settlements such as Laguna and Carmel. At the end of the 19th Century, artists began moving to the West Coast in droves to paint unique landscapes under the bright Californian sunlight.

Today these pictures are highly prized. If you collect California Impressionist paintings, you will be searching for, at the top end, paintings by: Edgar Payne (1883 - 1947), Grandville Redmond (1871 - 1935), William Wendt (1865 - 1946), and Guy Rose (1867 - 1925). But there are hundreds of fine, lesser artists who painted beautiful California landscapes at the same time. Examples by the following Californian artists are worthy of investment: Anna Hills, William Swift Daniels, William Griffith, Joseph Kleitsch, Elmer Wachtel, Colin Campbell Cooper, Benjamin Chambers Brown, Alson Skinner Clark, and George Gardner Symons, to name only a few.

AMERICANS IN PARIS

Americans in Paris from 1850 to 1900 formed their own artistic style. They mixed techniques from the Barbizon School with the Impressionist movement, developing the American School in Paris. These Americans abroad became known as "Expatriate Artists." They flocked to Paris, especially after the American Civil War, to study with the emerging Impressionist Masters, like Monet, Renoir, Sisley, Bazille, and Pissarro.

So many Americans were painting in Paris during the last half of the Nineteenth Century, that the *Gazette Des Beaux-Arts* offered this comment ". . . the United States, so young a country, could be so rich in works of painting, especially works of the French School. It is not by the hundreds but by the thousands that one must count them." And Henry James wrote, "It sounds like a paradox, but it is a very simple truth, that when today we look for 'American Art,' we find it mainly in Paris. When we find it out of Paris, we at least find a great deal of Paris in it."

The list of talented Americans painting in Paris and in the French countryside during the late Nineteenth Century is legendary. If you want to collect this School, look for paintings by Frank M. Boggs, Daniel Ridgeway Knight, Frederick Arthur Bridgman, Theodore Robinson, Charles Sprague Pearce, Irving Ramsey, Mary Cassatt, John Singer Sargent, William Thorne, Childe Hassam, Frank Weston Benson, William Leroy Metcalf, Elizabeth Nourse, Ellen Shepherd, and hundreds of other expatriate artists. Since they have grown in popularity among American collectors during the past 30 years, prices for expatriate art have risen accordingly.

WOMEN ARTISTS OF BOSTON

Women artists of Boston in the late 19th and early 20th century form another School of art you might want to collect. Look for paintings by Marguerite Stuber Pearson, Lilla Cabot Perry, Marie Danforth Page, Annie Hurlburt Jackson, Margaret Foote Hawley, Nelly Littlehale Murphy, Gertrude Fiske, Agnes Anne Abbot, Polly Thayer, Margaret Fitzhugh Browne, Laura Coombs Hills, Alice Ruggles Sohier, and Elizabeth Vaughan Okie, to name a few. Many other fine Boston women artists can be found.

OTHER SCHOOLS OF ART

Many other Schools of art exist which you can collect. Consider paintings from the Old Lyme School, in Connecticut, or artists of "The Eight," some of whom formed the Ashcan School that depicted urban life. Other possibilities include the White Mountain School of Art in New Hampshire and the Hudson River School of Art. The best known Hudson River School Art include paintings by Thomas Cole, Frederick Church, Asher B. Durand, John W. Casilear, John F. Kensett, Sanford Robinson Gifford, Jasper F. Cropsey, David Johnson, Alfred T. Bricher, James Hart, Samuel Colman, George Inness, and early Albert Bierstadt, to name only a few. Scores of lesser artists associated with the Hudson River School also created works of art worth collecting as investments.

Continue studying art, reflecting on what touches your soul, and you will find a School of art to collect.

GALLERIES

Now that you've decided what you want to collect, seek out galleries that exhibit works by artists from this School. The Internet can provide you names of art galleries in your city. You can be specific and search for galleries under Old Masters, Impressionist Art, or Hudson River School Art. Then go to the gallery's Web site and take a virtual tour of their inventory. Of course, a personal walking tour of the galleries in your city is better and possibly a profitable way to spend a Saturday afternoon.

Once inside a gallery, continue discovering, as if in a private museum specializing in your favorite art. There you'll have a chance to meet the gallery director personally. After your second visit, you'll be greeted by your first name, probably offered a cup of coffee, even taken to a private viewing room. Think you'd get that kind of respect in the Metropolitan Museum of Art?

GALLERY AS MENTOR

Galleries are excellent sources for learning. A gallery director and his staff should be experts in the art they represent. The director of a gallery established for many years knows most, if not all of the artists in the School it represents. The owners or directors of some reputable galleries qualify as art experts, and can reliably authenticate works of art. Rarely can they afford to make mistakes. It's their business and reputation not to. A gallery will see hundreds of paintings a year in a specialized School, acquiring many of them, so the staff knows well what is bought and offered for sale.

If you buy a painting from a "reputable" distinguished gallery, its authenticity, which should be your first concern, is almost certain. This does not, however, relieve you of your responsibility under due diligence. (See Chapter 8, "Provenance, Due Diligence, Forgery, *Catalogues Raisonnés*.") A reputable art gallery will *always* guarantee a painting's authorship in writing; if they won't, don't buy that work. Something is wrong. There's hardly an acceptable answer for why a gallery won't guarantee in writing a painting's authorship. Better galleries even guarantee to buy back a painting if you tire of it or want to buy another painting.

Whether you're a prospective collector, investor, or dealer, once you know your budget (see Chapter 4, "Investing in Art"), be up-front with the gallery. Let them know your price range. In certain cases, a gallery may let you buy a work over a period of time, often without interest charges. Also, let them know that you're interested in learning about art in general, and specifically in the art the gallery represents. Ask questions about price, value, condition, artist rankings within a School, and which artists to invest in. Inquire about how to build or round out a collection; and which artist's work is likely to appreciate most rapidly. If the gallery perceives you as being sincere, and a potential customer, usually the director will be glad to share knowledge with you. Remember, you want to learn from dealers and experts who know what they're talking about. A well-established reputable gallery is a good place to start.

AVOID BEING RUSHED

Don't rush or allow yourself to be rushed. Take your time when conducting business. A reputable gallery will always afford you enough time to buy a work of art under non-stressful conditions. Be wary of the gallery that gives you a full-court press, trying to force a painting on you. It is not adhering to ethical practices.

PLACE A HOLD ON A PAINTING

Place a hold on a painting whenever you think you *might* want to buy it but need time to do research. You should always verify the price the gallery is asking. Unless you know the artist's work well and what he sells for at auction, ask the gallery to place a 48-hour hold on the painting. Most galleries will accommodate you, so the painting will be waiting for your return.

Even though you're considering buying a painting from a reputable gallery, you still have to research the artist's auction records and confirm the price. Unless you know the gallery director like a brother, you can't take anything for granted. Appropriate diligence is every buyer's responsibility. Don't hesitate to make a counter offer if you want to buy the painting, but think it's over priced.

EXPANDING YOUR KNOWLEDGE:

If you decide to collect and invest in Hudson River School paintings, as an example, and you live near New York City, you might want to visit Questroyale Fine Art Gallery at 903 Park Avenue. At Questroyale you'll be able to view the very best Hudson River and Luminescent School paintings available on the market. The friendly gallery staff can provide you catalogues and literature, and even help acquaint you with lesser artists of the Hudson River School. Here you might find a painting you can afford (www.questroyalfineart.gallery.com).

PARIS STREET SCENE PAINTINGS

Paris street scene paintings can be seen by visiting Rehs Galleries at 5 East 57th Street in New York City (www.rehsgalleries.com). Here you'll be able to see Paris street scene paintings by artists such as Eduardo Cortes, Luigi Loir, and Antoine Blanchard, and other fine investment quality art by European and American artists. Owner, Howard Rehs, writes a very instructive, free online newsletter about the art market. Visit Rehs' Web site, and its gallery when in New York City.

BELLE EPOCH AND BARBIZON PAINTINGS

Belle Epoch and Barbizon paintings can be examined by visiting, for example, Schiller & Bondo European Paintings at 19 East 74th Street in New York City (www.schillerandbondo.com).

OTHER FINE ART GALLERIES

Obviously, not all fine art is sold only in New York City. Other fine art galleries are located throughout the United States. In Dallas, W. J. Morrill Ltd., sells British, American, and European investment art (www.wjmorrill.com). In Boston, Vose Galleries sells only American art (www.vosegalleries.com). Also in Boston, Childs Gallery sells investment quality European and American paintings, including a wonderful selection of Woodstock, New York, artists (www.childsgallery.com). In Florida, The St. Augustine Gallery sells American and European paintings (www.staugustinegallery.com.) In California, Garzoli Gallery sells investment quality American art (www.garzoligallery.com). In Washington, D.C., Guarisco Gallery has fine academic and Impressionist paintings (www.guariscogallery.com). In Pennsylvania, Gratz Gallery sells investment quality art from the Brandywine and New Hope Schools (www.gratzgallery.com). The list of fine art galleries that are reputable is seemingly endless. Find one near you that specializes in the art you want to collect.

Should you ever have a question or doubt about the legitimacy of a certain gallery, contact a senior associate at The Art Dealers Association of America in New York City at 212-940-8590 (www.artdealers.org).

THE DOWNSIDE OF WORKING WITH A GALLERY

Price is always an important consideration, and it's the major downside in working with a gallery. You'll pay, in one way or another, for those "guaranteed" works of art. Ultimately you may pay for all the mentoring and free information, the free coffee, and the private viewing room. Buying art from a retail gallery can cost you as much as 30 to 100 percent more than buying art from a private dealer. The upside is peace of mind and assurance that you're buying authentic artworks. You also have access to "fresh" examples, expert knowledge, and a chance to return a painting for another, generally more expensive one, should you tire of the first. But these services are not free.

TEA SESSION ART WITH A MENTOR

If you form an Art Investment Club, as described in Chapter 4, consider inviting an art dealer to your weekly tea sessions. In this way your learning experience will be deeper and your knowledge can grow exponentially.

Case Example: Tea Session Art

Many years ago this author met weekly with a friend and his wife in their living room to discuss art. In an informal setting over tea, we discussed our latest acquisitions, which in those days were rather minor examples. But we thoroughly examined the three or four paintings we brought weekly, week in and week out, for several years.

Meeting on Saturday mornings at 10 a.m., our sessions usually lasted an hour or two at the most. After some time we learned how to look at art with a critical eye. We examined all aspects of a painting: front, back, and frame, from subject to signature. We began to get a "sense," and a "feeling" for notable art, then better art. We also learned how to bargain and ask key questions: "How much you pay for that?" "Do you want to sell it?"

"Where'd you find that?" "What do you have to get for it?" We would study indistinct signatures with a magnifying glass, debating whether the artist's name started with an "E" or an "F," or possibly a "P."

In this way we began to buy paintings from each other, sharing information, and educating each other and ourselves about art. Those Saturday morning tea sessions were invaluable learning opportunities.

READING THE TRADE PAPERS

In order to be serious about collecting, investing, or dealing in art, you must study trade papers and art magazines. Reading about art and antiques will increase your knowledge of fine art and get you thinking about how to make money in art. It's essential to keep abreast of who's buying what, for how much, and who the sellers are. You need to learn which auction rooms are best for you regarding purchases and consignments, and where to find the occasional sleeper.

Trade papers and magazines are packed with advertisements of people wanting to buy and sell art. You'll need to know who they are.

If there is homework that must be done to successfully deal in art, it's reading one or both of the trade papers listed below. Also, certain art magazines are considered essential reading.

TRADE PAPERS

You'll find dealers in a trade paper who specialize in the art you collect. If you're looking for a particular artist or painting to round out your collection, you should routinely search the trade papers.

For the art dealer, reading the trade papers is absolutely essential. A savvy art dealer will conduct business right out of a trade paper. Some dealers add as much as $100,000 a year to their income by mining the gold hidden in art trade papers.

Two significant art and antique trade papers on the East Coast of America are: *Maine Antique Digest,* published monthly and costs $43 for 12 issues (call toll-free 877-237-6623 (www.maineantiquedigest.com); the other important trade paper is *ANTIQUES And The Arts Weekly* (also known as the "Newtown Bee"), published weekly, and costs $67 for 52 issues. Call 203-426-3141 (www.newtownbee.com).

These trade papers cover more than just obituaries and new gallery openings. They're filled with industry news, relevant articles, and selected regional auction results. Each issue contains hundreds of advertisements of paintings for sale and artworks wanted. Attorneys often advertise important estate sales in these trade papers. The jewel of all art news is, of course, "auction announcements." These trade papers will inform you of when and where valuable paintings are being auctioned. See Chapter 9, "Buying Art," for ways to mine gold in trade papers. *The Maine Antique Digest* is a gigantic rag paper and will take most of the month to read. It retails for $3.75 per issue; you can buy it at most chain bookstores, such as Books-A-Million, Borders, and Barnes & Noble.

FOREIGN TRADE PAPERS

Art dealers sometimes need to advertise in British trade papers to attract the largest audience of buyers for an English painting. An excellent British trade paper in which to advertise is *Antique Trade Gazette,* with representatives in New York. Telephone 845-266-4980, (www.antiquetradegazette.com). For the collector or dealer who has a French painting to buy or sell, the best French trade paper is the *Gazette Hotel Drout,* telephone 33.1.48.00.20.80, gazette@gazette-drout.com. To auction in Paris, you'll want to consign your work to *Drout,* at www.drout.com; telephone 33.1.48.00.20.20.

AMERICAN ART REVIEW

The *American Art Review* magazine is recommended reading. It's published bi-monthly, and costs $23.50 for six issues, or $5.95 per issue in bookstores. You can subscribe to *American Art Review* at www.amartrev.com, or telephone 760-738-1178.

American Art Review is coffee-table art at its best. Each issue contains more than one hundred high-quality pictures of American paintings. But it also offers in-depth articles on different Schools of American art. These featured articles provide a cultural, historical, and political context for each School of art. Discussions are supported by high quality pictures and artists' biographies. Studying these pictures and reading the articles on various American Schools of art are indispensable ways to learn both.

Treat yourself to 12 back-issues of the *American Art Review* (last two years). If you have formed an art club (see Chapter 4), hand out several issues to each member so they can study them. If you remember the details of only one School of art from each issue, and only five artists' names from each School, by the end of one year, you will have acquired a substantial knowledge base in American art. After reading all your issues, exchange them within your group to continue learning about American art.

ART MAGAZINES WORTH READING

Reading fine art magazines is an excellent way to stay on top of industry news and art events. The following magazines are excellent choices:

- *Art & Antiques* magazine
  www.artandantiques.net
- *Art & Auction* magazine
  www.artandauction.com
- *Antiques & Fine Art* magazine
  www.antiquesandfineart.com

- *Artnews* magazine
  www.artnewsonline.com
- *Antiques* magazine
  www.themagazineantiques.com
- *Art+Auction* magazine
  www.artandauction.com

These excellent art magazines also are available for sale at major bookstore chains, such as Borders, Books-a-Million, Barnes & Noble.

AUCTION CATALOGUES

Auction Catalogues are more than just impressive coffee-table art books. They're an invaluable source for price information and photoarchival reference, and a crucial learning tool for advancing your art education.

Auction catalogues at Christie's and Sotheby's now cost between $30 and $40. (Certain "old" and "rare" art bookstores have excellent non-current copies at much cheaper prices. Also, monographs and auction catalogues can be purchased at flea markets and online.) Of course, if you have a painting up for sale at Christie's or Sotheby's, you're entitled to a free catalogue. Although possibly costly, for $30 you get approximately 250 high quality photographs of important American or European paintings which collectors and investors are currently buying and selling. That's exactly what **you need to know: what collectors and investors are buying and selling today.**

You can establish your buying goals and quality standards based on the representations found in auction catalogues. What's more, Christie's and Sotheby's also give you a free estimate of 250 paintings. Now, *there* is a valuable service, especially since it's free. Finally, you get a color picture of the artist's work. So when you have an opportunity to buy a painting by the same artists, open your catalogue and compare pictures. Be aware that these color reproductions are usually, but not always very accurate. If the quality in the painting you want to buy matches the quality in the picture in Christie's catalogue, you've got a green light to buy it, providing the price and condition are right. Every painting represented in Christie's and Sotheby's catalogues is "authenticated" and "guaranteed," unless otherwise stated. (See "Explanation of Cataloguing Practice," at the back of each catalogue.)

> You want to buy paintings other collectors and investors are buying and selling, thereby assuring you a market when you decide to sell your painting.

Christie's and Sotheby's major sales are in April and October. Choose the American or European sale that represents the art you want to collect, and buy that catalogue. (For Christie's, call 212-703-8080; Sotheby's, call 212-606-7350.) Better than ordering the catalog, *attend the auction.* Be part of the excitement!

TEST YOUR APPRAISAL KNOWLEDGE

Have someone put tape over the price estimates in your catalogue so you can't see the printed estimates. Then research several paintings. Now try to come up with your own price estimate. The catalogue will give you all the information you'll need in order to estimate a painting's value: subject, size, medium, support, attribution, signature, date, condition, and a color photograph of the painting. It will also give you the provenance history. After you have read Chapters 6 and 7, "Research and Appraisal," you should be able to estimate a painting's value, and no doubt come close to what the experts say. Always try to test your knowledge.

SPOT A TREND

Compare actual hammer-prices with pre-sale estimates to determine if an up or down trend is developing in the art market. After an auction, ask for "auction results" which will be faxed or mailed to you. If you attend the auction, as the sale progresses write the actual hammer price next to the estimate printed in the catalogue. If the painting passed, and did not sell, so note it. If an estimate for an oil painting by, for example, John Jameson (1842 – 1864) is $30,000 to $50,000, and it sells for $210,000 (Phillips de Pury & Luxembourg, New York, May 2002), you have to question *why.* Did the auction room make a mistake in its estimate by 80 percent, or is Jameson's work suddenly in demand and taking off? The latter is more likely the case. (Be alerted by such extreme variances, though. Occasionally, negative factors not publicly known are involved. Therefore, contact one or two foremost non-commercial experts on that particular artist and his work to gain critical information.) Investigate significant variances between auction room estimates and actual hammer prices. If you can figure out the trend, you can stay ahead of the curve; and you will find profit at the end of your rainbow. (See Chapter 9 for a discussion on *Back Room Deals* and *Negotiating After the Auction is Over.)*

BUILD AN ARTIST FILE

Build a file for the artist you're interested in. Cut out and save articles and pictures from magazines and trade papers that highlight your favorite artist. One dealer did this for the painter William M. Hart (1823 – 1894) as a way of learning when he was new in the art business. For many years the dealer collected pictures of Hart's paintings and information about Hart's life, including the years he traveled abroad and the years he painted in various locations throughout the United States. Today this dealer is a recognized expert on William M. Hart.

BECOME A RECOGNIZED EXPERT

With commitment and dedication, turn your passion for art into a quest for knowledge. Become a recognized expert—become a *connoisseur.*

4

Investing In Art

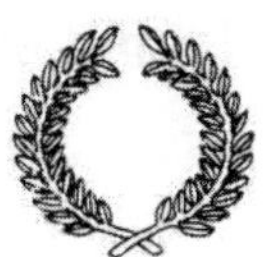

If you want to become the "millionaire next door," you'll have to invest in appreciating assets such as art, not in consumer products.

It's interesting but not surprising, that Thomas Stanley and William Danko in their highly acclaimed book, *The Millionaire Next Door,* identify "Auctioneers" as Prodigious Accumulators of Wealth (PAWs), as opposed to UAWs (Under Accumulators of Wealth). UAWs are people who *look* prosperous, but despite expensive suits, fancy cars, and flashy jewelry, UAWs usually are low net-worth people. They're big consumers, not wise investors.

When Stanley and Danko studied millionaire-occupations, "auctioneers and appraisers" were consistently at the top of the PAW list. In fact, when all auctioneers were surveyed, more than 35 percent of them were found to be millionaires.

> *Auctioneers hold a higher proportion of their wealth in appreciating assets than do other high-income producers, and they invest in categories in which they have expertise.*
>
> **—Stanley and Danko**, *The Millionaire Next Door*

ART IS A SOUND INVESTMENT.

Since auctioneers hold a higher proportion of their wealth in appreciating assets (art and antiques), and invest in what they have expertise in (art and antiques), we can assume that art and antiques are sound investments because auctioneers disproportionately are more likely to become millionaires. The key word in this assumption is having *expertise* in what you invest in.

ART vs. OTHER INVESTMENT STRATEGIES

Before we consider art as an investment strategy, let's first look at other asset investments such as stocks and real estate to see how they perform over the long run.

STOCKS

The majority of American investors place their hope in the stock market to stay ahead of inflation and have their money grow. How successful have Americans been over the last 80 years investing in stocks?

80 Years Of Stock Market Results	
YEAR	**ROI**
1928 – 1929	17.7%
1930 – 1939	5.3%
1940 – 1949	10.3%
1950 – 1959	20.8%
1960 – 1969	8.7%
1970 – 1979	7.5%
1980 – 1989	18.2%
1990 – 1999	13.3%
S&P 80 Year Average	13.4%

A 13.4% return on investment over 80 years is not very impressive. In only three out of eight decades did returns exceed the S&P average.

The stock market remains a risky business. You have little control over your investment in the stock market, other than to leave the money in or pull it out. And which mortal knows when to do that?

Illustrating how risky the stock market can be, the Dow Jones Average fell 1,200 points in just 30 days in the summer of 2002. That means 12.5 percent of America's investment in Wall Street was obliterated in 30 days. Expunged! Billions of dollars were lost; people's dreams of financial security and early retirement were over in a flash. Gone! 2001 through 2003 were not beneficial years for investing in the stock market as hundreds of thousands of people lost their life's savings.

No one knows when the stock market will plummet or crash. But with wise art investments, the road is never so bumpy. What's more, art can offer a higher potential return on investment than the stock market.

REAL ESTATE

Real estate can be a sound and conservative investment compared to the stock market. However, it's much slower to appreciate than art. Historically, real estate has appreciated at only 6.5%, and gold at only 4.4%. Nevertheless, many people have bought homes, fixed them up, and sold them for a profit. The rental market can be profitable too, but it can be labor intensive. A "fixer-upper" is not for the average investor, certainly better suited for the handyman with a heavy toolbox and a pickup truck. Just try to gut-out a house, upgrade the electric and plumbing, install a new heating system, and put on a new roof, not to mention find reliable tenants. Of course, forget weekends, because that's when you mow the lawn, fix faucets, and knock on doors to collect rent.

ART IS A TANGIBLE ASSET

Investing in art is hands-on and occurs in present time. It's not like investing in stocks and bonds or pork-belly futures where you own paper certificates. As an investment, the art trail leads right to your living room wall. It's visible and tangible, there to be seen and enjoyed. With art, your investment isn't hidden in a wall-safe behind a painting. Your investment *is* the painting! Art is also transportable, redeemable, and a bearer instrument. It can be lent to a museum, carried to your summer home, or used as collateral against a loan.

Compared to real estate, investing in art is clean and simple. You can buy an investment-grade painting for, say $10,000, and hang it on your dining room wall where it becomes dinner conversation for the next 10 years. Then, whenever you're ready to retire, take the painting off your wall and sell it for $50,000. And you make this incredible profit legally, without stress, sleepless nights, or stock market hiccups.

> Regardless of which party is in power, what the tax rates are, or how many CEOs are sent to prison for cooking the books, your investment in art will always be safe and profitable.

HOW MUCH PROFIT CAN YOU MAKE IN ART?

You can make more money investing in art than in almost any other investment. While no two art transactions are exactly alike, and each painting has its own profit margin, similarities do occur in putting together art sales. Let's look at the results of three art deals that out-performed the stock market. The dealer who put these art sales together (we'll call him John Painter) bought and sold three paintings in six months, and made 750% profit on his investments.

1			
Painting	**A**	**B**	**C**
Artist	**Jules Rozier**	**Louis de Schryver**	**M. de Vlaminck**
Buy	$2,000	$7,000	**$75,000**
Sell	$6,000	$31,000	**$115,000**
Profit	$4,000	$24,000	**$40,000**
% Profit	200%	340%	**53%** ∞
The profit from three paintings is: $4,000 + $24,00 + $40,000 = $68,000 ÷ $9,000 = 750 % Profit. (Painting C, by Maurice De Vlaminck, was **bought with no money**. See Appendix 1, "Making the Art Deal," for details on this sale.)			

As in real estate, John knew that **you make your money when you buy,** not when you sell. Once you purchase a valuable painting, other than cleaning or restoration, only time can improve your investment. You can't improve a painting's appearance, increase its square inches, give it a new facelift, or even a fresh paint job . . . well now, that will never do!

So John was patient and bought wisely, achieving success with these three paintings. Certainly 750% profit beats a 13.4% profit, which is what the stock market averaged over 80 years.

The above examples, however, are not always typical. After all, not every day can one buy a $75,000 painting with *no money down,* and then sell it two weeks later for a $40,000 profit. However, such an occasion can and does happen, and you will see how John structured this art sale when you read Appendix 1, "Making The Art Deal."

EXPECT 25% RETURN ON YOUR ART IVESTMENT

Many art transactions are structured where you sell a painting before you buy it; this is not uncommon. In fact, one of your buying strategies requires asking yourself before you buy a painting, "How much can I sell this painting for, and to whom?" (See Chapter 10, "Selling Art.") Know this information and have a sense of what the ROI will be *before* you buy a painting. If intuition tells you the ROI will be less than 25%, consider passing it up. A 25% ROI should be your goal after factoring in the cost of sales and transaction costs. In time, this will not be difficult to achieve, and with experience your ROI estimates will become amazingly accurate.

On the other hand, when you invest in stocks, you have absolutely no control over a company's ROI. In fact, you have no clue as to what the ROI will be. You're entirely dependent upon the stock market, the nation's economy, the CEO, and his management team: the operations director, purchasing manager, the sales and marketing departments. It's too easy for these variables to let you down. With art, however, you have maximum control at minimum risk.

ART VALUES INCREASE OVER YEARS

Ian Jackman, in his book, *Artist's Mentor*, reports that Mark Rothko kept records of how many paintings he sold each year and for how much:

- 1957: 17 paintings; average price $1,700
- 1958: 13 paintings; average price $2,400
- 1959: 17 paintings; average price $5,400
- 1960: 11 paintings; average price $7,500
- 1961: 8 paintings; average price $12,000
- 1962: 7 paintings; average price $18,000

In 2003—some 40 years later, Rothko's "No.9" (White and Black on Wine) sold for $16,359,500. Not bad for a Modernist. In 1913, Ralph Albert Blakelock's "Moonlight" sold for $13,900, the most ever paid for a painting by a living American artist, reports Questroyal Fine Art, in its Fall 2004 Volume: "Important American Paintings." Today, Blakelock's high record is $3,525,750. The record for a work by an American-born painter is $27,502,400 for George Bellow's *Polo Crowd* in 1999. And the prices keep going up. (Note: Ralph Blakelock was committed to an asylum in 1899, and like his contemporary, Vincent van Gough, he was most forceful and prolific during his years of confinement.)

ART INVESTMENT FUND

A group of Southwest investors is starting an Art Investment Fund that will act and perform like any other mutual fund. Soon people will have the opportunity to own shares in art instead of investing in pharmaceutical companies or pork-belly futures. I recently talked with the director of the fund, and we agreed that the ROI from art can and should be 30%. This would be extraordinarily high compared to ordinary mutual funds. Of course, there will be management fees and administrative costs, but 30% ROI is extremely attractive, and possible with art. Even higher returns are available to the private dealer.

PRICE AVERAGING

The success of a mutual fund is based on the average performance of the companies in the fund. For example, 10% of the companies in a portfolio might actually lose money, 30% might break even, and only 60% show varying degrees of profit. The companies that lose money and the companies that break even greatly weigh down the profit-average of the overall fund. Still, the director of the art fund believes his fund will return 30% profit. This is because his fund will only select artworks that are winners, avoiding mediocre paintings—and so must you. Even with art, if you have to "average," the ROI might be only modest. The Hudson River School, for example, which in recent years has risen sharply in value, when measured as a "School" only averaged about 15 percent ROI. It's true this School out-performed the stock market. Still, 15% ROI is nothing spectacular. But "price averaging" won't affect you, because you're not going to buy *every* Hudson River School painting offered at auction. You're looking to **buy only one painting** in a season—perhaps in a year, and you're going to wait until you're offered, or find, a painting that will give you an uncommonly high profit, maybe even spectacular results.

BUY ONLY DISTINGUISHED ART

Do not buy decorative or collectible art and hope it will enrich your portfolio. It won't. Don't waste years holding on to a decorative piece expecting it will one day grow into investment art. It won't. **Start with investment art.** Be patient: (1) make sure equity is in the painting before you buy it (buy below market value), and (2) make sure the market for the artist's work is strong enough to *pull* the painting into higher price ranges. Remember, the goal of this book is to ensure that 100% of your profits come from 100% of your art transactions. In other words, there should be no disappointments among the paintings you buy. Make money on every art transaction, from every painting you buy.

Unless you buy a collection of paintings, you will not be dealing with "averages." Even a collection of art, however, should produce handsome profits. When buying a group of paintings, consider offering a group price that is at or below what you expect just one, or possibly two of the better paintings would fetch at auction. Let that one painting pay for the collection; all the others will be profit.

However, if you buy a group of paintings and wind up with a decorative piece, sell it quickly, as profitably as possible. Don't fool yourself thinking you can raise the level of quality of decorative art by keeping it. You can't. Admit a buying experiment went wrong. Better invest your money in investment art that always has a high growth potential.

BUILDING A RETIREMENT FUND WITH ART

Art dealers turn over paintings for a quick profit. However, a wise dealer will **hold onto one worthy painting a year as a long-term investment** for his own retirement. If you're a new investor, consider buying a $5,000 painting by a well-listed but under-appreciated artist every year to ensure financial comfort in old age.

Instead of putting $5,000 a year, for example, into a 401(k) retirement plan, buy art as described above every year, hanging it on your living room wall. Enjoy it. After 10 years the painting should be worth $25,000, perhaps more. That's 20% profit per year for 10 years, which is 400% return on investment. That is achievable. Then, whenever you're ready to stop working, retire a $25,000 painting each year to augment your social security pension. Here's how it will look:

Art Portfolio Retirement Plan				
YR R1	YR R2	YR R3	YR R4	YR R5
$25,000	$25,000	$25,000	$25,000	$25,000
YR R6	YR R7	YR R8	YR R9	YR 10
$25,000	$25,000	$25,000	$25,000	$25,000

Total invested over10 years: $50,000. Total return: $250,000. Return on investment: 400%. (R1 is the first year of retirement.)

HOW MUCH TIME WILL YOU NEED TO INVEST IN ART?

The answer is five to seven years. However, the longer you hold onto an appreciating asset, the greater will be your return on investment.

- **The collector**, who has no timeframe in mind for selling a work of art, and might keep a painting indefinitely, stands to realize the biggest profit gain. By example, John Whitney's painting "*Garcon la Pipe,*" by Picasso, bought in 1950 for $30,000, sold in 2004 for $104 million.

- **The investor**, on the other hand, definitely has a timeframe in mind for selling a painting, usually five to seven years. Five to seven years is sufficient time for an economic cycle to recover and peak again, providing ample opportunity to resell a painting at maximum profit, even one that was previously bought at auction. A painting purchased at auction is considered again "fresh" to the market after five years. Without a fresh painting to offer the market, you may well have difficulty achieving a high ROI from a work that was auctioned only recently. Remember your unfresh painting will be viewed internationally since major auction sales are posted on the Internet for the world to see. Anyone considering buying your painting would, in the course of doing research and due diligence, see exactly how much you paid for the work at auction. Forearmed with this knowledge, the buyer would gain bargaining power, while you would lose the benefit of having the purchase price kept secret. An investor can, of course, sell a painting at any time, even after only one year, naturally realizing a smaller profit.

- **The dealer** is not limited by time. Generally speaking, a dealer will sell a painting for the best price at the earliest opportunity. Since he constantly works his strategy, including a lead-generation program, he *always* has potential buyers in mind for an artwork. In fact, the wise dealer thinks about future buyers before he buys a painting. The collector and investor, on the other hand, can have many years to enjoy an artwork before thinking about a potential buyer.

HOW LONG SHOULD YOU LEAVE YOUR MONEY IN AN INVESTMENT?

Consider how long to leave your money in an art investment in order to double it. At 10%, money doubles every 7.5 years, but with art we're looking for a higher return than that. At 20%, for example, an easy way to calculate how long it will take to double your money is to divide the ROI (20%) into the number 72. Hence, 72 ÷ 20 = 3.6 years. A 25 % ROI would be 72 ÷ 25 = 2.9 years. It works with any number. Just divide the ROI percentage into the number 72, and you'll see how many years it takes to double your money.

If you don't have enough time to double your money, perhaps you shouldn't be in that investment. For example, if you're heavy in stocks and intend to retire in, say three years, you might not even be able to recoup a loss if the stock market takes an unexpected dip, much less double your money. Retiring in three years and still heavy in stocks, consider transferring your money into something more predictable. Putting everything into a money market, however, at 1 % may be safe but is not a profitable strategy either. Understand how to buy art, putting 10 or 20 percent of your money into paintings, say up to $50,000, would be a safe and wiser investment, providing you know how to buy art. (See Chapter 9, "Buying Art.")

GETTING STARTED

The successful art dealer is buying paintings all the time, which means he needs to be spending money every week. Investors and collectors have the luxury of being able to take their time buying art.

HOW MUCH MONEY WILL YOU NEED?

How much starting money you will need, depends upon your investment strategy and motivation—and how much you have set aside or can raise to buy art.

At whatever entry level you begin, consider starting with at least $2,500 or $3,500, better yet $5,000, $10,000, or more. If you're willing to put $10,000 into an art investment, clearly you have to be an experienced art buyer. Most likely, you have been buying and selling art long enough to have made successful art transactions at the $5,000 level. Buying art is not about hoping or wishing you'll get lucky. If you don't have expertise and knowledge investing in art, don't gamble. Buying art is risk taking, but doesn't have to be reckless, only calculated. Do your research carefully. Then plan a deliberate buying schedule.

Art Buying Schedule		
Buyer	**Example Buying Schedule**	**5-Year Plan**
Dealers	One painting every month	60 works
Collectors	One painting every 6 months	10 works
Investors	One painting each year	5 works

No set schedule for buying art is necessary. Regard the above as a comfortable schedule for each category of buyer. The dealer works full time, so buying one painting a month isn't hectic for him; nor is buying one painting every six months too much for the collector, or one painting every year for the investor.

Finding the right painting to buy takes time. Explore the Internet, auction rooms, art magazines, and trade papers. Talk with dealers and visit galleries, shows, and antique stores while at the same time developing your stable of pickers and knockers. Don't become impatient. Avoid settling for mediocre art. Wait for the choice painting. Stay focused; then act decisively. Have your money ready or know how to raise it.

FINDING YOUR POOL OF MONEY

Some dealers have $100,000 stashed away in a mayonnaise jar just waiting for the right painting. Others don't have $500 in cash; sadly they have to walk away from opportunities because they don't have available money, and don't know how to raise it.

But certain doctors, lawyers, and teachers have money to invest. A doctor who knows that you have had successful experience buying and selling art, might find your investment idea appealing. If there's a worthy painting available for purchase, but you don't have the money to buy it, **don't walk away from it.** *Make a deal. Don't be shy.*

Meet with your doctor friend and suggest, "I have an opportunity to buy an excellent painting by Emile Gruppe (1896 – 1978) for $5,000. It's a full-size painting. The subject is Gloucester Harbor fishing boats. It's in excellent condition, and from the right period, dated 1958. I believe it's a steal. However, I don't have the money to buy it myself, or I would. Would you like to be a partner with me on this painting? You put up the money, and I'll do all the marketing, advertising, and selling. I already have three buyers in mind. It should sell for $10,000. We'll split the profit, $2,500 each. You'll have your money back in less than 90 days and that's a 50% return on investment. What are your thoughts?" Chances are you'll get your $5,000. When you do, live up to your word. Do a splendid job.

After two or three successful $5,000 sales with the doctor, he'll soon trust you buying a $25,000 painting with his money. He may well recommend you to others. Your ultimate goal is, however, *financial independence* like the "millionaire next door." So be sure to save your money, and keep one distinguished painting each year for your own retirement.

FORMING AN ART INVESTMENT CLUB

In forming an Art Investment Club, you and a friend each invest, say $6,000 (or four friends invest $3,000 each); here's how to profitably invest $12,000 in art. The example below assumes you will sell paintings every year for about 50% profit (not average paintings), and invest profits into the next year's buying schedule, year after year for five years.

Aggressive Buying Schedule					
YR 1	YR 2	YR 3	YR 4	YR 5	Distribute
$12,000	$18,000	$27,000	$40,000	$60,000	$90,000
Buy 2 $6,000 Works	Buy 3 $6,000 Works	Buy 3 $9,000 Works	Buy 4 $10,000 Works	Buy 3 $20,000 Works	Distribute Club Profits

Achieving the above results does demand significant experience in addition to sophisticated art-buying skills, to be learned in Chapter 9, "Buying Art."

Buying art aggressively, however, requires more than hard work: to be able to walk by mediocre paintings in search of more profitable ones takes discipline, time, and patience. Remember, however, the purpose of forming an art investment club is not only to make money, but also to learn and to have fun. A group of friends going together can enjoy the process of researching auctions, galleries, and museums, then during dinner discuss values and decide which painting to buy. Club members can join in choosing which paintings to hang in their homes, sharing artworks by rotating them over the investment period.

WHICH ART TO BUY?

Buying criteria are the same for all paintings and Schools of art, as shown below:

Buy:

1. examples of outstanding not mediocre quality (anyone can get average ones). It is better to buy the best quality of second-tier artists than poor quality of first-tier artists.
2. artworks with equity in them (buy below market price).
3. paintings only by well-listed artists (who sell consistently well at auction).
4. works by artists who exhibited during their lifetime, for example, at the Royal Academy in

London, at the Salon in Paris, or the National Academy of Design in New York.

5. paintings by artists who were prolific, painting hundreds, even thousands of works during their lifetime.
6. works by artists who started, or belonged to a recognized School or movement, who painted contemporaneously with the founders of the movement, or at least participated early in the School.
7. examples with sound commercial prospects.
8. paintings by artists whose School of art remains highly collected and in demand, e.g. Hudson River School, Brandywine School, California Impressionism.
9. artworks representative of an artist's *oeuvre*, his central theme paintings: Thomas Moran's Grand Canyon scenes, not his Venice or India pictures.
10. works with excellent physical and artistic characteristics:

    - High quality workmanship.
    - Pleasing subjects that other people buy, sell, and collect.
    - Condition that is very good to excellent
    - Full size, 24" X 36" (big is better than small, generally).
    - Framed appropriately in a Period frame, preferably handmade, hopefully signed by the frame maker.

Omission of two or more of the above elements might cause serious concern, perhaps even reason not to buy a particular painting. The more you come to fulfilling the buying criteria, the stronger are your chances of buying worthy investment art.

WHERE TO START LOOKING

In Chapter 3, "Becoming a Connoisseur," explore how to identify your specialty—what School of art to collect, and possibly invest in. It will be the School, style, period, theme, subject, or artist that interests you most, strikes the imagination, and pleases your eye. It can run the gamut, varying from 17th century Dutch paintings to early 20th century California Impressionism. Whatever School, Period, or style of art you choose as a specialty, in your search for the best painting, you'll come across many other works that offer opportunities to make a profit. Decide whether you can afford to walk away from a quick profit, say of $5,000 or more. If not, become an ad hoc dealer for this one painting; buy it, sell it, take the profit, and continue looking for your prize painting.

FINDING AN ART ADVISOR

Consider seeking the advice of an expert, someone to guide you on the acquisition of a major art purchase. But where do you find an art advisor? "Ask Around. Inquire at museums, galleries, and auction houses; ask collectors, professors, and associations for names of advisors," suggests Margaret Littman (*Art & Antiques Magazine,* March 2003.)

HAVE A GOAL

Know what you're looking for. Are you interested in art as a collector or an investor? Know what kind of art you want to collect, and what your budget is. Do research and know the basics about the School or period of art you want to collect. Knowing what makes a work of art or artist valuable will help to make more meaningful conversations with advisors.

EVALUATE EXPERIENCE

Having a Yale Art History degree and speaking three foreign languages, though they can be helpful, don't necessarily qualify an advisor to be *your* advisor. He must also have operational knowledge and street experience. He must know the trade from the inside, and have a pulse on market opportunities such as when a collector plans to retire an important work of art, or the de-accessioning of an entire collection. Your advisor must also be able to negotiate favorable terms and conditions, including guarantees. He must be able to research a provenance, ensuring that the title and ownership of a work of art will pass free and clear of all encumbrances to you upon full payment for the painting. Ask questions.

COMPATIBILITY

You must be able to relate and communicate with your advisor, having energy and enthusiasm in common.

INTEGRITY

Integrity is most important. Check around and get references. Make sure your advisor is respected in his industry and held in high regard by his peers. Decide if you want to pay a retainer fee, percentage of sales, or an hourly rate, making your contract in writing.

DUE DILIGENCE

Notwithstanding your selection of an advisor, pursue your own due diligence. Read this book in its entirety, and proceed cautiously, but with curiosity and excitement. Where *is* your prize painting?

WHERE TO FIND AN ART ADVISOR

For more information on finding an art advisor, consider the following sources:

Am. Society of Appraisers
555 Herndon Pkwy. #125
Herndon, VA 20170
703-478-2228
www.appraisers.org

Appraisers Assoc. of America
386 Park Avenue, # 2000
New York, NY 10016
212-889-5404
www.appraiserssoc.org

Architectural Arts Co.
6410 Dykes Way
Dallas, TX 75230
972-392-2121

Corporate Art Consultants
200 E. 33Rd St.
NY, NY 10016
212-683-5611

Chubb Collectors Services
55 Water Street
NY, NY 10041
877-602-4822
www.chubbcollectors.com

Programs in the Arts
10 Astor Place, Rm. 502-D
New York, NY 10003
212-998-7137
www.scps.nyu.edu

Tactical Considerations

Keep these issues in mind when considering investment-quality art, suggests *The Robb Report* (August 2004):

- The worst time to buy a piece of art is immediately after a highly trumpeted sale, especially of a work in the same category.
- Transaction and holding costs over a 30-year period may run as much as 25 percent of the price we pay for an artwork at auction. [Author believes this to be extremely high.]
- Insurance costs run approximately $1 to $1.50 a year for every $1,000 of market value.
- Seek the counsel of a reputable advisor, preferably someone who will work on a fee basis. Always check references.
- Employ a curator to catalogue acquisitions, and seek occasions to exhibit, buy, and sell.
- [Buy the best quality examples of second-tier artists over poor examples of first-tier artists.]

5

Research and Appraisal: Technical Examination

The technical examination deals with the investigation of forensic data as the first step in the overall process of research and appraisal. The technical examination will help you understand important facts about a painting's history: materials used, techniques employed, and possibly even about the artist himself. Understanding this data can be helpful in determining if a painting is authentic or not.

APPROACH TO EXAMINATION

The basic approach to research and appraisal work is (1) gather relevant information, (2) investigate data, (3) evaluate findings, and (4) reach conclusions based on technical analysis and logical assumptions.

Conducting a technical examination is usually the job of the conservator or conservation scientist. But it also remains the subject every collector and investor must know in order to successfully buy art. Let us glean as much as possible from the technical examination.

TECHNICAL EXAMINATION

Let's assume you have chosen a painting to buy because of its outstanding quality. You are familiar with the artist's work or the School of art. After you make an assessment of the painting's condition, size, and subject, you then must determine if the signature is genuine and the painting authentic. Even if the painting is unsigned, but the quality of work is extremely superior, the painting warrants further investigation. But before you delve into directories and price guides, first conduct a technical examination to gather as much forensic information as possible.

AGE VERIFICATION

Verifying the age of a canvas can help determine if a painting is accurately dated and therefore possibly authentic. If a painting is dated 1749, or is undated but signed by an artist who painted in 1749, or its School was active in 1749, the forensic data must support the conclusion that the painting was executed about 1749 or something is wrong.

For example, tacking margins (canvas border that is wrapped around a stretcher) and the state of the fabric should be consistent with the given date of the painting. This would include the nails, techniques, and materials used in stretching the canvas. The tacking margins on an old canvas tear easily. New canvas is strong and flexible. (See "Strip Lining" below for remedies of weak tacking margins.)

Understanding the different kinds of supports, stretcher systems, grounds, paint properties, and varnish coverings along with knowing when they were invented and used can aid you in determining a painting's age. If the support is canvas, examine carefully the original canvas or linen (not a relining) to determine whether it's hand woven or machine made. If hand woven, you'll spot irregularities in the weave; if machine made, the weave will be precisely regular and the painting therefore dates after 1750. Keep in mind, the best place to start a technical examination is with the support itself.

SUPPORTS

The "support" is the structure or surface on which an artist paints a picture, and it is usually wood or canvas, but can sometimes be paper, cardboard, Masonite, or metal. Let's look at several supports and the preparation process involved in making a support ready for painting.

WOOD PANELS

Artists have painted on wood panels since before the calendar was invented. Wood panels were the preferred support for painting in Europe through the 15th century. They were still being used in the 18th and 19th centuries, and continue to be used today. Panel identification alone, however, cannot verify authorship; but it can help date and place a painting.

The construction method for joining panels was, for example, different in southern Europe where soft woods were used, from northern Europe where hard woods were typically employed. Conservators in different countries also chose different cradling techniques to preserve warped panels, so it is possible to identify an Italian restoration from a Spanish one. If you have a painting apparently signed by a 17th century Dutch artist on a soft wood panel like poplar, but with Italian-style cradling on the back, you have reason for concern: the technical evidence suggests a southern European work and not a Dutch painting.

Even though a wood panel might be centuries old, the painting on it still can be quite new. Transferring a complete painting from one support to another has been done since the 18th century, but it is usually from a panel or canvas to a canvas, rarely from canvas to wood. Under close examination you can see original saw marks in wood panels. A cut made with a hand-held saw looks quite different from a cut made with a mechanized saw whose regularized circular saw marks are clearly not hand-cut.

AMERICAN OILS ON WOOD PANELS

American artists in the 18th century often diagonally scored wood panels to give the surface a textured or twill look. Of course when craquelure occurred, patterns still followed the properties of the wood, but not in fabric or twill.

SIZE

Size is a water-based glue. It's the first application, which seals a panel or canvas. The next layer, gesso, is a chalk-like ground suspended in a glue or oil and applied over the size. The final preparatory layer is "priming," a fine, clay-like inert material, often colored. Grounds that cover the tacking margin can reveal color at the edge of the canvas or panel, which can be compared to known examples of the artist or period. Grounds applied to wood panels were generally thicker than grounds used on flexible canvas. Some Schools of art, mainly naïve or folk art by unschooled artists, didn't know better and rarely used gesso priming or protective varnish at all. These supports are generally susceptible to damage.

GESSO

Gesso is a plaster-like chalky substance used to "hold paint." The support surface is whitewashed with gesso before the artist adds paint. The process of applying gesso varied from country to country in both texture and color, depending upon the period or School of art. These details are best examined by X-radiography. When such findings are added with other forensic information, the conclusions reached are more accurate and definitive.

CANVAS SUPPORTS

Fabric supports have been employed since the 15th Century, the first of these supports were probably tablecloths, napkins, and handkerchiefs; even nautical sails, and later window shades were used. Art supplies took a new turn in the 18th century when fabric was manufactured specifically for oil painting. Linen weave was preferred to cotton, and still is today. After an artist chose a fabric or wood support, it was usually prepared with size, gesso, or priming materials, sometimes all three layers. Then it was ready for easel painting. Until the 18th century, economy and convenience influenced support selection more than anything else. Artists simply painted on whatever surface was available, or on what they could afford at the time. The 19th century saw a greater variety of artistic expression, both in the United States and in Europe. By then, art supplies were manufactured for the masses.

MILLBOARD

Millboard is pressed paper with a rough surface to imitate canvas. First introduced in the early 1800s, millboard is now a generic term that includes academy and canvas board. As the name implies, students used academy boards in art schools, an inexpensive product well suited for quick paint sketches.

Academy board became popular with professional artists in the 1840s. They were compact and easily portable, and many famous artists used them. When railroads expanded the territories, artists looked for lighter more transportable materials as they took to on-site painting in distant places, especially in the 19th century when oil paints in tubes were widely produced. However, academy board tended to twist and warp under heavy layers of paint, and after drying, the paint cracked and flaked easily.

Canvas board was introduced in the 1870s. It consisted of overlapping canvas that was glued to the reverse side for extra support. It became popular with students and professionals alike in the late 19th and early 20th century, and remains in use still today. You can't dismiss a painting as "student work" just because it's painted on canvas board. It could well be a $50,000 painting by a famous artist.

MANUFACTURER'S MARKS

18th and 19th century merchants called "colormen" sold art supplies. Manufacturer's marks were often stamped on the back of canvas boards, sometimes connecting certain artists or Schools with the support. An excellent resource to identify the date of manufactured artist's materials is, *American Artists' Materials, Volume II: A Guide to Stretchers, Panels, Millboards and Stencil Marks*, edited by Peter Hastings Falk.

DAMAGE TO CANVAS SUPPORTS

Fabric supports are affected by moisture and atmospheric conditions. Expansion or contraction of a support can cause the upper layers of paint to start to slide over the undercoating of gesso. Once sliding begins, paint can separate from the support, the whole structure becoming unstable. Deterioration can proceed rapidly. Flaking paint and lifting edges diminish the value of a painting significantly. Sometimes lining is the best remedy for a damaged painting.

LINING CANVAS SUPPORTS

Conservators have been lining canvas supports since the 17th century. Lining is the process of attaching a new canvas to the back of a weak or damaged canvas. When the lined canvas in turn becomes weak or damaged, the liner is removed and the original canvas is then "relined."

17th century linings were affixed to canvas supports with animal pastes and glues. By the 19th century conservators had turned to the use of wax and resins to affix linings to canvas supports, and wax and resins are still used today, including synthetics. Extreme care must be taken when affixing a liner to the back of an original canvas. Most linings are affixed with adhesives under heat and pressure. Excessive heat or pressure applied to the lining of a painting, such as by a flat or steam iron, can *crush* the impasto on the front side and flatten raised edges. This kind of damage permanently devalues a painting.

STRIP LINING

Strip lining is the process of affixing strips of new canvas along the weakened edges of the original canvas. Old canvas can have dry and brittle tacking margins, and the frayed edges can tear and pull away from nail fasteners. Sometimes only strip lining is required to strengthen a canvas and reattach it to the stretcher.

PATCHING

A canvas patch can be used to cover a small cut or puncture hole in a canvas. When very large patches are used to cover, say, five percent or more of the original canvas, sagging can occur from the sheer weight of large patches. Sagging is undesirable. Over time sagging will become visible on the front side of the canvas.

EXCESSIVE LINING

Some conservators reject employing patches and opt for complete lining, which is an invasive and costly procedure. Of course, full lining becomes required when damage is extensive. However, at times when damage is minor, unnecessary lining is often performed, not unlike unnecessary surgery in a hospital. If you have a one-inch cut, why would you line the entire canvas?

STRETCHERS

Stretchers are wood frames on which canvas is stretched, then fastened with nails. Stretchers can frequently offer clues as to the School, period, or even the artist who painted the picture. In past centuries successful artists ordered custom made stretchers, which sometimes bore the logo, stamp, or trademark of the manufacturer. By the 19th century, however, expandable stretchers were widely available. The best stretchers were adjustable and could be “keyed out” to expand unevenly. By tapping wedges (keys) into the corners of a flexible stretcher, one could take up slack caused by seasonable humidity, thereby making the canvas tight again. Directories are available that can help you identify the dates and locations where stretcher manufacturers operated. (See *American Artists' Materials, Volume II,* by Peter Falk.)

STRAINERS

Strainers are fixed wood frames on which canvas is stretched. Artists in the 17th and 18th century unfortunately used these strainers. Important and fragile paintings on such strainers may well require these frames be replaced with adjustable stretchers. But by the 19th century expandable stretchers had been invented, allowing artists even today to prefer stretchers over fixed strainers.

HARDWARE

Nails used in the tacking margins to secure a canvas to the stretcher can reveal important forensic clues. Pre-machine made nails are recognizably distinctive and irregular, therefore possibly traceable to certain periods and locations.

STAPLES

Staples have been available for a long time. Obviously not all paintings stapled to a stretcher were mass-produced on an assembly line in Taiwan. Invented in 1866 by the Novelty Manufacturing Company, staples were first used in bookbinding. But by the early twentieth century, artists could paint on canvases stapled to stretchers. So don't dismiss a painting just because you see staples; you might overlook a $50,000 Californian Impressionist painting.

MASONITE

Masonite, on the other hand, has not been around as long as some people might think. Invented in Laurel, Mississippi, in 1924 by William H. Mason, Masonite was a product of the Great Depression. When money and art supplies were scarce, particularly in the 1920s and

1930s, many artists began painting on Masonite, which served well as a paint support. Remember though, if you buy a painting on Masonite that is dated, for example, 1895, you do have a problem. Masonite wasn't invented then. However, Masonite has served widely as a backup support; many valuable antique paintings on canvas or paper have been laid down and glued to Masonite. It's not uncommon to find an authentic, signed and dated 18th century painting laid down on Masonite manufactured in 1940.

LABELS AND MARKINGS

Canvas, stretchers, and frames, even brushes, palettes, and art supplies will often bear visible manufacturers' marks and stamps. These marks and stamps are important clues to help you identify the School or artist associated with the painting you are researching.

GALLERY LABELS

Feel encouraged when finding an old gallery label attached to the back of your painting, *providing it's original,* and was put there by the gallery whose name the label bears. Beware of the dealer who collects important gallery labels, then affixes one to a painting you are about to buy.

If what you find is a legitimate label, and part of the painting's provenance, then hope it's an old label from one of America's major art galleries, such as Knoedler and Company, Duveen Brothers, Newhouse, Paul Rosenberg, Rosenberg and Stiebel, Wildenstein, and French and Company, or an old label from a major British or European gallery. In London, look for Leonard Koetser, Colnaghi and Company, J. Leger and Son, Marshall Spink, and William M. Sabin and Sons. In Amsterdam, Douwes Brothers and Peter de Boer. In Munich, Julius Boehler. In Florence, Mario Bellini. In Paris, Durand-Ruel and Duveen.

These art galleries are world renowned and have helped shape the art world during the 20th century. Some of the world's most important paintings have been bought, sold, or brokered through galleries, including works by Da Vinci, Raphael, Titian, Rembrandt, Vermeer, and Rubens. Great artworks from every School, including the Impressionist Masters, have been sold through such galleries.

The directors of these galleries are regarded as authorities and experts in their specialties. The prestige and respect given these galleries makes your painting, bearing their labels, most likely the work by the attributed artist. Even if your painting is unsigned and bears a label from a distinguished art gallery, its attribution is secure if the provenance and firm opinions by accepted and renowned experts on the artist accompany the painting. If you like the painting, you've done your research and due diligence, and the price is right, buy it if you can afford it.

PRESERVING HISTORICAL DATA

Every conservator and art collector needs to preserve historical data. Do not erase or destroy historical marks or stamps; take every precaution to preserve writings on the backs of panels, canvases, and stretchers. Artists often signed their names, inscribed the date, location, or title of a painting on the back of a canvas or stretcher. For instance, inscriptions that could point to a specific artist include, "*Rue Madeleine, Place de l'Opera,*" 1888, could indicate a painting by Childe Hassam (1859 – 1935), or "October on the Juniata River," 1879, could be a painting by Sanford Robinson Gifford (1823 – 1880), or "The Grand Canyon," 1921, could be a painting by Thomas Moran (1837 – 1926).

RECORD HISTORICAL DATA

All information pertaining to a painting becomes part of the provenance of that painting. Take photographs of the front and back of a painting before sending it to a conservator for restoration, especially if lining is going to take place. A new lining will permanently cover up all marks, stamps, and writing on the back of the original canvas.

HISTORICAL INFORMATION STAYS WITH A PAINTING

Copies of documents, such as letters from the artist, bills of sale, or records of conservation work can be placed in a business-size envelope and taped to the back of the frame (never on the canvas). In this way documents associated with a painting's provenance go wherever the painting goes.

PAINT AND COLOR

From 14th to the 17th century, artists had to manufacture their own paint. They experimented continually, and were as much scientists as creative artists. They cooked and mixed animal and plant parts with egg yokes along with various liquids to develop a medium that flowed (tempera). Tempera produced bright colors, dried quickly, and lasted for ages. Producing paint wasn't an easy process: it took countless trials and endless testing. One day it was egg yokes only; the next day egg whites only; then linseed oil, olive oil, and oils from various nuts, etc. Not until the 18th century could artists buy fully prepared paints in a variety of colors. Before that time, Western Europe was a virtual laboratory of artistic experimentation. This artistic experimentation gave meaning to the word "Renaissance—*rebirth,*" and was one of the driving forces that brought the Continent out of the Dark Ages. The Renaissance ushered in a new era of artistic and cultural discovery (starting roughly in the year 1350 and extending to the triumphant sculpture, painting, and architecture of Michelangelo).

TEMPERA PAINT

From the Dark Ages (400 – 1100) to the early Renaissance (1350 to the early 1400s), artists used pigments found in plant and animal matter to color the pictures they painted. In the third quarter of the 1400s, the technique of oil painting was introduced into Italy from Flanders, first via Sicily by Antonello da Messina (1430 – 1477), and then to Venice in 1475. (The Renaissance Period lasted roughly two hundred fifty years, from 1350 to 1600, and overlapped with the late Gothic and early Baroque Periods. Most Renaissance paintings, however, were executed in oils.)

OIL PAINT

Artists began experimenting with oil paints in the 14th century. They added drying agents to linseed and nut oils to achieve an oil-based paint that dried relatively quickly after coming in contact with air. Flemish artists Hubert and younger brother Jan van Eyck (1385-1441) are credited with inventing oil-based paints, and no doubt the van Eyck family improved the process of paint-making; however, oil based paints were previously developed by Flemish painters of miniature manuscript illuminations before the van Eycks were born. (Three of van Eyck's masterpieces, "The Adoration of the Lamb," completed in 1432; "The Arnolfini Marriage," completed in 1434; and "Annunciation," completed in 1436, all were executed with oil paints.)

OIL PAINT TEXTURE AND VISCOSITY

What came out of Flanders in the 15th century was a translucent oil paint that rendered the illusion of reality in intense, brilliant colors. The texture and viscosity of oil paint allowed artists to work with flowing paint to produce shades of colors and gradations in tones unachievable with tempera paint. Oil paint also permitted wet-in-wet painting *(alla prima)*, which was popular among 16th century Venetian artists, where color played a more dominant role than form. Conversely, Florentine artists emphasized drawing over color. Oil paint also allowed artists to make compositional changes right on the canvas (*pentimenti*). Impressionist artists three hundred years later would adopt many Venetian techniques that gave rise to color and spontaneity.

After its introduction in the late 1300s in Flanders, oil paint became the preferred medium for artists during the next six hundred years, to a large extent replacing the dull, flat surface of tempera paint. Tempera paints continue to be available today along with oils. Acrylic paints became popular in the mid 20th century.

DAMAGE TO OIL PAINT

Damage to paint occurs naturally through aging, from evaporation of media such as oils, chemical reactions to paint properties, and from moisture, humidity, environmental contaminants, and physical impacts. Nothing lasts forever; everything undergoes change. The discoloration of a protective organic varnish, for example, can easily be corrected, but damage to layers of underlying paint, or the undercoating of gesso, are often permanent, only repairable by extensive and costly conservation. During recent decades, synthetic varnishing, which is more stable, has steadily replaced former organic varnishing.

From its discovery in about 1350, and for the next 400 years, the process of making oil paint was experimental and ever changing. Master artists taught their apprentices the current understanding of chemical reactions in paint properties. In the 14th century no one knew for sure how one chemical would react with another. No one knew what effects humidity and moisture would have on supports, gesso, layers of paint, or on protective varnish. Conclusions were hard to reach, and success stories rarely were shared with the outside world, as modern communications had not yet been introduced. So the advances achieved in paint-making through experimentation, for example, in Flanders, might not have reached Madrid, Spain, for another seventy-five years. Not until the 18th century did the British Government commission a panel of experts to study the chemical properties of paint and the aging process of different paints, varnishes, and supports. The study's findings helped establish standards that were shared with the Society of British Artists. By the 19th century, paints were made with compatible properties and uniformity in manufacturing. Longevity of canvases was improved while the array of brilliant colors for the artist's pallet increased.

COMMON DAMAGE TO PAINT

"Craquelure" is the term applied to surface cracks in a support, be it canvas or wood panel. Cracks in a painting's surface occur naturally over time. In fact, if you have a one-hundred-and-fifty year-old painting without craquelure, be concerned, for you might have a modern forgery. Just as it's hard to find an 18th century painting or earlier that has never been lined, it's unlikely you'll find a 19th century oil painting without some surface cracks. A regularly patterned craquelure appears predictably in oil paintings one hundred years or older, as the oil bonding the particles of color partially dries out. Cracks will appear in patterns differently depending upon how the paint properties react, upon the method of applying gesso, the stretcher system and the support itself. Damage can also occur if moisture or humidity comes in contact with the support, thereby loosening the bond between the gesso and the first layer of paint and causing the paint to move, shift, or slide over the support. Sometimes you will see water stains on the reverse side of a canvas, perhaps caused by dripping water in a damp basement; this will almost certainly cause flaking and eventual paint loss. However, minor cracking and diminished color brightness in a century-old painting should be expected and is not considered damage unless abnormally severe.

Color brightness found in some oil paints fade faster than others and is referred to as "fugitive colors." This is particularly true of "lake" paints (dies mixed with pigments). Some paints weaken in sunlight, and become transparent to the point where canvas shows through the paint. Over-cleaning an oil painting by an amateur or poorly trained restorer can skin a painting and expose the grain of the canvas. These kinds of damage will have an adverse effect on a painting's value.

EVALUATING TECHNICAL DATA

A close examination of technical data will help you understand (1) the age of a painting, which can help you determine its authenticity; (2) possible attribution to a particular artist or School, from the materials used, the style of painting, and from deciphering marks, labels, and inscriptions; and (3) a painting's physical condition. Being able to attribute a painting to a particular artist or School, and knowing a painting's condition is excellent or very good, will figure heavily in your determination of the painting's value, and whether or not to buy it.

THE TECHNICAL CHALLENGE

The challenge for you is to learn what the technical signals tell you about a painting and to be able to evaluate forensic information quickly, even on the spot. "Patina," for example, is a coloration change that occurs naturally over time. All canvas, including panels, stretchers, and frames, gradually change color from oxidation. It's the natural aging process. With practice you'll be able to quickly confirm if a painting is, for example, from the 19th century or not. This confirmation process can be made in a glance or a matter of seconds. A five-second look at the back of a canvas or stretcher should be enough time to satisfy you that the painting is, for example, an 1870s work.

Once you have confirmed the painting is from the period it's supposed to be from, you can turn to the front side and begin to evaluate the picture: the quality of work, the subject, and the signature. Later, you can return to the reverse side for an in-depth technical examination.

You should learn about using ultra-violet light to examine the painted surface of an original picture. A "black light" can reveal old damage, non-original inpainting, non-original accents, even false or strengthened signatures or monograms.

When you are considering buying a painting you will not have weeks or months to evaluate every technical concern. Fine paintings have a tendency to sell well and quickly. Nevertheless, never feel pressured to buy a painting if you feel uncomfortable about some aspect of its technical characteristics or authenticity. When in doubt, pass it up.

CONSERVATION TIPS

Canvas on supports can become slack or taut, while wood panels can warp and crack. Paintings generally do well in temperatures between 70 and 75 degrees Fahrenheit, with relative humidity between 40 and 60 percent.

BACKING A PAINTNG

Backing a painting with protective Fome-Cor (or archival non-acidic board) is **the single most important preservation step you can take to protect your painting.** The protective backing should cover the entire back of the picture, being screwed into the stretcher or strainer and not into the frame. Do not leave air-vent holes. A protective backing will slow the effects of environmental damage and protect the painting from accidental punctures and tears.

DISPLAYING A PAINTING

Displaying a painting in direct sunlight can cause damage to paint pigment and organic varnish. Generally, display paintings on interior walls rather than on perimeter walls, which can be uninsulated and subject to temperature fluctuations. Those hung on perimeter walls must have corner buffers or spacers at the bottom left and right back corners to keep the picture from touching the wall. Heat from an incandescent lamp hanging too close to a painting's surface can also cause damage. It is better to use indirect or recessed lighting to illuminate a painting.

HANDLING PAINTINGS

Handling paintings requires special consideration. Careless handling can cause puncture holes and tears. Move paintings as little as possible; always use two hands to carry a painting, with the image side facing you. Before moving your painting or any artwork, know in advance where you are taking it, and move anything out of the way that might damage the art or trip you. If you have to store a painting, put it in a dry closet (preferably climate controlled), not in a damp basement or hot attic. Be sure to store paintings with a piece of cardboard over the image side (you already have protective Fome-Cor over the back).

FRAMING A PAINTING

Framing a painting is the occasion to make sure the fit and finish of your artwork are just right. Ask your framer to pad the rabbet (the part of the frame that touches the painting) with felt. This will help prevent abrasion. Try to avoid using nails altogether. Driving a nail through a valuable frame and into an antique stretcher is an invasive and potentially damaging process. Use mending plates instead, which are screwed into the frame, and then bent over the stretcher to hold the painting in place. Also avoid using "eye" rings to string picture-hanging wire; instead use "D" rings, which should be screwed into the frame, never into the stretcher or strainer. Replace old rusted wire with a coated wire of the appropriate strength. Always hang a painting on a hook (or two for heavy paintings), never on a nail.

DUSTING YOUR PAINTING

Dusting your painting twice a year should keep it free of dust particles. Avoid contact with flaking paint and lifting edges, and only dust with a very soft, sable-hair makeup brush. Never clean a painting yourself; don't try to use home cleaners or commercial solvents to clean a painting since serious damage can occur. Always consult a conservator for professional cleaning and restoration work. Find a conservator at www.aic.stanford.edu.

This chapter provides only an overview of the technical examination. For an in-depth discussion on paint properties and the conservation process, read *Seeing Through Paintings: Physical Examination in Art Studies,* by Andrea Kirsh and Rustin S. Levenson (Yale University Press, 2000), which was a major source for this chapter. For the serious art collector, investor, and dealer, I highly recommend this excellent book.

6

Research and Appraisal: Printed Resources

Research and appraisal are at the heart of successful art buying. Do this well and you'll make a profit. Skip this process or overlook an important detail and you'll likely pay for your mistakes.

Research and appraisal studies incorporate all of your art training. Here you need to combine instincts with knowledge to determine if a painting is authentic or not, and whether to buy it or pass it up.

Through research, we systematically study and investigate all aspects of a work of art. We evaluate the information collected by weighing, comparing, and reasoning in order to reach logical conclusions. Finally we appraise art by setting a price on a painting in order to establish its replacement cost or its fair market value.

For example, a large oil painting representative of the best work of illustration artist Stevan Dohanos (1907 – 1994), would be appraised differently depending upon the purpose of the appraisal.

- **Replacement Cost** is the "best market," and therefore the retail price at a distinguished gallery, say, $25,000 (which also is the insurance value).
- **Fair Market Value** is what the IRS might allow for tax or gift purposes, say, $15,000.

To successfully research and appraise art, you will have to know how to do four things: (1) conduct a Technical Examination (covered in the previous chapter), (2) do a Resource Data Analysis (look up printed and computerized information), (3) get Expert Opinion (check with museums, galleries, or scholarly sources), and (4) do a Market Value Analysis (find out who's buying and selling what you're interested in, and for how much). These are broad disciplines that require specialized knowledge, but not a Ph.D.

PRINTED RESOURCES

Among many kinds of art reference books, we limit our discussion here to three categories: (1) Auction Price Indexes, (2) Biographical Information, and (3) Monographs and Exhibition Catalogues. Of these three, auction price indexes are the most meaningful to your research. Knowing auction price records is essential in order to buy and sell art successfully.

Most art dealers began their career researching a painting in a public library. However, spending too much time researching art at a local library might not be suitably productive. You'll soon learn that it pays to own a few art reference books of your own. Nevertheless, you would be wise to develop a good relationship with the art librarian in your city, particularly one at a university with a strong art history department. From time to time, you will be calling on her for help.

Every collector and investor has reference books at home, particularly in their special areas of interest and collecting. You won't need the 34-volume set of the

Dictionary of Art, by Groves Press ($8,800 list price) in order to research a particular painting, though that would be nice. But you will need a few basic reference books.

ARTPRICE INDICATOR

Whether you're an experienced dealer or just starting out, an excellent reference book to own is *Artprice Indicator*, which will only cost you $19.95. The *Artprice Indicator*, at 1,750 pages, lists over 50,000 artists' names, and includes the description and price results of multiple works by an artist sold at auction. An excellent resource book; it's inexpensive enough to keep a copy in your car or shoulder bag, to be used at auctions, while traveling on vacation, or for your home library. Measuring only 4 ½" X 7", this single reference book and a $5 magnifying glass (*loupe*) can put you into the art business for under $25. A limited supply is still available by filling out the order form on the last page of this book.

Caution

Artprice Indicator *offers an important word of caution, which is worth repeating, and applies to all appraisal estimates: "Never use price guides or abbreviated auction price references such as* Artprice Indicator *to appraise or value individual works of art. They are useful for approximating prices in pressure situations, but not suitable for exclusively making final determinations as to what artworks are worth on the open market. For example, if you discover a painting in an antique shop priced at $200 and find three listings for the artist in* Artprice Indicator, *all in the $2,000-$3,000 range, the painting could well be a bargain. On the other hand, be cautious when you're researching a specific Picasso print, and* Artprice Indicator *lists only one auction record for this work; while, in fact, thousands of Picasso prints have been auctioned in the past decade." Search out other auction records, in price index books and online* *databases before making a final determination of a painting's market value.*

RESEARCHING SIGNED PAINTINGS

If your painting is signed and you can read the signature, even if you don't recognize the artist's name, you should be able to determine within a few minutes whether you're dealing with a major or minor league artist. Simply open your price reference book and turn alphabetically to the artist's name. It's that simple. If your artist is a "listed artist," even of modest reputation, you will find his name listed, and the price his work sells for at auction. If his work typically sells for under $5,000, you have a painting by a minor artist. You can still make a profit with this work; for example, if you buy it for $500 and sell it for $2,000. But you would not buy this painting on speculation. It's only decorative or collectible art (under $5,000), and will not appreciate significantly. You would only buy this painting if you knew someone who collected the artist or subject matter, and you were confident he would pay $2,000 for it. Otherwise, pass it up. You should look for bigger fish.

If the artist you're researching typically sells for over $10,000, then do smile, that is, once you've authenticated the signature. If this art typically sells for over $25,000, you can let out a shout of joy. However, if your artist sells for over $50,000, well, you're in the big leagues. You're dealing with a major artist. Not yet world class, but major. (See "Sample Price Rankings" in Chapter 2, "Valuing Art.") If this artist isn't listed in your price index book, don't give up right away, especially if you feel the painting has superior quality. Check other reference books.

DAVENPORT'S

If you own *Davenport's* extensive listing, go to it first, and check alphabetically to see whether your artist's name is listed. If you don't own *Davenport's,* don't worry. It's not the most important art reference book in the world, and it costs $199. But this book does list even very minor artists, which other references sometimes omit. *Davenport's* is limited by not showing multiple price entries for an artist's work. Generally, it lists only one or two price references for each artist, and usually the highest price is cited, which won't help you formulate an understanding of the average price for an artist's work. You must be able to compare your painting with other artworks by the same artist, i.e. size, subject, and price, and what they sell for at auction. Only then can you make an intelligent comparison, placing an appropriate value on your painting. The auction price indicated in *Davenport's* could well be a fluke. It could be the highest price the artist ever achieved at auction, say, $12,000, and might never achieve again. A deeper search might reveal the "average price" for the artist's work at auction is only $700, so why pay $12,000? Yet many "sellers" use *Davenport's*, usually to their advantage.

Two Kinds of People Use *Davenport's,* the inexperienced collector and investor (if it's the only reference book he has), and the shrewd art dealer who tries to sell you a painting for more than it's worth. Some dealers will offer a painting for sale, and say, "Look, the artist is listed for $4,700," and they'll show you a listing in *Davenport's.* (Probably the highest price the artist ever achieved.) Then he'll give you a *special price*: "But you can have this painting for $1,200." It might sound like a good price, but don't be fooled. The painting might not be worth $500, even though *Davenport's* lists the artist for $4,700. A "one-time" high auction record is no guarantee the value of your painting is even close to the *Davenport's* record. Generally speaking, you'll need to know more information than *Davenport's* offers in order to make an informed decision about the market value of a painting. Beware of the seller who justifies his price by showing you a listing only in *Davenport's.*

Researching Unlisted Artists. If your artist is not listed in *Davenport's,* chances are he's not listed elsewhere either, because *Davenport's* lists almost everything that has paint on it. But don't give up right away if you can't find the artist's name listed in a price guide. Try at least one other price index book and then do a Google (explained in Chapter 7). Remember, you're buying art based on *quality of work*, not on name alone. So if an unsigned artwork really is outstanding, you still might want to buy it. If it's that excellent, it probably was painted by a listed artist, maybe even an important artist. Your job now is to connect the painting by attribution to its creator. If you never attribute your painting to a particular artist or School of art, your painting will remain a decorative piece—a "furnishing picture." You will only be able to sell this painting as decorative art, not as collectible art, and certainly not as investment art.

Davenport's should only be one of many price index books you check.

ARTPRICE INDICATOR

Next, check your *Artprice Indicator.* As mentioned above, the *Artprice Indicator* costs $19.95, and is an excellent reference book. It lists over 50,000 artist's names, and shows multiple price records for an artist's work. It gives a basic description of each example sold at auction. It will show if the painting sold was a still life, landscape, or portrait; media (oil, watercolor, pastel); support (canvas, board, panel); size in inches and centimeters, and whether the painting was signed, unsigned, or attributed. It also lists the date and location of the auction; for example, "Christie's New York, 1998." Knowing where an artist's work previously sold at auction can be helpful should you decide to sell your painting at auction. The auction room can notify its customers who might be interested in bidding on your artwork. Their successful experience with your artist is an excellent reason for you to consider consigning your artwork to them.

MAKE COMPARISONS

Make a comparison between the painting you possess—size, subject, date, etc, and a similar work sold at auction. Be sure to use like elements in your comparative analysis. Don't compare the price of a floral still life with a genre painting of children playing, even if the size and other factors are the same. If your painting is the one with children playing, it should be worth much more than a still life by the same artist. Similarly, if the size of your painting is 9" X 12", it is probably worth much less than a painting measuring 24" X 36" by the same artist. Make price adjustments for variances between the painting you're holding and the one listed in the auction record book.

Compare your painting with auction results found in several price guides. Then try to estimate the price your painting might fetch at auction. Since your estimate will be based on a technical analysis and logical assumptions, it should closely approximate a professional appraisal. Be conservative. If your painting might fetch $15,000 to $20,000 at auction, plan on $12,000 and be delighted if goes higher. On the other hand, if you're selling at auction, also be conservative, especially when establishing price estimates. For example, if you think your painting should bring $20,000 at auction, don't set your estimate at $15,000 to $20,000, and certainly not higher. Try $10,000 to $15,000, or even lower, like, $7,000 to $12,000. It's better to have a modest estimate than an impressively high one, which usually scares bidders away. You want bidders to participate; lower estimates encourage competitive bidding. Don't worry; the bidding will quickly rise to meet the painting's true value. (See Chapter 10, "Selling Art," for a discussion on auction strategies.)

ART PRICE ANNUAL

Next, check your *ADEC Art Price Annual* to see how your painting might compare with other paintings sold at auction. The *Art Price Annual* has slightly more listings, but is very similar in format to the *Artprice Indicator*. The big difference is price: $195 compared to $19.95. (See the order form on the last page of this book.)

HISLOP'S PRICE GUIDE TO FINE ART

Hislop's Price Guide also is an excellent reference book, costing only $20. *Hislop's* is useful because it averages auction prices for you, so you don't have to locate and examine multiple records or do the calculations. Hislop's lists 25,000 artists' names; for each artist it tabulates findings under five columns: (1) number of works sold in a year, (2) total value of all works sold, (3) lowest price achieved, (4) median price achieved, and (5) highest price achieved. Knowing the median price for an artist's work is extremely helpful; it gives you an immediate sense of probable value. An entry might look like this:

John Leslie Breck (1860 – 1899) American					
Media	Qty	Total Sales	Lowest	Median	Highest
Oil	4	$379,500	$22,000	$58,750	$240,000

Here we see that four Breck paintings were auctioned in the year 2000, and the total annual sales were $379,500. We also see the lowest price achieved was $22,000; the highest $240,000; and the average price for a Breck oil painting at auction was $58,750. If after all your research, you can confidently say that your painting by John Leslie Breck is in very good to excellent condition, medium to full size, and is listed in the *oeuvre* of Breck's work, you can assume your painting is worth $50,000 to $60,000, possibly more. With this information, you can determine how much you'd be willing to pay for a Breck painting, or what price you might ask when selling it wholesale or at auction.

It should be noted, in fact, that John Leslie Breck's artworks are extremely valuable and highly sought after. In 2004, a large oil by Breck was retailing for $800,000 at a distinguished New York City gallery.

Comparative pricing is fundamental when buying and selling art. And *Hislop's* does the averaging for you. However, it only shows pricing. *Hislop's* fails to give a description of the artwork. You'll have to check other reference books to compare canvas size, subject matter, and where a painting sold at auction. Costing $20,

Hislop's is available through most chain stores such as Barnes and Noble, Borders, and Books-a-Million.

BIOGRAPHICAL REFERENCE BOOKS

A biographical reference book provides historical information about an artist's life and career, but adds little to understanding a painting's accurate value. Therefore, a biographical listing alone is never adequate reason for investing in a painting. You particularly need price index information to buy an artwork. However, having biographical information about an artist's life can help sell your painting. Moreover, you will become more knowledgeable and persuasive.

Even if your artist's name is "listed" in a biographical reference book, he may not be listed in a price index book, which is more important, at least in terms of money. A biographical listing generally details the dates your artist lived, where he was born and died, what schools he attended, where he apprenticed, and with whom he painted. Some biographical listings indicate awards and prizes, and those exhibitions and shows that included his art, such as the Salon in Paris, the Royal Academy in London, or the National Academy of Design in New York.

Biographical reference books are slowly being replaced by Internet databases. For example, Googling will probably turn up a raft of information about your artist's life. Nevertheless, many collectors and investors have at least one biographical reference book, particularly in their specialty, such as *Old Masters, Hudson River School Artists, or 20th Century Illustrators.*

THE BENEZIT

The French *Benezit*, extending to 14 volumes, is one of the oldest art dictionaries still published. Listing mostly European artists, especially French, it's often quoted by way of reference. For example, a dealer might offer you a painting for sale, saying, "*Look*, the artist is listed in

Benezit." Pushing Volume 9 in front of you, he indicates the page, and says, "He was born in 1688 and died in 1752." And you should be thinking, "*So what*!" That information has little to do with the $5,000 price tag on the painting. You really need auction price results. Get more information.

MANTLE FIELDING'S

Mantle Fielding's Dictionary of American Painters, Sculptors and Engravers, lists 13,000 biographies, one of which will probably shed light on your American artist. For example, under the name "Church," both Frederick Edwin Church (1826 – 1900) and Frederick Stuart Church (1842 – 1923) are listed, both receiving about the same amount of space. Both entries contain the same basic information: where and when the artists were born, where they went to school, whom they painted with or studied under, when they opened their studios, what medals they won, when and where they died. According to *Mantle Fielding's*, there would appear to be no difference in stature between these two artists; but in fact significant differences separate the two painters. Now, let's look at *Hislop's Price Guide*. Here you'll see that the average price for a painting sold at auction by Frederic Stuart Church was $3,500, while the average price for a comparable painting sold at auction by Frederick Edwin Church was $3,800,000. Clearly, your painting needs to be by Frederick Edwin Church. The difference in value is the amount of zeros: thousands or millions of dollars.

Important information can be hidden in a biography, which sometimes determines outcomes and results. In the above example, key to Frederick Edwin Church's enormous success as a painter, in addition to his exceptional abilities, was his training under Thomas Cole, who founded the Hudson River School. That bit of information is like the difference between studying under a weekend painter, or the likes of Leonardo Da Vinci. Frederick Edwin Church studied under a master painter, and he became a master painter.

Biographical information also can help you compose a descriptive ad to sell your painting, for example, one by William M. Hart, who was born in Scotland, immigrated to America, and painted with many Hudson River School luminaries.

William M. Hart

1823-1894

Seashore Morning: oil on canvas, 16" X 20", signed and dated 1862. This beautiful seascape was painted off the Long Island coast just after Hart returned from Scotland. Best known for his Hudson River School landscapes, Wm. M. Hart is a listed artist with established auction records, and his paintings hang in the Metropolitan Museum of Art.

$15,000

ART DICTIONARIES, DIRECTORIES, AND ENCYCLOPEDIAS

There are many art dictionaries, directories, and encyclopedias, both online and in print format. Depending upon your special interests or need, you might find useful information in the following resources:

- *Dictionary of British Artists*
- *Dictionary of Victorian Artists*
- *Dictionary of Contemporary Artists*
- *Dictionary of Woman Artists*
- *Dictionary of Artists in America*
- *Directory of Museums*
- *Dictionary of Afro-American Artists*
- *Dictionary of Russian/Soviet Artists*
- *Dictionary of Native American Painters*
- *Dictionary of Illustrators*
- *Dictionary of Auction Houses*
- *Who's Who in American Art*

SIGNATURES, MONOGRAMS, AND SYMBOLS

The Encyclopedia of Artist's Signatures, Symbols & Monograms ($199) lists 25,000 cross-indexed examples. This publication is enormously valuable in identifying an artist's signature; many depository libraries carry a copy of this encyclopedia. Also try www.signaturehelp.com.

BUILDING AN ART LIBRARY

Collect reference books and resource directories whenever you can, if they're available at a reasonable price. Art reference books can be bought at flea markets, country auctions, used bookstores, and online. Try collecting reference books pertaining to your School of interest; your level of expertise will be related directly to the depth and scope of the resources you have available to study and examine.

BARGAIN BOOKS

Art books can illustrate complete Schools of art, such as Pre-Raphaelite, Hudson River, Renaissance, French Realism, and British Portraiture. These can be bought inexpensively if you purchase closeouts, overstocks, and remainders. Some of these books may be shopworn or have a scuffed cover, but you can buy a $75 art book for $12, sometimes less, if you shop carefully. One excellent source for bargain books is Edward Hamilton Bookseller, Bargain Books, at www.hamiltonbooks.com.

MONOGRAPHS AND EXHIBITION CATALOGUES

Not only beautiful books to look at, monographs and exhibition catalogues are an invaluable resource for examining the details of an artist's work or examples represented by a School of art. If you attend an auction, such as Christie's or Sotheby's, buy their catalogue, now up to $35, especially if it contains outstanding examples in your specialty. It's expensive, but worth the beauty and education, particularly due to their exquisite color reproduction. However, if you consign an artwork to a major auction room, be sure to request a free copy of their catalogue. After the auction, request its price results be sent to you either by fax or email, or go online and download them. When you receive the price results, update your catalogue by annotating the hammer price achieved beside the printed estimate. Study trends and price variances. In this way you will develop a deeper knowledge of art values, and you will begin to remember artists' names. Keep expanding your art library. Keep expanding your memory.

PERSEVERANCE IN RESEARCH PAYS OFF

Turning over every stone sometimes is necessary to find what you're looking for. A prime law in exceptional collecting and/or investment art buying: **don't give up one search short of success**. The following case example takes researching in coffee-table art books to the extreme, but as it demonstrates big profits can be a result.

CASE EXAMPLE: Mistaken Attribution

"*Gypsy Encampment*" was the title Dixon & Dixon gave to a painting exhibited in their Atlanta gallery. They attributed the unsigned work to the "Barbizon School," priced at $11,500 for the large landscape painting. There was only one problem: the picture didn't look *Barbizon.* It was an interior forest scene of a gypsy encampment, but just didn't look like the Fontainebleau Forest, where Troyon, Dupre, Rousseau, and Daubigny painted. This work appeared too refined, too detailed, the trees too green, and the sky too blue. The landscape had too much depth, clarity, and openness in it to be Barbizon. Masterfully painted, this canvas looked more British than French.

It was late Saturday afternoon, and the dealer asked the gallery manager if she would "hold" the painting until closing time at 5 p.m. The gallery agreed. The dealer then took a picture card off the tear-sheet beside the painting, and headed right for the Barnes and Noble Bookstore in downtown Atlanta. He selected eight or nine picture books on British Art, Victorian Art, Pre-Raphaelite Art, and British Landscape Paintings, and carried all of them to the café. In a comfortable chair with a *café latte*, he began flipping through the pages, in one book after another. He was looking only for an example of similar work, not necessarily by the same artist, but perhaps from the same School. He wanted to know with certainty that the painting in the gallery was from this or that School of art. Then he could more aptly appraise its value.

The *café latte* was gone. The dealer was getting tired. Finally, on page 249 of the last book, *The Pre-Raphaelite Landscape* by Allen Staley, he saw the *exact* painting! There it was, the "Gypsy Encampment." Only it was titled, "Thinking of the Future," by Henry Mark Anthony.

Staley's write-up of Henry Mark Anthony and this particular painting was substantial. Regarding this exact painting exhibited at the Royal Academy in 1845, William Michael Rossetti, the preeminent art critic of his day, in his review, called Anthony "the most outstanding landscape painter in England." Moreover, Ford Madox Brown's diary was full of praise for Anthony—"like Constable, only better by far."

The photo caption under the picture in Staley's book then read, "Present location unknown."

"I'd like to buy the *Barbizon* painting," the dealer said when he returned to the gallery. "But your price is too high. Would you accept $5,000?" The woman looked at him, and he could see she wanted to make a deal, perhaps to make up for an otherwise dismal day. "Six thousand dollars," she said. He agreed. Walking out of the gallery, he left Atlanta with a beautiful Pre-Raphaelite painting. The status of the painting's location changed from "unknown" to the dealer's house. He was delighted indeed with his discovery.

In the above case example, luck and taking advantage of being in the right place at the opportune time played a big part in the discovery of a missing

Henry Mark Anthony painting. Correcting the misattribution from Barbizon to Pre-Raphaelite, however, took knowledge, instinct, and perseverance.

In the next chapter, Chapter 7, "Research and Appraisal: Computer Databases," we continue our discussion of research techniques. Finally, we conclude our discussion of research in Chapter 8, "Provenance, Due-Diligence, Forgeries, and *Catalogues Raisonnés.*" Then we'll concentrate on "buying" and "selling" art in chapters 9 and 10.

After his amazing discoveries, Albert Einstein was asked about his intelligence, his ancestors, and from whom he might have inherited his genes? He replied:

> I know quite certainly that I, myself, have no special gifts. Curiosity, obsession, and dogged endurance, combined with self-critique, have brought me my success.
>
> ***—Albert Einstein***

And so it is with art research.

"The only sensible way to regard the art life is that it is a privilege worth paying for."

—**Robert Henri** (1865 – 1929)

7

Research and Appraisal: Computer Databases

Welcome to the computer world! Just imagine buying or selling art today without the aid of a computer and the Internet. Most of the information you'll need to research and appraise art is available online. Of course, you must maintain a print library as a back-up, but familiarity with the Internet and knowing how to store and retrieve digital images on your computer are essential. You'll use the Internet extensively in research, and later for transmitting and receiving digital images of paintings you want to buy and sell.

In this chapter we'll look at four important Internet resources: (1) Google.com, (2) Artnet.com, (3) Askart.com, and (4) Europe's website for art, Kunstmarkt.com. Most art dealers use these Web sites for fact-finding and auction price research. Let's look at each site individually.

GOOGLE.COM

www.Google.com is arguably the most popular search engine in the world for doing research; here you'll find answers to most of your questions about art. Always be specific with your inquiry; get right to the point. Don't type, "Find me an East Coast buyer for a John Lafarge painting"; "John Lafarge gallery," will get better results.

Most of your inquiries or concerns about art will relate to (1) artists' biographies, (2) where to sell art, (3) where to buy art, and (4) support information about art, such as how to find a curator, conservator, subject expert, museum, gallery, or *catalogue raisonné*.

Google.com is a good place to start. (Auction records are best researched in an art price database, discussed below in detail.)

ARTIST BIOGRAPHY

If you haven't found your artist's name in a reference book, type in the artist's name at Google.com. Chances are you'll turn up a raft of useful information about the artist. Having complete biographical information enables you to make an informed decision about your painting, including where to sell or consign it, what museums might be interested in buying it, and where to find an expert to authenticate it. Knowledge gives you business advantage, so dig in and find out as much information as you can about the artist or School of art.

You must persevere in your research. If your Google turns up no results, try variations of an artist's name. For example, (1) Vlaminck, (2) M. Vlaminck, (3) M. de Vlaminck, and (4) Maurice de Vlaminck. Don't give up after the first or second page of your Google; scroll through pages 3, 4, 5, and 6, etc., you might find what you're looking for on page 7. Also search the location or state where the artist was born or died. Then try the School and artists with whom he painted. And finally, re-check the signature to make sure you have the correct name spelling. Consider the opinions of others.

One Dealer made an exhaustive search for an artist named Frank Eccinton, and came up empty handed. Stubborn in his pursuit, he even researched Mormon Church Genealogy Records, but couldn't find a trace of the name anywhere on the planet. One day the neighbor's teenage son looked at the painting and declared the name to be Egginton not Eccinton. Sure enough, Frank Egginton was a prolific though minor British watercolorist who painted Irish landscapes.

Another Web site to mark as a favorite is www.Artcyclopedia.com. Here you'll find 125,000 records of great works of art, including detailed information on sixty or more Schools of art; everything from Barbizon to Baroque, from the Harlem Renaissance to the High Renaissance. Print out what you need. Build your arsenal of art information.

Another great Web site is www.yourartlinks.com. This site has over 4,000 art links on the World Wide Web, covering more than sixty categories of art information.

A superb Web site for art history research is www.witcombe.sbc.edu. Also try www.bc.edu and www.dart.fine-art.com for more art links on the World Wide Web. Many universities offer excellent art research information. Here are four outstanding Web sites:

- *UCLA*: www.library.ucla.edu/libraries/arts.
- *Stanford University:* www.sul.stanford.edu/depts/art.
- *Yale University*: www.library.yale.edu/art.
- *New York University:* www.library.nuy.edu.

Be imaginative and resourceful when using the Internet. Persevere; you'll find just about anything you'll need to know about art on the Internet.

SELLING ART

Where to sell art is a dilemma many new collectors and investors face. They haven't quite figured out who's buying what, or how to find serious buyers. However, a simple Google search can provide links to qualified buyers for your artworks. For example, try "Old Masters gallery London," or "Impressionist Masters gallery Paris," or "Modern Masters gallery Chicago"; then offer these galleries your painting.

If you wish to sell a Californian landscape, for example, by Edgar Payne (1882-1947), your first question might be, "Who's buying Edgar Payne paintings?" A good prospect would be dealers and galleries who *sell* Edgar Payne works of art or the California School. Google for "Edgar Payne art dealers," or "Edgar Payne art galleries," or "California Impressionist galleries." Your search will likely reveal many dealers and galleries buying Edgar Payne works of art, including their names, telephone numbers, and Web sites. Simply call up these dealers and galleries and begin negotiating. (See Chapter 10, "Selling Art.")

Most every artist from mid-level to first-tier ranking would have dealers and galleries wanting to buy their artworks. The Internet can help you identify who these buyers are. If you're selling a painting by a master artist, simply Google "Matisse dealers" or "Picasso dealers" or "Mary Cassatt dealers." You'll find galleries and dealers all over the world interested in buying your painting. After finding a potential buyer for your painting on the Internet, however, be very careful to protect your asset. Never send a painting to someone you don't know, expecting to see a check in the mail.

If your painting is by a minor artist, however, valued under $5,000, you might not find a dealer or gallery for this artist on the Internet. There just isn't enough stock, currency, or interest in the artist's work. If there were, somebody would have a Web site up expressing interest in buying his work. There are, however, regional collectors who buy artworks even by minor artists, so always check the Internet. If you can identify the subject matter, try searching, for example, under "Ohio Folk Art," "Pennsylvania landscapes," or "World War II art," if that's what you have. Google will turn up buyers and sellers for just about any kind of art.

BUYING ART

Guess what? The same dealers and galleries that sell California Impressionist art, like Edgar Payne's work, also *buy* California Impressionist art like Edgar Payne's paintings. Just reverse the above process to find potential sellers for the art you want to buy. Ask the same dealers who would buy your artworks if they have any paintings for sale by your favorite artists, or if they know someone who does.

CONTACT MANAGEMENT

Always network. If you don't get a positive result from an inquiry, ask the person with whom you're talking if they know someone who can assist you. Don't hang up the phone until you get the name and telephone number of at least one other person who can help you. Persist, persevere, persuade, but be polite.

As an art dealer, you'll talk with dozens of people every day, networking and coming up with new telephone numbers and Web sites. Keep records. Develop a contact management system so you can retrieve important contact information whenever you need it. Consider using a contact management software program such as *ACT!, GoldMine*, or *Microsoft Outlook*, or keep accurate notebook records, and bookmark all your favorite Web sites. This book suggests many popular art Web sites but you will discover new ones on your own, and we hope you will share them with us. We want to include your recommendations in future editions, inviting you to email your favorite art Web sites to Rondavis77@aol.com.

SCHOOLS OF ART

You can research a School of art by doing a simple Google search. For example, under "Pre-Raphaelite Brotherhood," you will find the school's history, also art dealers, galleries, museums, and a list of the School's major artists. Here are some excellent links to Schools of art:

- www.Askart.com
- www.Atcyclopedia.com
- www.YourArtLinks.com.

Study the specific School of art in which you have interest. Become a recognized expert. The World Wide Web is full of historical and technical information about your School of Art sufficient to lead you down the path of connoisseurship. Find the museums and galleries that specialize in your favorite School of art; visit them, again and again. Study and research. Meet with curators, historians, and art dealers who are expert in this School.

INVESTIGATIVE RESEARCH

All research leads to a comparison of data and information. The computer can store millions of pieces of information, enabling you to compare one record with another that will lead you to a conclusion. The final decision, however, of what is or is not authentic, rests with experts and not computers. Ultimately, the scholar, art historian, or connoisseur must weigh the evidence, preferably together, and decide whether an artwork can or cannot be attributed to a particular artist.

Collect as much information as possible about your artist; then compare it with as many records and expert testimonies as you can in order to determine whether your painting matches the work of a recognized master. The computer can assist, but you must make the final decision.

ART DATABASES

Most serious collectors, investors, and dealers use an art database to research biographies and auction price records before they buy or sell an artwork. Two excellent databases are Artnet.com and Askart.com; most art dealers use one or both of these databases. Both databases are fee-based member services, but each also offers free information that can help you make wise choices about buying or selling art. **Consult these databases daily for free information**. But only subscribe to them when you require pay-for-information, for a one-time use, such as just before going to an auction (see below).

The major difference between the two databases is that Artnet.com covers both European and American Artists, while Askart.com covers only American artists. Both sites require that you have a credit card to subscribe to member services, but no payment or credit card is required to browse either site or to download free information, which is abundantly available. Both sites have a different fee-base structure depending upon your use as an individual, professional, gallery, or museum. Let's look at how you can cost-effectively use these databases to your advantage.

ARTNET.COM

Artnet's auction database is the most comprehensive illustrated electronic archive of fine art auction price records in the world. It lists 185,000 artists, and has price records for more than 2 million lots sold at over 500 auction houses.

Artnet costs $29.95 per month for 10 searches, and rolls over each month unless you cancel your service. So that you don't forget, after sign-up, go right to "edit profile" and cancel your service, which means that after 10 searches are completed, you won't be billed $29.95 for another 10 searches, unless you sign up again. Unused searches do not accumulate, so use all 10 searches within the 30-day time frame. Let's see how $2.95 per search can be a wise investment.

AUCTIONS

If you intended to bid on a $20,000 painting at auction, it would pay for you to invest $2.95 ($29.95 ÷ 10) to learn about the artist and his work *before* going to the auction. For $2.95 you can access Artnet's database and view up to 100 example paintings by the artist, learning what each one sold for at auction. This study exercise is tantamount to comparing neighborhood home prices before you make an offer on a house you want to buy. It's a smart thing to do.

HOW TO BENEFIT FROM EXPERT OPINION

Artnet downloads auction results following major sales at Christie's, Sotheby's, and other large auction rooms, then makes pricing information available to its subscribers as a paid service. Christie's and Sotheby's have already authenticated all the images you will see on Artnet's database. Otherwise these paintings would not have been approved for sale at auction. For the sake of comparison, you can assume that every digital image on Artnet's database was authenticated by an expert at Christie's or Sotheby's or some other reliable auction room, and most probably is 100 percent "right." Therefore, what you see posted on Artnet's database is a reliable example representing the artist's work. Now compare your painting with the 100 images posted on the Internet to see if there's a match of quality, workmanship, technique and subject. Hold one painting up to the other, and compare carefully. If your painting looks nothing like what you see on the database, be very careful; you might not want to bid on this painting. If your painting looks *"right,"* continue your research and compare auction price records of similar works (size and subject). Then estimate the price you think your painting will fetch at auction.

The possibility exists that one or two paintings out of 100 by an artist sold at auction might be forged or copied. This might happen at a small auction house where an appraiser failed to give a painting careful evaluation, but it's unlikely to happen at a major auction room, such as Christie's or Sotheby's, where a team of experts vets every painting before going to auction. So feel assured comparing your painting with images posted on Artnet's database, which almost certainly are authentic and representative of the artist's work.

GAINING EXPERTISE

You'll become quite expert after studying one hundred paintings by a particular artist, which is what Artnet affords you to do for $2.95. You also can print color copies of a sample painting, or all 100 if you like, and discreetly take them to the auction room for comparison.

If it's a big auction with many paintings worth bidding for, you might want to use the entire subscription allotment to research 10 artists. In this case, spending $29.95 to gain confidence and valuable information about 10 paintings you want to bid on, is a small cost of doing business possibly yielding large profits for you.

ASK THE EXPERTS

Finally, before you buy any expensive painting, ask the experts: Christie's 212-636-2000, and Sotheby's 212-606-7000. Speak with a department specialist in 19th Century American Art, European Moderns, Old Masters, or whatever School or Period you have, and mention the name of your artist. Tell her you're "considering" selling your painting at auction, if it's worthy art. Ask for an evaluation of your work of art, and an e-mail address; then send her a digital image with a description of your painting. Usually you'll have a preliminary estimate back within 72 hours (free), and an offer to auction your painting in one of its venues (if it's worthy art).

GALLERIES

Over 1,300 major galleries are registered on Artnet. You can access these galleries free in three different ways:

- **By Gallery.** Type in a gallery name, and find its location, telephone number, e-mail address and director's name.

- **By Location.** Type in a location, and find out how many galleries in that city are registered with Artnet, including international locations. For example, type in Belgium and find major galleries in the cities of Antwerp, Berchem, Brussels, Knokke, and Zeebrugge. Do the same for New York City to find major galleries there, including addresses, contact information, and the kind of artworks they represent.

  Having contact information for five or six Belgium galleries makes it easier when you're trying to sell your painting by Gustave de Jonghe (1829 – 1893). Simply call up the gallery and start negotiating.
- **By Artist.** Type in an artist's name and find which galleries represent that artist in which cities and countries.

These features make it easier to identify galleries that buy works by your artist, and you learn how to contact new buyers.

ARTISTS

Over 16,000 artists' works, almost all of investment quality, are offered for sale at galleries registered with Artnet. You can view them free—all 16,000. Check to see which galleries are currently selling artworks by the artist you're about to purchase. Then call the gallery to find out the asking price of its painting by your artist. You will then know what your example might retail for in a distinguished gallery. You also might be able to sell your painting to the same gallery (possibly even before you buy it). Tell the director that you have a painting for sale by an artist it already represents. Describe your painting and offer to send them a digital image. If your work is by an artist the gallery frequently sells, the director might offer a fair wholesale price for your painting. *Make a deal. Don't be shy.*

RESEARCH
Artnet allows you to access Groves *Dictionary of Art* for artists' biographies and related art information, the most comprehensive art encyclopedia yet, in English. It also links you to museums and other art sites.

MAGAZINE
Access Artnet's free online magazine, newsletter, and reviews to see when fairs and art shows are coming to cities near you.

ASKART.COM

Askart is the other excellent Web site for researching paintings. It gives access to more than 35,000 American artists, most likely listing your artist among them. Askart is easier to navigate, offering features not found on Artnet. Askart gives you *unlimited* use of its database, not limiting you to only 10 searches as on Artnet. You can research as many artists as desired for the monthly fee. The monthly subscription fee is $21.90 for unlimited use, $19.50 a month for automatic renewal, or $11.95 for a 24-hour day of unlimited use. Dealers and institutions have special subscription plans that include features for advertising their galleries and artworks. To avoid automatic renewal, edit your profile and cancel your subscription as soon as you register or you'll be charged another $21.90, unless, of course, you want to signup for another month's service.

ARTIST TABLE OF CONTENTS
Askart provides a free opportunity to tour its site, therefore do so. Note the wealth of information available free and also what is available on a subscription-fee basis. The tour uses two artists as examples, Edgar Payne and Herman Herzog, because they receive the most inquiries. A Table of Contents is provided for all 35,000 artists. Let's look at Edgar Payne's:

Edgar Payne (1883-1947), California artist, known for mountains, harbors, and figures.

Table of Contents		Click and Find
Artworks for sale	13	13 dealers sell paintings by Edgar Payne
Artworks Wanted	15	15 dealers wanting to buy works by Payne
# Dealers	42	42 dealers specializing in Payne's artwork
# Museums	21	21 museums holding paintings by Payne
Biographies:	Yes	Biographies on Edgar Payne are available
Active Bulletins	1	1 active bulletin with current comments
# Books	74	74 book titles on Edgar Payne
# Periodicals	36	36 periodicals featuring Payne's work
Image Gallery	536	536 color images of Payne's work to view
# Auction Records	489	489 auction results to study and compare
Graphs	Yes	Graphs showing Payne's price economics
Magazine Archives	Yes	Magazine Archives available
Record Price:	2003	Record Price $347,200 achieved 07/26/03

Askart.com can help considerably in the sale of your American painting. Find the artist alphabetically, then click and review the Table of Contents for your artist. In the above example, you'll find 15 collectors interested in possibly buying your painting by Edgar Payne, included are their telephone numbers and contact information. Call these interested buyers, make a deal. If you're buying Edgar Payne paintings, 13 collectors are listed to sell you their paintings and 42 dealers willing to assist you with the sale or purchase of an Edgar Payne painting. You can also look at 536 color digital images of Edgar Payne's works to study and 489 auction results to compare with the price of your painting.

The artist's Table of Contents can help you decide whether or not to bid on an Edgar Payne painting.

DIRECTORIES

Askart also offers free access to directories for Museums, Dealers, Auction Houses, Professional Associations, and an Art Glossary, including Dealer Artworks for Sale. All this is available free at Askart.

SHORTCUTS TO FINDING A *CATALOGUE RAISONNÉ*

UCLA's Art Library Web site, www.library.ucla.edu, offers excellent help finding a *catalogue raisonné* for an artist. Unfortunately, all *catalogues raisonnés* are not found in a single directory or research location. Sometimes difficult to find, they are not consistently identified in library catalogues. These sources are described in the title by other terms or phrases such as the German "*werkverzeichnis* . . . ," or "the complete works . . . ," or "the paintings of . . . ," etc. The following guide will give you some assistance in identifying whether or not a *catalogue raisonné* for your artist exists. Try the following keyword searches:

- Keyword search for *catalogue raisonné* and artist's name, e.g. **catalogue raisonné Picasso.**
- Keyword search for *werkverzeichnis* and artist's name, e.g. ***werkvereichnis* Chagall.**
- Keyword search for complete paintings and artist's name, e.g. **complete paintings da Vinci.**
- Keyword search for other media such as complete drawings, prints, sculpture, e.g. **complete etching Rembrandt.**
- Keyword search for complete catalogue and artist's name, e.g. **complete catalogue Cezanne.**
- Keyword search for complete works and artist's name, e.g. **complete works Reynolds.**

WHAT IF THERE IS NO *CATALOGUE RAISONNÉ* FOR AN ARTIST

Many artists, even famous ones, do not yet have a *catalogue raisonné* published for their body of work. Some never will be published. Nevertheless, you can still determine if your painting is authentic or not.

FINDING A SUBJECT EXPERT

Start by Googling for museums holding paintings by your artist or the galleries and dealers that represent this artist. Make a keyword search for a dealer and artist's name, e.g. Hermann Herzog dealer, or, Albert Bierstadt gallery. Search free at Askart.com or Artnet.com. For example, in 2004 Askart shows 122 museums that hold paintings by the artist Childe Hassam, listing their addresses and telephone numbers. Call the museums or galleries in your area to inquire who is the subject expert for your artist or School of art. Then make an appointment to meet with that person. Ask if you can bring along a painting to be viewed (but *not* appraised).

You're trying to find the most qualified person who is an expert on your artist. The expert's credentials, experience, and reputation must be impeccable. He must be considered superior by his peers, in galleries, auction rooms, and academia.

When you find this expert, don't be surprised if he's reluctant to evaluate your painting. We live in a litigious society. Many scholars and institutions have been sued for discrediting a painting's authenticity and then rejecting it. In fact, most museums and institutions have policies that forbid curatorial staff from offering price estimates on works of art. But many experts will offer an opinion, and you're looking for one *in writing.* Realize that the private expert will charge a fee for a written opinion, authentication of attribution, or art historical assessment. Such expert scholarly services are not free, but will substantiate considerably the worth of your work.

EXPERT TESTIMONY

Another way to have your painting accepted is to find a subject expert to examine your painting. This could be an art historian, museum curator, or a recognized dealer at a renowned gallery. Approval by a major auction room, such as Christie's or Sotheby's also can confer authentication, but such endorsements usually come without a guarantee, and it's not as strong as the approval that comes from a recognized expert.

A curator is still your best source for help in finding a subject expert or a *catalogue raisonné* for your artist. (See Chapter 8, "Provenance, Due Diligence, Forgery, and *Catalogues Raisonnés*" for a detailed discussion on this subject.)

CASE EXAMPLE: Finding an Expert For a Minor Artist

A dealer found a painting of a woman standing in front of a bedroom dresser looking at her reflection in a mirror. A candlestick, brass dish, and a Buddha statue ornamented the dresser top. The artwork was an exceptional oil painting, 16" X 12", unsigned, and the dealer paid $60 for it.

The only thing the dealer knew for sure was the painting's age: circa 1950s. With that, he researched New York City galleries specializing in art from the 1930s to 1950s, and sent them a digital image. One response came back quite positive: "Looks like the work of Agnes Richmond."

Agnes M. Richmond (1870-1964) was an accomplished artist, but her paintings never achieved recognition or commercial success. Her high auction record is only $9,000. She lived in Brooklyn, New York, for a period of time, painting extensively between 1920 and 1960. Her depictions included many interior apartment scenes, such as the subject matter in this painting.

The dealer Googled for the National Museum of Women Artists in Washington, D.C. (www.nmwa.org), and contacted the Chief Archivist who found an obscure record of a gallery in Georgia that once exhibited Agnes M. Richmond's paintings and listed the name of the gallery's curator. The dealer then did a national search on www.switchboard.com and finally located the former curator, who indeed was an expert on Agnes M.

Richmond. He agreed to look at a digital image and offer an opinion.

Not every research project turns up the results you're looking for. The expert's e-mail ended any hope of this painting being of, or by Agnes M. Richmond: "*I do not think it is an Agnes Richmond painting. It's too rough, clunky, rounded forms, too Ashcan School-like and not enough impressionistic touches. I do not recall A.R. using ornaments such as a Buddha, candelabra, or brass dish. There's a self-portrait in a Florida private collection, and this is not a portrait of Agnes Richmond, which leads me to believe it is not by A.R. because it is definitely a self-portrait. Sorry I could not be more helpful.*"

Identifying the name of the artist of this unsigned painting would indeed be satisfying; like putting a tombstone on an unmarked grave, it brings final rest. But some people's identities remain known but to God, such as the artist of this self-portrait.

The dealer did not, however, consider the research project a loss. He expanded his business base. He now had a new contact in a New York City gallery that specialized in paintings from the 1930s to 1950s—the kind of artwork he frequently came upon. He also opened a door in the National Museum of Women Artists in Washington, D.C. What's more, he developed a working relationship with a new art expert and a former curator. These contacts will be important to his art business and will bear future fruit.

Best of all, he still has this strong, accomplished self-portrait of the woman looking at her reflection in a mirror, which always will intrigue him.

THE CURATOR

We end this chapter as it could have started, by acknowledging the curator. In fact, the subject in every chapter of this book is the specialty of the curator. A curator is the best ally you could have in the art business. Curators are incredibly knowledgeable about art, which is why they run our nation's museums and oversee vast fortunes in public and private art collections. Curators are highly educated, usually with a Ph.D. in art history. They continually study art, conduct research, collaborating with other curators and art historians. They have the best pulse on what's happening in almost every aspect of art. They have to: it's their business and career. A curator will almost certainly know the answer to your art questions, or know how to find the answer. What's more, curators will be able to make introductions for you, perhaps with a personal reference. If you can't identify who the expert is for your artist, or can't find a *catalogue raisonné* for your artist, ask a curator.

Curators, however, are always busy with museum affairs; dealing with patrons and charitable gifts, meeting with board members, and coordinating exhibitions. It won't be easy to enlist their time in your research project, but it doesn't hurt to ask. One way to get to know the curator in your city is to become a member of your local museum and participate in various social, cultural, and education events. (See Chapter 3, "Becoming a Connoisseur" for ways to join a museum.) Another way to get to know your curator is if you own a painting by an artist that would fit into a current or future exhibition: offer to lend your painting to the museum. Lending a painting to a museum is a win-win situation. It establishes visibility for you, and it helps the museum. It also adds credible reference to the provenance of your painting—now including the museum, which should translate into raising the painting's appraised value. Your painting could be worth more coming out of a museum exhibition than going in. Moreover, the museum pays insurance for your painting while it's on loan.

However you do it, get to know curators. They can be of great help to you.

KUNSTMARKT.COM

This German Web site is added parenthetically at the end of this chapter because the above *American databases*, particularly Artnet.com, are used by most art specialists, including those in Europe. Nevertheless, Kunstmarkt.com offers excellent art research information. If you go to this Web site, click on the American flag on the left side of the Home Page to translate contents from German to English.

The *Kunstmarkt* database offers eight major categories of art information: "Magazine," "Art+Capital," "Knowledge," "Artists," "Art Buy," "Auctions," "Galleries," and "Addresses." If you click on "Addresses," for example, then click on "Auctions," you will find contact information for European auction houses; in Belgium there are 11, in Germany 104, Denmark 3, Finland 1, France 2, Great Britain 4, Italy 5, Monaco 1, The Netherlands 7, Switzerland 15, Spain 1, Austria 1, and Israel 1.

If you need to consign an artwork to a European gallery or auction room, this site will be very useful to you.

8

Provenance, Due Diligence, Forgery, *Catalogues Raisonnés*

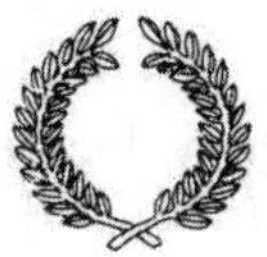

Potentially too much is at stake for you to risk not to have a working knowledge of provenance, due diligence, forgery, and *catalogues raisonnés.* Even though these issues generally concern the scholar and art historian, you also need to understand how these issues can impact your art business, for good or bad. Ample research information is available so you can buy and sell art legally, confidently, and profitably. Let's look at each issue in detail.

PROVENANCE

Provenance originally meant "place of origin," but today more generally means "history of ownership." Technically, a provenance traces a work of art from the time it leaves an artist's studio right up to its present owner and location, recording all the stops and transactions along the way. A provenance weaves together a record of ownership. That time span can be fifty years or five hundred years.

A documented provenance largely serves two purposes, (1) to support a claim for rightful ownership of lost, stolen, or looted art, and (2) to add legitimacy and authenticity to the purchase or sale of a work of art. You will most likely be concerned with the latter, but it's important to understand the former, as well as the scholarship involved in provenance research, and where the best Web sites, databases, and records are kept.

DOCUMENTATION

Museums are most concerned with provenance research because their inventory might include objects of cultural property that, under current laws and conventions, would have to be returned to the country of origin if it were found to be illegally located in the United States. Whether a work of art is an Old Master painting or a flea market special, proper diligence is always required when buying art. Unless the acquiring party can prove "good faith," or plead ignorance, an object of art can be confiscated under UNIDROIT Conventions (International Institute for the Unification of Private Law), and returned to its rightful owner. A museum, for example, would not be able to plead ignorance in order to escape its obligation of due diligence.

Gaps in provenance always raise suspicion. Scholars and researchers continually try to stitch together gaps in a provenance with bits and pieces of historical information. Nowadays, when a museum discovers an artwork in its inventory without a provenance or with a serious gap in the provenance, the museum will post that artwork on its Web site for the world to see. Since World War II when art looting was systematically carried out by the Nazis as well as misappropriated by Allied forces, the art world has attempted to come clean—to be transparent. If your family has a rightful claim to looted art, begin checking gaps in provenance records posted on museum Websites. (Also be sure to register your stolen Old Master with the local police, with INTERPOL, the Lost Art Register, and with the FBI if it's valued over $2,000. See below.)

CASE EXAMPLE: A Gap in Time

A collector once submitted a beautiful painting by George Innes to a competent restorer for a new canvas lining. The restorer took more time than originally estimated, but eventually returned the painting fully lined, and the painting went right back on the collector's living room wall.

Several years later the collector was stunned when he discovered that his beautiful painting by George Innes had just been sold in a New York City auction room. The painting on his living room wall was a copy, and not the painting he submitted to the restorer.

A skilled forger doesn't take long to make a complete new painting of an important artwork and make it look old. Distinguishing a carefully painted fake from the original can be indeed difficult especially if the canvas was lined at the owner's request. Without an original bill of sale, provenance, documentation, or a conservation contract, the collector had no proof that he ever owned an original painting by George Innes.

A painting that suddenly appears in the marketplace with a one hundred year gap in its provenance, where no one knew its whereabouts, will understandably raise red flags and cause concern. You need to have this painting re-authenticated. A specialist scholar, at a negotiated rate, will need to re-examine this painting to make sure it is still the original Old Master.

PROVENANCE RESEARACH

The Los Angeles County Museum of Art has an excellent Web site at www.lacma.org/Provenance/documentation, which offers information on how to read a provenance, related links, and the following explanation:

> *Provenance research begins by assembling the information in the museum's* files—acquisition *and exhibition records, scholarly references, and correspondence. The information on each object varies, depending on the date and circumstances of the acquisition and past research on the object. The goal is to find specific names and dates that will identify when and from whom each owner acquired the work, and to whom and when each relinquished ownership of it. It is important to document the circumstances of that transfer—sale, inheritance, or gift. Exhibition catalogues, which identify the owner at a specific date, sale catalogues, especially those annotated with names of buyers and sellers, collection catalogues, and* catalogues raisonnés *(monographic books with lists of all the known works of an artist) are important sources of information. Other clues may be found in photo archives and scholarly articles about the artists and/or collectors. Papers and business records of collectors and dealers are very valuable sources of information, but they are often limited by the availability of the records, as well as by the willingness of dealers to reveal their sources. Digging deeper, the researcher may look for wills, insurance inventories, and other personal documentation.*

WHAT GOES INTO A PROVENANCE

You're trying to piece together a trail of names of owners who bought and sold a work of art, perhaps spanning several hundreds years, in order to determine when the transfers of ownership took place, and whether it was by a sale, inheritance, or gift. To close any gaps between owners in a provenance, you might have to research library references, auction house catalogues, museum databases, and historical data.

Perhaps the best place to start your research is with The Getty Provenance Index. The Getty's six databases of ownership records are available at its Web site, www.peidi.getty.edu. The Frick Museum in New York City is an excellent source for art information, its library having over 70,000 auction catalogues dating back to the 17th century and over one million images in its photo archives. The Frick Library at www.fresco.frick.org/screens/provbib.htm will provide links to many other museums, libraries, and art research databases. Other excellent Web sites for provenance research are The National Gallery of Art at www.nga.gov/collection/collect.html, The Art Institute of Chicago at www.artic.edu, and The National Archives at www.nara.gov/research/assets/bib/lotart.html.

PAYING FOR PROVENANCE RESEARCH

If you're prepared to buy a world-class painting and pay a world-class price, you should have it authenticated by a world-class authority, someone who will guarantee that the painting will be included in a *catalogue raisonné*.

CASE EXAMPLE: Importance of Provenance

Two versions of the "Little Soldier," painted by Eastman Johnson (1824 –1906), both comparable in size, quality, and condition, and of the same subject, had very different results at auction. One sold at Christie's New York for $85,000. Seven months later the other version sold at Doyle New York for $607,500. The difference was provenance: the latter was owned by John B. Stanchfield, the attorney who defended millionaire Henry Thaw in the notorious murder case that inspired the Broadway musical "Ragtime." Notable owners add value.

DUE DILIGENCE

Due diligence is a two-edged sword, obligating both the buyer and the seller. Special problems arise when a third party is involved, like a thief. The three parties in a due diligence dispute are: (1) the rightful owner, (2) the thief, or someone who facilitates an illegal transaction involving stolen art, and (3) the innocent acquirer who buys a painting in "good faith." The law is somewhat imprecise and requires interpretation; nevertheless, each party has an obligation to fulfill under due diligence statues.

The thief, of course, goes to jail if he can ever be found. Usually, he's never heard from again. The dispute is left to the rightful owner and the innocent buyer to settle. A judge usually has to decide how much due diligence is enough, and determine if you did "enough" to protect your interest, as law requires. Let's see what you can do to avoid disputes in your art transactions.

RIGHTFUL OWNER

In the case of stolen art, the law allows a rightful owner to recover his artwork from an innocent acquirer who bought the painting in "good faith," without compensating the buyer in any way. However, much depends on whether the rightful owner exercised due diligence after discovering his art was stolen, and when, exactly, he discovered his art missing. Common law statues allow a rightful owner six years for recovery of stolen art, but such right can be breached by a lack of diligence on the part of the rightful owner.

DATE OF DISCOVERY

The question arises, when does the six-year limitation begin? Do the six years begin when the rightful owner discovers an artwork missing or when the theft actually took place? It depends. Let us assume an artwork is discovered missing from a museum, and records show the last inventory taken by the museum was twenty years ago. In this case, no one knows when the theft actually took place. A judge might decide the museum should reasonably take an inventory every four years and bar the plaintiff in the above example from seeking remedy due to a lack of diligence. The thief might have sold the painting at auction ten years ago. Under common law, the party who bought the painting in good faith would normally have to return it to its rightful owner, unless he can prove such rightful owner did not exercise due diligence after discovering the artwork missing. So the innocent buyer might still be able to keep his painting.

HOW MUCH DILIGENCE IS ENOUGH?

The rightful owner in the above example (the museum) should update its custody and security policies and take inventory more frequently. Moreover, a diligent curator should be checking major auction rooms to monitor the sale of similar works of art.

If a valuable antique is discovered missing, the rightful owner should immediately report the item missing.

File a report with:

- Local police.
- Art Loss Register: www.artloss.com.
- FBI: www.fbi.gov/majcases/arttheft/art.
- INTERPOL: www.stolenart.net.
- Museum Security Network: www.museum-security.org.
- Holocaust Art Theft: www.wjc-artrecovery.org.

If a rightful owner is diligent in reporting stolen art, as above suggested, he will go a long way in protecting his rights under law, shifting the burden of proof to the buyer. Let's see what the buyer can do to protect his rights under law.

GOOD FAITH BUYER

If you're buying investment art valued over $10,000, especially if valued over $50,000, and either the provenance or the seller is suspect, shaky, or unbelievable, then you should check art theft resources on the Internet to see if the artwork has been reported stolen. The above Websites are where a diligent owner might register stolen art. A judge might uphold your right as a "good faith" buyer in a dispute if the result of your search is negative, and you can prove you diligently tried to find out if the artwork was stolen. The judge might even allow you to keep your artwork (providing the owner exhibited a lack of diligence). On the other hand, if a buyer acquires artworks from a known thief or questionable source, where reasonable doubt about title exists, the buyer could forfeit his right to protection under the law. He might well be ordered to return the painting to the rightful owner.

LIMITATION OF RIGHTS

Uniform Commercial Code 2-725 gives a buyer four years from date of purchase to bring suit for breach of warranty.

CASE EXAMPLE: Rosen v. Spanierman

Spanierman's in New York City is a reputable art gallery and in 1968 sold a painting represented to be by John Singer Sargent. Spanierman continued to report to the buyer on the painting's increasing value in subsequent years, until 1987 when the purchaser learned from Christie's that the painting was not by John Singer Sargent. The painting turned out to be a complete fake, and the buyer brought suit against Spanierman Gallery. However, in this case the court found that the date of discovery was not as relevant as the date of purchase. The buyer should not have waited 19 years to have the painting authenticated. The court decided that a prudent person would have had the painting re-appraised within four years of purchase, and therefore refused to allow the plaintiff remedy. Since the buyer failed to exercise due diligence, "future performance" was not a relevant factor.

Verify your valuable art for authenticity within four years of the purchase date to protect your rights under UCC laws.

OBLIGATION UNDER DUE DILIGENCE

Both parties are obligated under due diligence. The sooner and more thoroughly you report stolen art the better; and the more thoroughly you make sure the artwork you want to purchase isn't stolen, the better off you'll be. Keep accurate records.

KEEPING RECORDS

Start a folder for each artwork you acquire, keeping related documents and records there. The buyer should insist that the seller or transferor provide a bill of sale for every painting bought. The buyer also should insist that the seller provide the name of the rightful owner before any transaction is consummated. Short of that, the seller must warrant and state that as an agent of the owner he has the right to convey title and ownership to the buyer.

FORGERY

Art legend indicates that Jean Baptiste Camille Corot painted 2,000 pictures in his lifetime, 5,000 of which are in the United States. The professional forger has had a field day releasing "newly discovered" masterpieces on an unsuspecting and unknowledgeable public, while fooling many scholars along the way. Let us begin our discussion on forgery by first looking at a celebrated case example of a master forger at work.

CASE EXAMPLE: Master Forger

Dutch painter Han Van Meegeren (1889-1947) was arguably the best-known forger of the 20th century. At the end of World War II, an Allied art commission (set up to recover looted art) discovered a previously "unknown work" of Jan Vermeer in the collection of Nazi Field Marshall Hermann Goering. Goering was an obsessed art collector. His collection, however, was missing one Old Master, and he coveted a painting by Jan Vermeer. So Meegeren created one for him. The story goes that

Meegeren traded his forged Vermeer to Goering for 200 lesser, authentic Dutch paintings already stolen by the Nazis, which Meegeren brought back to Holland. The bill of sale for the Vermeer painting was found among Goering's records and traced back to Meegeren, who was charged in May 1945 with selling a Dutch national treasure (the forged Vermeer painting) to and collaborating with the enemy. Selling a national treasure and collaborating with the enemy were serious crimes, and brought a much stiffer prison sentence than that of forgery. So Meegeren confessed to forging the Vermeer painting; and rather than "collaborating with the enemy," he argued that he tricked the Nazis. However, the tribunal didn't believe him. The work was simply too good, therefore the experts believed the painting was an authentic undiscovered Vermeer which Meegeren had sold to Field Marshal Goering. Selling a Dutch national treasure to the Nazis during World War II was tantamount to treason.

To prove his innocence, Meegeren first had to prove that he was guilty of forgery. To do this, he had to paint another "Vermeer" in his prison cell, which the authorities allowed him to do. In all, Van Meegeren is now recognized by Vermeer experts to have painted 14 forgeries of Vermeer and also fake examples by Pieter De Hooch, several of which had been proclaimed masterpieces by scholars before learning that they were imitations.

What one of the world's most preeminent art experts, Abraham Bredius, said when first seeing the "discovered" fake Meegeren Vermeer: "What we have here is a—I am inclined to say THE masterpiece of Johannes Vermeer." (See www.mystudios.com for more information on the Meegeren case, and other general art facts.)

The easiest faking occurs when a forger takes a genuine period painting of a lesser artist, preferably from the same School (say, a talented student or studio assistant of, for example, Corot), and forges a more distinguished name onto the canvas. The forger then sells the painting as an original work by the artist of greater stature. In this case, creating an "aged look" is not necessary, as the canvas, stretcher, and materials used are already age-appropriate for the master's work. Often though, the faker will paint in certain additional accents to existing details to "improve" the unauthentic canvas. Such added improvements, including a bogus signature, initials, or monogram can be revealed by examination under ultra violet light.

A newly "discovered" artwork might even come with a certificate of authenticity, which should not be taken at face value. It's easy to create academic stationery signed by a scholar attributing an artwork to a Master. Call the expert; fax him the certificate; ask if he signed it. But even if he did, he could be wrong. If you still have concerns, take the painting to another expert. Even among specialty experts, one may have a better "eye," a more discerning ability. Moreover, be wise concerning the eye of the specialty expert, who may lean conservatively to protect his reputation. Keep in mind when you seek the advice of an expert, particularly in terms of a commercial rather than educational context, he will charge for expertise services.

COPIES

Copies are too easy to make and present little challenge for the skilled forger. As with any painting you buy, check Internet archival photos to see if the same or a very similar painting already exists, and if so, with whom. A brazen copier might leave the original painting in a museum and try to sell you his copy. Finding copies, however, is not absolute proof of fraudulent behavior. Gilbert Stuart, for example, painted dozens of original paintings of George Washington. Ronald D. Spencer's book, *The Expert versus the Object*, tell us "When you see a duplicate painted by the Master, it's called a replica. When you see a duplicate painted by a copier, it's called a forgery."

A successful forger would be unlikely to copy an Old Master. Instead, he'd create a whole new masterpiece in the hand of the Old Master. In fact, he might invent a new period for the Old Master, where no examples exist for comparison. For example, Vermeer's early work was of religious subjects and his later work, genre scenes. A skilled forger would create a painting in Vermeer's "transitional" period (there was none) in the style and technique of Vermeer's hand, but slightly different from his earlier or later work. How do they do this?

FORGERY TECHNIQUES

The forger studies the Master's work, practicing and experimenting for years until his work matches the Master's hand. During this preparation time, the forger gathers materials from the period, such as canvas, stretchers, and paints. He grinds pigments as the Master did, using brushes made of the same materials. Some forgers even decorate their studios with period antiques to put themselves in the Master's frame of mind. To avoid X-radiography detection, the forger strips away all remnants of the original painting.

After creating an artwork indistinguishable from the Master's hand (except to an experienced expert), the forger has to create the necessary age to fool the experts. Dark varnish would be added, and the finished product baked to perfection in an oven. The forger then would roll the dried painting until the right crackle effect was achieved, and finally the cracks were filled with India ink to fool the best experts.

SELLING A FORGERY

A forger can add credibility to a fake masterpiece by creating a believable provenance, then giving the painting to an unsuspecting attorney or dealer to sell for him. For example, creating a provenance for a fake painting by Jean Francois Millet (1814-1875), might read like the hypothetical example below:

> *A young French girl living on the edge of the Forest Fontainebleau received the painting as a wedding gift from her great-grandmother who ran a boarding house where the artist lived when he painted in the village of Barbizon. That woman gave the painting to her daughter as a wedding gift when she married an American soldier after World War II, who subsequently moved to Cleveland, Ohio, in 1948. This woman never had children, and when she died in 2001 the attorney representing her estate sold the painting at auction in Chicago, where it fetched $67,000.* (Not bad for a forged painting with a completely fabricated provenance.)

So as not to perpetuate fraud, some collectors who learn they unwittingly acquired a forged painting without recourse, might have the forged name removed (painted over), and sell the painting as a decorative "unsigned" work at a loss. Learning from his experience, though bitter, the collector is forewarned. *Caveat emptor.*

CATALOGUES RAISONNÉS

If a *catalogue raisonné* lists your painting among an artist's work, it's proof that your painting is authentic, unless the word "dubious" or "fake" is associated with it, in which case you have the kiss of death on your painting. No reputable gallery or auction house will represent it; it will be very difficult to sell. If you find a *catalogue raisonné* for your artist, and then discover your painting was omitted from the publication, you'll have an uphill battle proving your painting is authentic, much less worth top dollar.

All this might seem of little importance to you and it is, unless you paid $200,000 for a painting by, for example, Fitz Hugh Lane; then some expert tries to tell you your painting is a copy or a forgery or a misattribution; your example at best is worth only

$3,000. Now a *catalogue raisonné* takes on practical importance: you'll no doubt start looking for another expert opinion and I dare say the dealer who sold you the painting, along with a successful trial attorney.

Catalogues raisonnés, however scholarly, are subject to error, sometimes even deliberate misrepresentation. Not all *catalogues raisonnés* are reliable or equal. A *catalogue raisonné's* veracity and authority is directly tied to the credibility of the scholar who examined the paintings.

WHAT IS A *CATALOGUE RAISONNÉ*?

A *catalogue raisonné* is a comprehensive listing of an artist's entire work, or work in a particular medium, with entries presented in chronological order. Details can vary but generally they include the date of work, size, medium, subject, condition, provenance, attribution, and last known location. Often, essays, analyses, and exhibition records also are included. The cataloguer creates an identification record for a specific artwork, like a painting's fingerprint, where decades or centuries later, a painting presented as the original can easily be confirmed or denied.

Producing a *catalogue raisonné* can take many years, even decades to complete. Some scholars spend their entire life working on a single artist's oeuvre. It's not a very profitable enterprise. Consequently, most *catalogues raisonnés* are sponsored by universities, museums, and institutions. Committees have replaced the lone cataloguer, where consensus is now sought among scholars, curators, and connoisseurs to determine if an artwork is authentic or not, and if it should be included in a *catalogue raisonné*. The consequences can be significant if a painting is omitted from a *catalogue raisonné*.

WHO SPONSORS A *CATALOGUE RAISONNÉ*?

Catalogues raisonnés are sponsored by families and estates of artists, by universities and museums, even cities and countries where an artist was born. The sponsor generally forms a committee, and funds scholars, historians, and connoisseurs to research and examine all the known works of an artist's oeuvre, which can take years of painstaking work. The "Committee" then decides which paintings are included in the *catalogue raisonné* and which are excluded. Such a discriminating process is required to best protect an artist's name and the value of his work.

In French law, however, the *droit moral* (moral right) is left to the wife of a deceased artist, or passed down to relatives of the artist, who decide what is or is not authentic. Fraught with self-interest, this practice has led in many instances to misattributions and false entries in catalogues raisonnés.

BIAS IN *CATALOGUES RAISONNÉS*

Some scholars' reputations have been compromised when dealers and collectors collude to influence outcomes. Notably, Renaissance scholar Benard Berenson was actually hired by British art dealer Joseph Duveen (1886-1939) to authenticate his Renaissance collection. Duveen was the quintessential art dealer selling paintings he didn't own to people who didn't want them, and sold many Old Master paintings to his American clientele. He built world-class collections for these "robber barons," the likes of Henry Clay Frick, William Randolph Hearst, Henry E. Huntington, Samuel H. Kress, Andrew Mellon, John D. Rockefeller, and Joseph E. Widener. In a time when Duveen's reputation grew as the premier art dealer of his day, the reputation of his hired scholar, Berenson, diminished, largely due to his apparent lack of probity and independent judgment. Nevertheless, Berenson is still regarded as a preeminent Renaissance scholar (especially early Renaissance). The Committee approach to consensus agreement is far more impartial and accurate.

THE CONSEQUENCES OF REVISING A *CATALOGUE RAISONNE*

The art field is always changing and self-correcting. New technologies and increased scholarship over the years have improved analytical processes. What once was thought to be an authentic masterpiece, might now be classified a forgery and therefore excluded from a *catalogue raisonné.* Obviously, such a revision or reconsideration can have catastrophic financial repercussions, and even life threatening results.

The renowned *Wildenstein Institute* in Paris probably sponsors more *catalogues raisonnés* than any other institution. Nevertheless, it recently had to announce the cancellation of the *catalogue raisonné* of Amedeo Modigliani's drawings, when threats were made to Marc Restellini (Modigliani drawing expert) because he had decided to omit questionable drawings from a new publication. Deciding to omit artwork from a *catalogue raisonné* can make a millionaire penniless overnight. On the other hand, including a new artwork in a *catalogue raisonné* can create a fortune for another owner. For a detailed examination of this subject, read *The Expert versus the Object,* Edited by Ronald D. Spencer (Oxford University Press, 2004).

SELLING A WORK OF ART SUBJECT TO AUTHENTICATION

Many paintings are sold subject to approval by an expert, or guaranteed inclusion in the next printing of a *catalogue raisonné.* Paintings sold for under $50,000 often are guaranteed by a handshake between dealers, but over $50,000, certainly for those over $100,000, buyers want a written guarantee by a recognized expert. As the dealer or seller's representative, you have to obtain the expert opinion; you should include the cost of obtaining the guarantee in the painting's sales price. The process can take time, and generally no money will change hands until the expert renders the guarantee.

Committees for *catalogues raisonnés* of European paintings generally convene in such cities as Paris,

Rome, Berlin, or Amsterdam. Sometimes meeting only twice a year to review paintings. They don't make it easy for you. Sometimes but rarely, the Committee will allow a consensus decision to be made from a 4" X 4" transparency. Otherwise, you will have to ship your artwork—at your expense—to wherever the Committee will meet. These expenses will not be cheap. But having the Committee approve your painting for inclusion in a *catalogue raisonné* can breathe life and considerable dollars into the sale of your painting.

INTERNATIAONAL FOUNDATION FOR ART RESEARCH

The International Foundation for Art Research (IFAR) offers a unique, impartial, and authoritative Art Authentication Research Service for works of art whose authorship is in question. IFAR draws on its own distinguished Advisory Council and an international network of eminent scholars and scientists.

Who May Apply. IFAR's Authentication Research Service is offered to individuals, art dealers, museums, and other institutions. IFAR will only examine a work for an owner or an agent officially representing the owner, or a prospective buyer with the owner's written permission.

Cost. IFAR charges an initial, non-refundable $250 deposit at the inquiry stage. This will be applied to the basic $2,000 cost if IFAR is able to undertake the research, and the client and IFAR agree to proceed. This price might sound steep, but if you're thinking of buying or selling a $50,000 painting, $2,000 is a bargain for the assurance and peace of mind you gain by knowing that your painting is authentic.

IFAR is an outstanding and distinguished art research foundation, offering many programs and services to its members, including the *IFAR Journal.* For subscription rates, membership fees, and other information, see www.ifar.org.

"It is in a museum that one learns to paint"

—**Pierre-Auguste Renoir** (1841-1919)

9

Buying Art

Finding valuable art and buying it at the right price is why you bought this book in the first place. Now it's time to put your investment money on the line and write a check. However, before we discuss where to find valuable art and how to successfully close an art transaction, let's first establish your buying strategy and rehearse your buying criteria.

BUYING STRATEGY

Determined by whether you are a collector, investor, or dealer, your buying strategy is your motivation for buying art. Each buyer has his own strategy and outcome objective. The collector buys what he likes, the investor what he requires, and the dealer what he can resell for a profit in the shortest amount of time. The case example below develops these three mindsets.

Case Example: Buying Expatriate Art

To collect Expatriate Art, particularly by the first wave of Americans who painted at Giverny, you would notify galleries and dealers that you're interested in buying a landscape painting by the likes of Willard Metcalf, Louis Ritter, Theodore Wendel, John Leslie Breck, Richard Emile Miller, or Louis Paul Dressar.

One day you receive a phone call about a painting by John Leslie Breck that is coming on the market. It's titled: "Flower Garden at Giverny," oil on canvas, size 16" X 20", signed and dated 1896, in excellent condition. You're shown a 4" X 4" transparency of the picture.

In the following scenario, no price was given by the seller's agent, yet the collector, investor, and dealer have to decide if they want to buy this painting and if they do, how much they would be willing to pay for it. They each study the transparency, admiring the vibrant colors in the flower garden at Giverny. Each covets this beautiful painting.

When they research the artist's auction records, they see four other paintings by John Leslie Breck that sold at auction the same year (2000). The lowest priced oil painting sold for $22,000, the highest fetched $240,000, and the average was $58,000. (See Chapter 6 for a discussion on *Hislop's Price Guide to Fine Art:* "John Leslie Breck".)

At askart.com they study the digital image of the actual painting that sold for $240,000, noting that it was much larger and in greater detail than the painting offered them. The average-priced painting ($58,000), however, looked quite similar to theirs, both in subject and size.

How much would the collector, investor, and dealer be willing to pay for this painting?

COLLECTOR

The collector would like to add the Breck painting to his collection, estimating its value at $75,000. However, because so few American Expatriate landscapes set in Giverny between 1887 and 1897 come to market, he's willing to pay a premium for this work, up to $100,000, possibly $125,000. At auction, he might bid X plus one more bid: X = $125,000. Within his budget, this painting would bring him great pride and pleasure.

INVESTOR

The investor would like to buy the Breck painting because of its desirable subject matter and the high demand for this School of art, which he believes will continue to increase in value. Breck's garden paintings are among his most prized works. The investor estimates the painting also is worth $75,000. However, for the painting to fit within his investment strategy (having pre-sale equity), he would have to buy it for under $65,000. However, believing this painting to be so outstanding, he's willing to pay top dollar, up to $80,000—possibly $90,000. In five years, the investor imagines the painting will be worth $250,000.

DEALER

The dealer would like to buy the Breck painting because he knows a collector who might pay as much as $125,000 for this work right away. Sufficient time also exists for the dealer to put the painting into auction in the spring sale at Christie's or Sotheby's in New York City. In this case the hammer price could go to $200,000, possibly more. In either case, this dealer needs a partner to buy the painting; and he feels comfortable advising investors to pay as much as $100,000 for it.

READY TO BARGAIN

If offered the John Leslie Breck painting, "*Garden in Giverny*," the collector, investor, and dealer, having researched the painting thoroughly, are now ready to bargain with the seller's agent. Regardless of whether the painting is offered at $25,000, $75,000, or higher, they are ready with finances and prepared to take negotiations to their personal threshold. They each know how much they're willing to pay for it. Such preparation is every buyer's responsibility. (See page 128 for an analysis of John Leslie Breck's artworks.)

BUYING CRITERIA

Your buying criteria will help establish standards for buying investment quality art, thereby assuring you of a profitable outcome. (See Chapter 2, "Valuing Art," for a detailed discussion on the below value elements.)

Buy:

- original paintings signed and dated by the artist.
- listed artists with multiple auction records.
- paintings by artists who produced a prodigious body of work in their lifetime, e.g., more than two hundred paintings.
- works by artists who had major exhibitions and showings in their lifetime, e.g., The British Royal Academy, The Paris Salon, The National Academy of Design.
- artworks by artists whose School of art remains highly collected and in demand, e.g., Hudson River School, Brandywine School, California Impressionist School.
- representative examples of an artist's *oeuvre,* his central theme paintings; for example, Thomas Moran's Grand Canyon scenes, not his Venice or India pictures.
- subjects that other people collect and invest in, e.g., children at play, women under parasols, genre pictures, mountain and vista landscapes.
- examples that are fresh and new to the market (have not been at auction in five years).
- representative paintings of the artist's highest quality.
- large size paintings, preferably 24" X 36", but generally not larger than 60 inches on any side.
- examples that are in good to excellent condition.
- paintings with an authenticated well-documented provenance.

- artworks that come with a free title, bill of sale, and a guarantee.
- and unsigned paintings that are outstanding (if reasonably priced), especially if accompanied by firm attribution from a renowned specialty scholar.

WHERE TO FIND VALUABLE ART

There is a food chain in the art world. You can make a profit dealing at the top or feeding off the bottom. In the game of art, paintings move up the art chain until they surface and someone gobbles them up. Some paintings miss the rising tide, however, remaining hidden for decades, even centuries, in the most unlikely of places. Valuable paintings can be found in country taverns, church rectories, wrapped in paper in garages and attics, abandoned in mini storage bins, and sometimes discarded as trash on the curb. Probably less than 25% of the people who own an antique painting understand its true value. To many people it's just a picture on the wall handed down from generation to generation. Some people are so unappreciative of art that they just give paintings away, or store them with Christmas ornaments in the basement.

After training your eye to identify valuable art, be assertive and ask the owner if he would like to sell his painting. Be confident! Create and take advantage of opportunities. The following paragraphs will help you understand how to find and buy investment art.

We begin at the bottom of the supply line and look at how paintings move up the art chain. A "knocker," for example, typically sells to a "picker" and a picker then sells to a "dealer," but not always. A knocker can skip a step by selling to a dealer who may then sell directly to The National Gallery in Washington, D.C.

Valuable paintings can be found just about anywhere. There is no restriction on where you can buy or sell paintings. Whether you're a bottom feeder or find your food at the top, success will depend upon your knowledge, skill, and willingness to swim in deep water with the sharks. (See Appendix 2, Where to Find Art.)

KNOCKER

A knocker is a person who knocks on doors, then asks if the house owner has any old paintings to sell. There aren't many knockers left; it's a dying breed. But some dealers stay active in the old trade, still knocking on doors asking, "Do you have any antiques or old paintings you want to sell?" Such prospecting can be humbling, but also bears much fruit.

The experienced knocker knows on which doors to knock, whether the big house up on the hill or the old farmhouse on the dirt road. Inside can be an important painting hanging in a country kitchen, the value of which the owner might have no idea. A knocker always takes off his hat; past success ensures being polite and friendly. If perceived genuine, the knocker might get to see an old oil painting, while perhaps sipping a glass of ice tea.

You never know what a person needs until you ask. Possibly selling that old painting over the fireplace is just what they've wanted to do. Perhaps they need money at this point in their life. Truth is, you'll never know until you knock and ask. *Make a deal. Don't be shy.*

Always have cash in your pocket and know what to say when you're inside. (See "Bargaining Techniques" below.) If you know a knocker, support him. Let him know you're a serious art buyer, and you'll pay substantial money for worthy paintings. If you haven't done it yourself, try knocking on a few doors. It's good to know what a knocker's up against.

PICKER

Picking is the second oldest profession in the world. A picker makes his living on the road, driving up and down the highway, stopping at antique stores to buy and sell merchandise along the way. He buys an old chair in one store for $10 and sells it five miles down the road to another store for $15. He then picks up another item, and down the highway he goes. A professional picker will stop at 15 to 20 antique stores and secondhand shops in a day. The next day he'll farm a new area, and by the end of a week an active professional picker will comb an entire region. He knows every shop owner by name. His notebook is filled with a list of merchandise his dealers collect. He's picking every day, looking for the *chochkas* and paintings his clients want. At the end of the day he knows exactly where to go to sell his antiques.

The picker has an excellent eye for quality merchandise. He knows what sells. However, he does not understand value, pricing, or market conditions. A picker works on a cash basis out of his pocket, quickly selling what he buys to dealers in his area. He generally sells at a price largely determined by what he pays for an item, regardless of its inherent value. A picker acts on instincts. Rarely does he research and seldom does he look for new markets, especially higher up the art chain. He stays in his own groove, buys cheap, adds a profit, sells quickly, and moves on. Over time, a skilled picker will feed many valuable paintings to a dealer. Make sure he knows what you collect.

Coaching the picker. Cultivate mutually beneficial relationships with pickers throughout your region, even out of state and internationally. Let them know you're a serious buyer, willing to pay a high price for quality paintings. In cash! Give out your calling card. Ask the picker to call you any time he has something to show. Encourage him to notify you first, especially when he sees a painting he thinks is important, even if he can't afford it. Tell him you'll pay a handsome finder's fee. Occasionally buy a painting from a picker even if it's not exactly what you're looking for, just to support him (providing it's inexpensive and you can move it quickly, even just to break even). Then coach the picker, "What I'm really looking for is . . . ," explaining the hallmarks of the art you buy.

Never bargain down a loyal picker. Try never to bargain down a loyal picker. Usually you're looking at a painting that's reasonably priced. Never degrade or belittle a picker's merchandise or speak condescendingly. If you're not interested in a painting, simply say, "No, thank you. It's not for me. But I appreciate your showing it to me." Then coach the picker on what you're really looking for. And again, remind him that you pay the highest price for certain compelling art.

Don't forget to send a Christmas gift to those pickers with whom you've done business. A $25 or $50 gift certificate is a nice thank-you for a picker who brought you two paintings that year, which might have made for you $15,000 profit. Be sure to keep the supply of quality art flowing your way.

Pickers are not listed in the Yellow Pages, but you'll meet them in antique shops up and down the turnpike. They come into antique stores showing their wares all day long and if you're there you can observe the transaction. However, never come between a storeowner and a picker in order to buy the merchandise the picker is selling. Wait first until the storeowner has declined the offer. You're a guest in the store; remember the picker belongs to the storeowner, not to you. If you're interested in the piece, ask the storeowner if it's OK for you to examine the merchandise. You also can negotiate outside the store. *Make a deal. Don't be shy.* Many outstanding collections contain valuable antiques that were bought from a picker in a parking lot.

Not everyone shares your interest or knowledge about art. Many people decline opportunities to buy paintings, even valuable ones, because they don't understand art. That's to your benefit. The art dealer, however, *does* understand art. He not only shares your interest for art, but also your art territory. He surely wants to share your customer base, too. Remember, the art dealer is your friend but also your competitor.

DEALER

Dealers move the art world, making it an exciting place to work. Some 80 percent of all artwork sold is estimated to move from one dealer to another. You're more likely to sell a work of art to another dealer than to anyone else. Higher prices keep getting added each time a painting is sold to another dealer (or profit made from it), until one day the painting runs out of dealer interest. Eventually the last dealer will have difficulty selling this painting for a profit; he might even have to take it off the market for a period of time. Paintings that come to the end of their profit potential end up on someone's wall, usually a collector who has paid top dollar for his painting.

Make sure you're on the front end of the buying cycle, and not the last dealer to buy a painting. You want to be near the painting's discovery, not advising the final buyer where to hang his painting. The price should give you a clue. If the painting's price is very high, you might be near the end of the buying cycle, or the seller is asking an unrealistically high price. You don't have to buy this painting. Or consider making a counteroffer, for example, say $10,000 lower to create a profit for yourself.

Knowing the dealer can help you understand the pricing dynamics. How honest is the dealer? Does he leave room for the next dealer to make a profit, or does he squeeze every penny out of a painting? Have you done business with him before? Get references, especially if he's from out of town. The art world is a small fishbowl. Somewhere, someone who can give a reference for him is bound to know the dealer you're talking with on the telephone. Perhaps a dealer on the West Coast knows a dealer on the East Coast who knows this person. If no one has ever heard of the dealer, then extra caution is required. If you're the seller, never release a painting to an unknown person without having money in hand.

DEALER INTEGRITY

Dealers are supposed to be professional; integrity is expected, moreover required. You have a right to ask a dealer frank questions, while being prepared to answer them yourself. You can ask a dealer if he owns the painting outright or if he's acting as a broker. If as a broker, and it's an important painting, remind him that you will require the seller's name on the Bill of Sale before money can exchange hands. Short of this, the dealer must warrant and state in writing that he has the authority to sell the painting on behalf of the owner. The seller's name is required for provenance continuance, which is explained in detail in Chapter 8. Ask if the painting has been "shopped around." Make sure it was not recently sold at auction, or "bought-in" (did not sell). If the painting is fresh on the market, where did it come from? Do not expect a dealer to reveal his sources for buying art, while never revealing your own. But you have a right to know if a painting came from an auction, collector, gallery, or another dealer. If asked the same question, you might reply, "I bought it from a picker or a collector," which could imply the painting has recently been discovered; therefore it would be at the bottom of the art chain. Disclosing that your painting came from another dealer could raise suspicion, signaling that profit has already been taken out of it, leaving less equity for you. Always check auction databases to see if the exact painting recently sold or was bought-in at auction. If it was recently auctioned and the dealer denied knowing this, then he's either lying or very inexperienced.

DEALER GUARANTEE

Reputable dealers will give you a guarantee, so ask for it. The guarantee ensures that the painting is by the artist the seller claims painted it, in the condition promised, or else the buyer's money is returned. This understanding is especially important for collectors and investors; a dealer also should insist on the same guarantee, in writing, of course. When time is a factor, a guarantee can be executed by e-mail, so long as the painting's description, price, condition, and deliverable promises are spelled out, and it is agreed that when the second party returns the e-mail to the first party, an enforceable contract is being put into operation. You must stipulate: "You agree to return my money without delay or question if the terms agreed upon as indicated above are not all met satisfactorily." If you agree to this, please type "I AGREE," and return this message to me." When you receive the e-mail, print it and file a hardcopy in your folder marked "AGREEMENTS." A sensible precaution would entail having an e-mail agreement with dealers you regularly do business with; it establishes a record of what both parties agree to. For complex agreements or high-value transactions, including dealing with multiple parties, a formal agreement would certainly be best.

DEALER CREDIBILITY—The Three Ts

You can influence how people talk about you. Your job as a professional is not only to buy and sell paintings, but also to manage people's perception of you. In the art business, your credibility is defined by your talk, tactics, and talent.

- **Talk.** Keep your word, always. Back up what you say with action. Once you give a price, make an offer, or shake a hand, never go back on your word. Your integrity is about keeping your word.

- **Tactics.** How you conduct your business matters. Do you leave money for the next dealer? Do you reward positive action? Do you give first right of refusal to loyal customers? Do you pay quickly, split profits fairly, and go back to say thank you? A client will surely remember your thoughtful gesture of going back to that old farm house, knocking on the door to say, "Here, Madam. I made more on the painting than I thought I would. Here's another $500."

- **Talent.** Nothing builds credibility like putting together a successful art transaction. When people see you raise $150,000 to buy a major artwork, regardless if the money is yours or an investor's, you build credibility in the trade. When that seller finds another important painting, he's coming right back to you; he knows you can come up with substantial money. Word gets out. More opportunities will come to you. Success builds on experience. Your reputation and credibility will grow as you perfect your own talk, tactics, and talent.

CHALLENGE vs. OPPORTUNITY

Some art transactions are complex, presenting a challenge: you have no money, no buyer in mind, and no clue for raising the money. It's OK; *don't panic.* Stop, and say to yourself: "This has been done before. I can do this." Then figure out a creative solution to make it happen**. Don't let the opportunity slip away.** Perhaps this is the occasion to call your mentor, and cut him in as a partner. You can come up with the money. *Make a deal. Don't be shy.*

GALLERIES

Galleries are at the top of the art chain. Unless you're a collector with considerable money, you won't initially be buying art in a major gallery. If you do, be prepared to pay for all the bells and whistles. Some galleries mark up merchandise 200 percent. If they buy a painting for $4,000, they try to sell it for $12,000, sometimes more. You pay for the costly retail space, guarantee of authenticity, and for the right to return a painting in exchange for a more expensive one.

A distinguished gallery offers exceptional art plus peace of mind, but at the highest price possible for the selected artist and work. The price of gallery artwork is almost always more expensive than comparable work bought at auction or from a private dealer. Ideally, you want a picker who will find the right painting for you. This is the least expensive and most rewarding way to acquire art. Better yet, find it yourself. Then one day you can sell the painting to a dealer or gallery. (If you buy from a dealer, it's unlikely you'll sell back this work to one, at least without suffering a loss.)

Now if you don't mind paying high prices, buy art at a major gallery. A renowned gallery, for example, would hardly risk selling you an over-exposed painting, one that has been shopped around or recently bought at auction. If the artwork isn't fresh on the market, a reputable gallery won't put the painting up for sale. If you lack confidence in your knowledge of art, perhaps you should buy art at a major gallery if you can afford it. Remember, however, a gallery's significant markup diminishes your profit. Therefore learn how to find your own artworks.

BUYING ART FOR THE NEW COLLECTOR

Spanierman Gallery in New York City exemplifies a reputable art gallery. It initiated a buying program called "Art for the New Collector: Re-Emerging American Artists, from $1,000 to $15,000" (www.spanierman.com).

Its New Collector II Program recently offered 19 paintings for sale: obviously all at retail price. Of these 19 paintings, using *Hislop's Price Guide* as a reference, 17 were priced *far above* the median price achieved at auction for paintings by the same artist; 2 were not even listed in *Hislop's Price Guide*; 7 were small enough to be considered a detriment to value; and only 3 of the 19 artists had auction records showing activity of more than 5 sales in the sample year. What's more, some paintings were very expensive considering the relative minor stature of the artist; for example, $35,000 for a painting by Gene Davis (1920 – 1985.). The average auction price for a Gene Davis painting in 2000 was only $2,900 ($3,400 for the very highest).

None of the nineteen paintings offered by Spanierman Gallery in The New Collector II Program meets our buying criteria for investment art. Nor do they meet, I'm sure, Spanierman's definition of investment art, because this gallery could, and does sell higher quality art, of course at even a greater price. What Spanierman classifies "New Collector's Art," is really for the beginner, although it's costly enough to be investment art. For example, the New Collector's Program at Spanierman's features a painting by Arthur B. Davies, size 6" X 9½", for $11,000, while the median price for an Arthur B. Davies painting sold at auction in 2000 was only $4,000.

If you invested say, $5,000 more wisely, you could have bought, for example, a painting by Charles Francois Daubigny at Slaon & Kenyon's Auction in November 2003, titled "Sunset By The Stream," size 12" X 18", for $5,200. Daubigny was a leader of the French Barbizon School, and a friend of Claude Monet. In fact, Monet lived on Daubigny's houseboat and was greatly influenced by him. A painting by Daubigny for $5,200 at auction would have been a much better investment than a 6" X 9½" Arthur B. Davies painting that retails for $11,000. Moreover, the Daubigny painting would have increased in value handsomely over the next seven years.

SELING ART BEFORE YOU BUY IT

Spanierman Gallery advertised seven works by Childe Hassam in the Summer 2004 issue of *Antique Magazine.* This is a fabulous offering; just one Hassam's painting, "Winter Nightfall in the City," sold at Sotheby's in 2000 for $1,400,000. But did Spanierman's own the seven paintings it was offering for sale? Evidently not. The small print in the advertisement read: "Sale pending previous sale," which means Spanierman first has to buy a Childe Hassam painting from the real owner in order to sell it to you. If the owner changed his mind or sold his Childe Hassam painting himself first, Spaneirman then would have to tell the retail customer, "Sorry, the painting is no longer available." Spanierman Gallery is not unlike other fine art galleries, selling works of art they don't own, or might have on consignment. Private dealers also "broker" paintings, which is not uncommon and is explained below in detail.

BUYING ART AT ANTIQUE MALLS

Antique malls offer booths to dealers who sell antiques or collectibles. Some dealers specialize in kitchen implements and country dishes, others in old furniture. All of them, from time to time throw in an old painting to add color and interest to their booth. However, where there are 40 or 50 dealers renting space in an old barn, at least one of them has an "eye" for valuable art. They're continually looking, just like you. That barn usually has been swept clean by the time you get there. There's nothing wrong looking through an antique mall, though, especially if it's the only show in town. But don't expect to find a valuable artwork there. You'll do better identifying the one art dealer there; give him your calling card and ask him to call you when he finds something special.

BUYING ART AT ANTIQUE STORES

Do consider browsing around an old antique store, especially one situated on a country road connecting two destination points, twenty or thirty miles apart. Passing by this isolated shop, people often drop off merchandise for sale or consignment; so when you come by, there's a chance you might happen upon a real find. Remember also in rural towns, especially in the South, that many prominent, old-time funeral homes have attached or nearby antique shops filled with belongings of the departed, which were used as barter to pay for funeral expenses. Occasionally you will discover surprisingly valuable art. If you decide to pick, however, Thursdays and Fridays are the best times to shop, that's when store owners put out their best merchandise for the weekend trade, which you'll want to beat.

BUYING FRAMES

Finding an exceptional period frame at an antique mall, perhaps even a valuable one, is more likely than finding a painting by a well listed artist, and why you should continually look for outstanding frames. Often a cheap print is sold in a valuable 19th century or early 20th century gilded frame, sometimes for as low as $20.

Experienced dealers often walk through antique malls looking only for period gilded frames. Keeping measurements of the frames they need in their wallets, when they see a rare, unique, or appropriate example, buy it just as passionately as they would a quality painting. They even buy frames for which they have no current use, provided they're period and in good to excellent condition, holding them for future artworks or reselling them to other dealers. As with paintings, condition is all important when buying frames. Many unique frames are signed or monogrammed on the back by the frame maker, causing some to be worth tens of thousands of dollars.

BUYING PRINTS

"Prints," including etchings, engravings, woodcuts, linocuts, and lithographs can have significant value. The majority of art dealers, including this author, know very little about limited edition prints, engravings, and etchings. Passing up every opportunity to buy them, we ignore prints, walking right by them in stores and antique malls. Many are priced as low as $5, just sitting on the floor of an antique shop; some could be worth $5,000, possibly more.

Unfortunately, prints as a genre are outside the scope of this book. Nevertheless, you are encouraged to learn how to identify and value prints, etchings, engravings, woodcuts, and lithographs. Some colleges and universities offer courses in art appraisal, including how to value prints. (See Appendix 3, What is a Print? There learn the difference between a Relief, Lithography, Screenprint, and an Intaglio, including etchings, the technique of Goya and Rembrandt.)

Gordon's Print Price Annual is arguably the best reference book for print auction records. A bit pricey ($265), it contains over 50,000 print auction records (www.gordonsart.com).

CASE EXAMPLE: Value of a Print

After negotiating a package price of $3,500 for several minor 19th century oil paintings, the dealer turned to the homeowner and added, "Oh, the price includes that *print* too. Throw that in."

It took several weeks for the dealer to sell the oil paintings, making a significant profit on his investment; then he turned to the Marc Chagall lithograph, of which he new absolutely nothing. However, since the print came out of an expensive home in a wealthy neighborhood, quite possibly the dealer thought it could have value. When the dealer had an appointment to meet with a Sotheby's expert on another subject, he took the Chagall lithograph along for a review. Much to his surprise, the print expert at Sotheby's authenticated the lithograph, and accepted it for auction. Sixty days later the Chagall lithograph sold for $4,200. This one print paid for the collection of oil paintings.

GETTING THE WORD OUT

If you're talking business with a knocker, picker, dealer, or antique shop owner, leave a calling card. You might have an all-purpose card printed with just your name, cell phone number, and your e-mail address. You can handwrite your interest on the back of each card: "Looking For Old Paintings."

WHERE TO FIND THE BEST BARGAINS

The best bargains will often be found in high quality unsigned paintings. These works are not easily attributable. Even professionals sell them cheaply in order to move on. This is where your trained "eye," intuition, and knowledge of art will give you an advantage over the competition. Because you can identify the School of art and possibly even the artist, and you know or suspect a signature might well appear after a professional cleaning, strongly consider buying a compelling unsigned artwork, if the condition is good and price is right.

If you're able to connect a distinguished unsigned painting with its artist and make the attribution stick, this will provide an exciting reward both financially and personally, because these are the paintings people often dismiss, sell cheap, or even give away.

THE LINED PAINTING

A lined unsigned painting demands a closer look, both physically and aesthetically. Whenever you turn an unsigned painting over and see that it has been professionally lined, study this painting closely. Ask yourself who would line this painting and why? Be curious, not skeptical. Regardless if it's a 17th century painting of the Madonna and Child or an early 20th century Modern, if it's lined, ask yourself why.

Lining a painting is an expensive conservation process that is performed to protect something worth preserving. Now no one protects something that is not of value. If someone has had a painting lined, quite possibly they know something you don't. Shouldn't you try to figure out the artist's name? That 17th century Madonna with Rose and Child could possibly be a painting by Simon Vouet (1590 – 1649), and worth much more than the $500 asking price.

This doesn't mean you automatically buy every lined and unsigned painting you find, but it does demand a closer examination of these artworks. Taking half an hour to study a quality unsigned painting is better than spending five minutes looking at a signed painting by a minor artist. Your potential fortune lies in the quality of this unsigned painting.

Among most usual reasons for lining a painting are (1) to repair holes, punctures, rips, tears, and severe abrasions which cannot be conserved properly with patches; (2) to reinforce original canvas severely weakened by water stains, or scorching by fire; and (3) to reinforce an original canvas which was poorly woven or extremely crude like burlap used in Spanish Colonial religious paintings, for example, from Cuzco, Peru, in the 16th century.

GETTING PAID FOR WHAT OTHERS DON'T KNOW

Like a lawyer or an accountant who is paid a professional fee for having specialized knowledge, expertise in art entitles you to earn money buying, selling, and brokering paintings. Whether buying a painting on e-Bay or at a country auction, your only advantage is in knowing what the seller doesn't know, and/or taking advantage of the time and circumstances. You've studied for this opportunity and you're prepared to invest cash, so why shouldn't you profit from the transaction?

However, there are dealers so knowledgeable that even when an experienced gallery owner sells a painting to one of them, the gallery leaves money on the table (under priced the painting), because the dealer would not have bought the painting unless there was equity in it. Be cautious if you're buying a painting from someone who clearly knows more about art than you; it could be costly. Bottom line is, you get paid for what you know.

TRAVEL THE WORLD FREE — BUYING AMERICAN ART ABROAD

American artists have flocked to European cities for two centuries to learn and to be influenced by European artists. The number of valuable American paintings left behind is staggering. They still hang in homes, hotels, and restaurants throughout Europe. People also move, resettle, and bring art with them, then leave it behind when they move again. Quality American art can be found in many countries in Europe, South America, and Asia, sometimes in the most unexpected places.

Placing a classified ad in a European newspaper could bring an American masterpiece out of a broom closet, and possibly into your collection. You might find a work of art that's worth all your trouble. It's also a fun and profitable way to travel the world, possibly free. A wise collector placed the following ad in the *New York Times:*

> Australian collector visiting New York City April 23-30, interested in buying high quality Australian art. Call 212-777-3333. Leave details.

A vigilant dealer called the New York City number and left his message: "I own an Australian painting by Nicholas Chevalier (1828 – 1902), and I would be happy to discuss the possible sale of my painting." It turns out the Australian collector placed the same ad in newspapers in San Francisco, Chicago, Boston, and in cities throughout Europe, having a local contact person take messages. When he arrived in the city where he had placed an ad, the collector returned phone calls. One day the New York City dealer received a phone call, and made arrangements to bring his painting to the hotel where the Australian gentleman was staying. Over lunch they agreed on a price and payment was made. The local contact person shipped the acquired artwork back to Australia (for which he was paid a fee), and the collector continued on his trip around the world. His next stop was Paris where, not doubt, Australian paintings were lined up for him to examine.

As an American traveling to Europe, you could do the same. Whether you're planning a trip to Paris, Tel Aviv, or Prague, place an ad in a local newspaper: "American collector visiting Paris April 23–30, interested in buying quality American paintings. Call: 097-00-34-77. Leave details."

You could also do the same if you were traveling to Wyoming, Montana, or Idaho. Advertise in a local newspaper stating that you're a collector looking for quality paintings by East Coast artists, or whatever School you collect. When you arrive at your destination, return phone calls and make arrangements to look at your favorite art. Be very careful, however, because a lot of art will come out of the woodwork, including possible fakes. Make sure you take a black light with you, and of course your *Artprice Indicator* guide. If you didn't bring your laptop, hopefully your hotel will offer access to a computer terminal where you can log on www.Artnet.com to retrieve archival examples of the artist's work to compare with the painting you've found. Internet cafés also allow you to research art databases while traveling abroad.

ADVERTISE IN SMALL COUNTRY NEWSPAPERS
Many small newspapers are syndicated through one publisher where you can advertise in a string of country newspapers covering an entire region for under $150. People are poor in rural areas of Upstate New York, Pennsylvania, Kentucky, and Ohio, and selling an old painting might appeal to a needy person's sense of hope or despair. Run an ad for several weeks and see what kind of gold comes out of the hills of rural America. You might be surprised.

COLLECTOR BUYING OLD PAINTINGS
Oils and watercolors, any condition
Cash! Call 555-333-4444

THE YELLOW PAGES
Many desperate people turn to the Yellow Pages first when they decide to sell antiques. A small boxed ad in the Yellow Pages can attract a surprising amount of business. The profit from one painting could easily pay the advertisement fee for many years. Placed under "Antiques," your ad might look like this:

PAINTINGS WANTED
Buying old antique paintings,
oils or watercolors, any condition.
Cash, Call 555-333-4444

"He is a poor disciple who does not excel his master."
—Leonardo da Vinci

FINDING VALUABLE ART IN THE LEAST EXPECTED PLACES

CASE EXAMPLES: Buying Art On the Road

In a small restaurant in Germany, an American tourist asked the proprietor, "I noticed a small painting on the wall in the back room; would you consider selling it? I'd love to have it. It would be a nice souvenir from Germany." A deal was struck, and the alert dealer took a fabulous painting back to his hotel, and back to America.

Checking into a Florida motel, an art dealer had to leave a $20 deposit at the front desk to open the telephone line to his room. Inside his room the dealer discovered a beautiful 1920s painting hanging on the wall over his bed; it was indistinctly signed. The subject was a young girl holding a calico cat in her lap beside a table with a vase of flowers. It was a beautiful picture. When the dealer checked out in the morning, the motel owner said, "Here's your $20, sir." The dealer replied: "Would you consider selling the picture in my room of the girl holding the cat in exchange for the $20? The woman looked out the window for a moment. The parking lot was empty—it was a slow night in Daytona. "Sure," she said, and put the $20 back into the cash register. "Take the picture. Enjoy it."

A real estate agent walked an art dealer through an empty 3-bedroom house in suburbia New York. An elderly gentleman stood quietly by in the corner of the kitchen; he lived next door. When the dealer returned a week later, the man informed him that his sister's house had been sold. The dealer expressed regret, and then asked, "I noticed there was an old oil painting and a Persian carpet in the hall. Would you consider selling them?" He did, and for $350 the dealer bought a 19th century painting by a listed Spanish artist and an antique Tabriz carpet. *Make a deal. Don't be shy.*

There will always be opportunities to buy art, but you have to mix discretion with perseverance. You don't walk into a friend's home and ask if you can buy the painting over the fireplace. And you don't ask a real estate agent to set up appointments to look at houses just so you can shop for antiques. But the truth is, an opportune occasion may occur when people move and sell their homes; ask if they would consider selling their antique paintings. Always be prepared. *Make a deal. Don't be shy.*

REAL ESTATE AGENTS AS PARTNERS

Establish relationships with real estate agents in your town, region, and state. They continually see valuable art in people's homes. Coach them on what to look for. An agent can casually mention, "I know an art dealer who pays top dollar for art like this. Would you be interested in selling some of your paintings?" Or an agent can give you a tip with a telephone number, which can translate into significant extra income for you and the agent. Be sure the agent knows he will receive a handsome finder's fee for his information.

TRADE PAPERS ARE HOMEWORK FOR DOLLARS

If you only do one homework project a month, let it be reading the *Maine Antique Digest,* or alternatively, the *Antiques and Arts Weekly* (*Newtown Bee*). These trade papers are filled with art news and opportunities: you'll need both to be successful in the art business. Many art dealers, galleries, and auction houses advertise in these trade papers. From just one issue you will be able to compile an impressive list of names and telephone numbers of buyers and sellers of art that will be useful for many years. You need that list in order to do business.

Read "Letters to the Editor," feature articles, and news releases to keep abreast of what's occurring in the antiques industry. Note the warnings about paintings that have been stolen, and about scams you should avoid. You'll also read legal rulings on buyers' and sellers' rights and obligations, and how to handle complex legal issues.

PAINTINGS WANTED

Dealers, collectors, and galleries place ads in trade papers for "Paintings Wanted," followed by a list of artists' names. If you own a painting by an artist on someone's list and you're ready to part with it, call the advertiser and negotiate a sale. It's as simple as matching your inventory with a name printed in a trade paper. If you don't own a painting that someone desires, but know someone who does, broker a transaction and cut yourself in on the profit. You will also see requests for regional art in trade papers, such as paintings from Indiana, Pennsylvania, California, and New England. When you're traveling in these regions, be especially vigilant. Because art from both coasts have been, as it were, *over farmed* in recent decades, Midwest art is now in strong demand. The best examples from Indiana, Ohio, and Michigan are highly prized.

Remember, a dealer or gallery that buys certain art, also sells the same art. So if you're a collector, you might find the painting you're looking for by contacting the dealer who also buys (and sells) what you're looking for. You could also advertise in the *Maine Antique Digest* or the *Newtown Bee*, asking dealers to contact you with offerings of certain subjects, Schools of art, or artist's work.

REPATRIATING ART

When foreign entrepreneurs of new economies come to power, invariably they buy back the best art from their country, which typically is located abroad (primarily in the United States). The best examples of art from the following countries are in high demand by collectors and national galleries: Russia, Japan, Korea, Philippines, Southeast Asian counties, India, Israel, Australia, and New Zealand. Caribbean and South American countries remain poor, and the best of their art is still being exported. Whenever these economies do stabilize and powerbrokers emerge, their art will be bought back—"repatriated," but at a very high price. Trade papers frequently report on these changing markets.

Investors and dealers, however, study trade papers primarily for opportunities to **buy art at auction**.

AUCTION OPPORTUNITES

Auction houses big and small advertise in *The Maine Antiques Digest* and *The Newtown Bee.* Look for investment-quality art coming up at auction near you, and also in out of the way places. Attorneys often put contents of an estate up for sale, which could include antiques and valuable old paintings. Rarely will an attorney move a sale to a distant city. Usually he'll consign everything to a local auction room, with instructions to advertise, generally, in *The Maine Antique Digest* and/or *The Newtown Bee.*

Competition for valuable art will be stiff at auctions near or in big cities, such as Boston, New York, Philadelphia, Dallas, Chicago, and San Francisco. But if the auction is 600 miles into the backlands of America, and you're willing to drive there, you have a better chance of coming home with a valuable painting. If you're a dealer, driving 600 miles once a month to make $10,000 is surely a profitable part of your job.

Auction houses too small to put up a Web site will have less competition than regional auctions houses that post online digital images. Regardless of how well a sale is advertised in trade papers, if the auction house does not have a Web site to view, most dealers will not show interest in art they cannot preview online. They'll choose to doubt the veracity of the claim that authentic paintings by William Galckens, Edward Potthast, or Ernest Lawson are actually being auctioned in such a remote location. But you'll call the auction house and inquire into the provenance, and ask the staff to e-mail you digital images of the paintings. Finding answers that satisfy you, you'll attend the auction. Once there, you'll be excited to learn the paintings indeed appear to be by Glackens, Potthast, and Lawson, and that there are no telephone bidders or competition in the room. What's more, the abstract painting signed and dated: "Ioannus XXXX111," which no one understood or showed interest in, you bought at its low reserve because you knew it was the work of John D. Graham (1886 – 1961). Clearly this was a trip worth taking; you ask the auction room to put your name on its mailing list for future auctions. (Remember, however, if such notable works are being offered not in a major city by renowned sellers, proceed cautiously.)

Reduced prices at auction. Attorneys and auction houses are interested in a quick sale. They rarely hold out for a high price, sometimes not even for a fair price. Many times valuable antiques are sold without the protection of a reserve.

CASE EXAMPLE: "House Sale" Auctions

Christie's and Sotheby's run "House Sales," generally in summer. They auction off art generally valued under $20,000, and also merchandise that did not sell in previous sales. The dog days of summer are an excellent time to buy art at Christie's and Sotheby's. The city is quiet. Most people are away for the summer. It's the perfect time to bottom fish. You might reel in an exceptional painting at a very reasonable price at a House Sale.

Christie's House Sale in July 2002 offered an English sporting painting by James (II) Barenger (1780 – 1831). It was 28" X 36," and it had a surprisingly low estimate: $5,000 to 7,000. What's more, the lot number and artist's name were printed in "red ink" in the catalogue, signaling there was no reserve on this painting.

An astute art dealer researched James (II) Barenger on www.artnet.com, noting that the same painting had been bought-in six months earlier at

Christie's main salon sale, when it had an estimate of $15,000 to $20,000 *with a reserve* (indicated by black ink).

The dealer concluded that the painting was part of an estate sale, and when it did not sell in the main salon, the attorney representing the estate directed Christie's to put the painting back in the next subsequent sale *without* a reserve, just to sell it.

The dealer arranged for a live telephone bid, and was surprised when the phone handler told him: "Congratulations! You bought the James Barenger for $2,500.

House Sales at Christie's and Sotheby's can be profitable, and a fun way to spend a summer afternoon in New York City.

EXPLANATION OF CATALOGUING PRACTICE

Always study the "Explanation of Cataloguing Practice," found in the back of an auction catalogue, where Christie's, for example, explains:

> *Unless otherwise indicated, all lots are offered subject to a reserve, which is the confidential minimum price below which the lot will not be sold. If any lots are not subject to a reserve, they will be identified with a symbol (red dot) next to the lot number, and the artist's name printed in red ink.*

Following are Christie's Explanation of Cataloguing Practice:

- **Pictures**
  Name or Recognized Designation of an Artist without any Qualification
  In our opinion a work by the artist.

- **"Attribution to . . . "**
  In our opinion probably a work by the artist in whole or in part.

- **"Studio of . . . "/ "Workshop of . . . "**
  In our opinion a work executed in the studio or workshop of the artist, possibly under his supervision.

- **"Circle of . . . "**
  In our opinion a work of the period of the artist and showing *his influence.*

- **"Follower of . . . "**
  In our opinion a work executed in the artist's style but not necessarily by a pupil.

- **"Manner of . . . "**
  In our opinion a work executed in the artist's style but of a later date.

- **"After . . . "**
  In our opinion a copy (of any date) of a work of the artist.

- **"Signed . . . " / "Dated . . . " / "Inscribed"**
  In our opinion the work has been signed/dated/inscribed by the artist.

- **"With signature . . . " / "With date . . . " / "With inscription . . . "**
  In our opinion the signature/date/inscription appears to be by a hand other than that of the artist.

BUYING STRATEGIES AT AUCTION

Auctions are significantly unpredictable social events that form a part of our economic society. Individual behavior and personal preferences often determine the outcome of auctions. Despite every participant having his or her own opinion as to an artwork's "true" value, the ultimate bid-price reflects variables such as exquisite to bad taste, what's "hot" or passé, even the negative effects caused by stormy weather or some calamity. Only when the hammer comes down is the price determined. Even then different results can occur in front of different audiences.

Regardless, if you attend an auction yourself or have someone represent you there, you want the winning bid. The best strategy is that which allows you to take a painting home at the lowest possible price.

Strategies abound for auction room success: where to sit, when to raise a paddle, and how aggressively to bid. It's all a matter of preference. Some auctioneers start the bidding high knowing it will come down; others start the bidding low hoping it will go up. Determining rules to remember are these: (1) know why you want the item (your motivation for bidding on it), (2) diligently research and appraise the item before the auction, (3) know and don't exceed how much money you're willing to spend, and (4) be familiar with the conditions of sale at the auction room (premiums, charges, buy-ins, and payment schedule).

COMMUNICATING AT AUCTION

Regardless of where you sit or stand in an auction room, make sure the auctioneer can see you. Don't hide behind a support column and don't visit the bathroom when your lot number is coming up. Stay focused on the business at hand.

At small auctions, the auctioneer will sometimes direct a sale to a friend or local dealer. If the auctioneer refuses to look your way, do whatever is necessary to attract attention to your raised paddle. Stand up if you were sitting down, step into the aisle, wave your arms, raise your voice, make a scene if necessary, but get the auctioneer to acknowledge your bid. Don't be intimidated. You don't want to drive home 600 miles without getting the painting you came to buy.

NEGOTIATING AFTER THE AUCTION IS OVER

Call the auction room after a sale to obtain results; pay close attention to lots that were bought-in. You may have seen a painting you liked either online or in a catalogue; if it was bought-in, find out why.

CASE EXAMPLE: Back Room Deal

A dealer called an out-of-state auction to inquire about the results of a painting he had consigned to the auction, and was disappointed to learn his painting did not sell. While on the phone, he inquired about another painting he was interested in, and was surprised to learn that it also did not sell. It was a large seascape by George McCord (1848 – 1909), with an estimate of only $3,000 to $5,000, which the dealer thought was extremely low for the quality of work. He inquired if anything was wrong with the painting and asked for a condition report. The dealer was informed that the painting had been professionally lined about forty years ago and that it was in very good condition. They had no explanation for the lack of bidding interest either in this painting or the dealer's own consignment. Knowing the reserve had to be less than $3,000, the dealer said, "I'd like to buy the McCord painting for the *reserve price.*" After a few minutes of waiting, he bought the George McCord seascape at the reserve price, paying $2,929 including buyer's premium. It was a steal. *Make a deal. Don't be shy.*

TACTICS AT AUCTION

Professional dealers often remain aloof at auctions, even avoiding other dealers they know. Blending in with the crowd, incognito, they act in the least way conspicuous. But you can rest assured they've previewed the art, studied the market, and researched certain paintings. They know exactly what they want to bid on and how much money they're willing to pay to take home a particular work of art. If their face is covered by a newspaper or their nose buried in a catalogue, don't worry, they're ready to jump into action at the first call of their lot number.

Dealers don't want you to know or see what they're bidding on, lest you bid on it too. Unless he's an outsider, most auctioneers know who the professional dealers are; they're even familiar with their paddle numbers. As a professional, make sure the auctioneer knows who you are.

UNSCRUPULOUS RINGS AT AUCTION

Most dealers act honorably and form independent bidding decisions. Some less scrupulous dealers, however, form "rings" or "pools" to bid collusively. For example, a group of four dealers might agree not to bid against one another in order to keep the price on a certain artwork low. One dealer will represent the group and bid on the painting. They will further agree to have a "private" or "secret" auction after the first auction, generally at a nearby diner or motel, to determine which dealer will take home the prized painting.

ROUND-ROBIN KNOCKOUT

The Round-Robin Knockout method of selection is best employed when dealers know each other, and perhaps regularly work as a team. In the private knockout, each participant must raise his bid higher than the previous bid in order to stay in the competition. Finally, bidding stops when someone is willing to pay the highest price for the painting.

The difference between the hammer price in the first auction and the final price in the knockout auction is the pool money divided among the players. For example, a painting bought in the first auction for $2,000 that fetched $5,000 in the knockout auction would have a net difference of $3,000. This $3,000 is distributed equally among the four dealers, or $750 each. Hence, the painting cost the highest bidder $4,250 ($5,000 minus his cut of $750). Had the four dealers been outsiders—strangers—quite possibly they might have driven up the bidding on this painting to $12,000. Obviously, sellers and auction rooms try to discourage and break up these rings.

A process that is more equitable for participants, albeit more complex, which is based on individual risk, is the *English Knockout.*

ENGLISH KNOCKOUT

In the English Knockout, participants submit a single written bid, much like a sealed bid, and the highest bidder wins. The lowest bidder drops out of the competition first. He is paid the difference between the hammer price in the first auction and his low bid, divided equally between the four dealers. The second highest bidder is paid in the same way, each time adjusting the pool of money according to the dealers who have dropped out, until the winning bidder prevails.

In the above example where the "ring" bought a painting in the first auction for $2,000, let's assume that in the English Knockout bidder A bids $2,500, B bids $3,500, C bids $4,500, and D bids $5,000. In this case, the dealers would split the pool money as follows: Bidder A would receive $125 (the difference between the first auction's hammer price and A's low bid, which is $500, divided by four dealers = $125 for bidder A). Bidder B would receive $458.33, which is one-third the difference between $2,125, the new cost of the painting ($2,000 plus $125 paid to bidder A) and B's bid of $3,500 ($3,500 minus $2,125 divided by three). Bidder C would receive $958.33, which is one-half the difference between the new cost of the painting, now $2,583.33 ($2,000 + $125 + $458.33 = $2,583.33), and C's bid of $4,500. The winning bidder, D, would pay $3,541.66 for the painting ($2,000 + $125 + $458.33 + $958.33).

BILL OF SALE

Ask for a Bill of Sale whenever you buy a work of art, even if the seller has to scribble a note on a piece of scrap paper. The Bill of Sale should indicate the seller's name and address, and include the artist's name and description of the painting: title, medium, subject, size, condition, framed or not, and any conditions of sale. The Bill of Sale must include the sale price, and state that the title and ownership of the painting passes free and clear of all encumbrances to the buyer at the time of sale. If the seller is not the owner, and refuses to divulge the owner's name, the seller must warrant and state that he has the authority to sell the painting for the owner.

THE LANGUAGE OF BARGAINING

Try out different ways of bargaining in order to discover your true voice. With experience you'll acquire naturalness. Learn which expressions enhance an art sale and which language to avoid. Dealers use the following expressions every day. Which is most effective for you?

- "How much would you accept for your painting?" (Too open-ended.)
- "What price would you take for your painting?" (It's an invitation for a high price.)
- "What's the best price you can make on your painting?" (No one likes to give a *best price.*)
- "How low can you go on your painting?" (No owner, of anything, wants to sell at the lowest price.)
- "How much do you have to get for your painting?" (Everyone has a price, and this one seems to get to the heart of the matter.)

"What (or "How Much") do you have to get for your painting?" is a question most owners are prepared to answer. It's generally their lowest price, below which no sale can take place. It's like the confidential reserve price at auction.

When offering a painting for sale, some dealers include a 10% or 15% cushion, or wiggle room to allow for negotiations. If you know the buyer well, then on certain occasions, state that the asking price is "firm," indicating no margin for negotiation.

PRESENT YOURSELF AS A NEW COLLECTOR

If you're buying at a location where no one knows you, and you've negotiated a fair price, like buying a listed artist for under $500, you don't need to divulge that you're an art dealer. Avoid saying, "I have a Tax I.D. Number, and I'd like a dealer's discount." It's better to pay the 7% sales tax ($35). Let the antique shop assume you're a collector. Retail shops like working with collectors; they'll probably call you the next time they have a special painting in the shop. However, if they learn you're a "dealer," the price of art will go up sharply. For low-end merchandise, leave your Tax I.D. Number in your wallet. On the other hand, if you buy an expensive painting, by all means use your Tax I.D. Number. That's why you have it. In a busy year, for example, where you buy $100,000 of art, sales tax savings of $7,000 (7%) represents an investment painting for your own retirement portfolio, which should be worth $25,000 after seven years.

DEALER TO DEALER

When you're buying in a store where you're known or you're dealing with another dealer, you can always say, "I have a client who would be interested in that painting. How much do you have to get for it?" This response implies the painting is not for you personally; yet you'll need to make a little profit yourself, so "give me a reasonable price." If the seller understands a third party is involved in the transaction, he might feel obligated to leave money on the table for the next seller. However, if the seller subsequently learns that you put the painting into auction for yourself instead of selling it to a client as you implied, your future bargaining power or entitlements with this dealer are over. You'll pay full price for the next painting.

HOW MUCH SHOULD YOU DIVULGE?

Divulge just enough information to stay honest. When a shop owner sees you examining a painting, you might be asked, "Are you a dealer?" To which you can reply, "I collect art. If I see a painting I like and it's reasonably priced, I'll buy it if I can afford it." The store manager then might conclude you're a knowledgeable collector, whom he'd like to keep on the special customer list. So you might get a fair, even a low price.

PROBING THE SELLER

Experienced art dealers sometimes ask what might seem like inane questions, such as, "Where did you buy the painting? How long have you owned it? Have you shown it to anyone else?" Gathering information, they're sharpening their bargaining position with you while formulating a plan to resell your painting. Dealers are always looking for an edge. If you slip or say too much, such as divulge the source or location of a painting, some art dealers will buy the work out from under you. Like the careless poker player who shows his hand, you can't blame the opponent for seeing your ace in the hole, then saying, "I'll pass," and dropping out, leaving you a smaller pot.

NEVER BE FIRST TO GIVE A PRICE, EXTEND AN OFFER, OR SAY HOW MUCH YOU'LL PAY FOR A PAINTING

If you inquire about the price of a painting and the seller asks, "How much will you pay for it?" **do not answer that question**. If you declare how much you'll pay for a painting, you *validated* the painting. You confirm for the seller that he has a valuable painting which before you showed interest, quite possibly he had no idea of. Secondly, you *appraise* the painting by saying how much you're willing to pay for it. Why would you validate and appraise a painting for a seller? And then buy it? Better for him to have the painting appraised elsewhere; then he can return to let you know his asking price. Once the seller states his asking price, you can always negotiate downward. However, once *you* extend the offer, you can never go down from that price. The seller can only negotiate upward.

It does not help your negotiating strategy if the seller knows how much you're willing to pay, especially after you've validated and appraised the painting for him. *Come on!* You have options. You can say:

- "It's your painting; you have to decide on the price." Or,
- "You know how much you paid for the painting; put a reasonable profit on it, and give me a price." Or,
- "Tell me how much you have to get for the painting." And finally, you can say,
- "Just pick a price. *Any price*! Tell me how much you want for the painting." (This will usually get the seller to name a price.) If the seller refuses to budge, you can say,

  "Obviously, you're not serious about selling your painting. Here's my telephone number; call me when you know how much you want for it. I pay the highest prices for art, but I have to know how much the seller wants."

  Be sure to call back in a few days. If the seller still refuses to budge, you can offer a price (not a ridiculous one) 25 to 50 percent below what you typically would be willing to pay for the painting. For example, if you would be willing to pay up to $10,000 for the painting, say,

  "I will offer you a fair price, which should allow you to make a good profit regardless of what you paid for your painting. I can pay you $5,000 and live with it; can you live with that price? He might accept it; or he might nudge you up to $6,500 or even

> $7,500, which is still 25% below what you are willing to pay for the painting.

Do whatever is necessary to motivate the seller to name his price. It's his painting! Once he does, unless it's a low price, consider not accepting it right away. Every reasonable asking price deserves at least one counter offer. But don't insult the seller, losing the opportunity to buy his artwork. If you're not prepared to counter offer, ask for 24 hours to consider. If pressed to make an offer, weigh in about 25 percent lower than the asking price. If the seller asked $10,000 for his Pennsylvania landscape by Hermann Herzog, you can counter with: "The painting is worth $6,500 to me. I have cash; would you accept $6,500 cash *right now*?" Expect to negotiate the difference, and probably pay $7,500 for the painting. **Don't let a valuable artwork get away, but don't pay more than a painting is worth.**

SPLITTING PROCEEDS

Examining a painting by Consalve Carelli (1818 – 1900), the dealer asked, "What to you have to get for this painting?" It was a picture of a horse-drawn carriage racing through the streets of Naples, Italy. It was an oil, 12" X 14", in excellent condition, and it looked authentic.

"Well, I don't know," replied the owner. "What do you think it's worth?"

"I'm not an appraiser, and I can't tell you how much to sell your painting for," said the dealer. "It's *your* painting; you have to decide that. I know of a client who might be interested in it. If your price is reasonable, I'll buy it. What do you have to get for it?"

"You're the expert," replied the owner. "You tell me what it's worth."

Over coffee, they went back and forth for an hour in the owner's kitchen. Finally the dealer suggested: "Look, why don't we 'partner' the painting. I'll do all the legwork. I'll do the marketing, advertising, and selling. I'll find a buyer, get the best price for the painting, and we'll split the proceeds. How does that sound?"

It seemed to work. "Fine," said the owner. "That's good with me."

The dealer was surprised. He signed a receipt and took the painting home. The dealer then diligently sought buyers for the painting, receiving one offer for $9,000 and another for $12,000. Of course, he could have sold the painting to the first offerer—he had nothing to lose, but he wanted to hold out for the highest price. He called a collector who had advertised for "Italian Painting" in *The Maine Antiques Digest,* and offered the work by Consalve Carelli for $18,000. The collector was interested and the dealer showed the painting. A price was reached, and the work sold for $17,500.

The original owner, however, was unhappy and he now resented the fact that he agreed to split the proceeds. The dealer kept his word, of course, and gave the owner $8,750, keeping $8,750 for himself.

What the owner failed to understand is that before he met the dealer, he had not a clue about his painting's value, and possibly could have sold it to a less scrupulous dealer for, say $1,500. Instead, he received $8,750.

The dealer had $5,000 cash in his pocket when he first met the owner and he was prepared to pay that amount for the painting if it were representative of the artist's work and in good condition.

In the end, however, the owner was not happy giving away half his money. The only way he could have avoided that was to acquire the knowledge and skills of an appraiser and dealer—what this book offers you.

CASH IS KING

If it's practical and safe, carry $100 bills with you on appointments when looking at art. Put the lowest amount you would hope to pay for the painting in one pocket, the extra cash in the other pocket. Then take out what you need to close the sale, as you need it. Many sellers will accept less than their original asking price if paid in cash. *Make a deal. Don't be shy.*

10

Selling Art

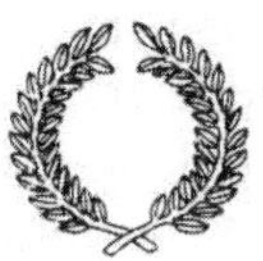

If buying art makes you feel good, selling art should make you feel better. For the collector and investor, selling art should mark the end a period of growth and prosperity, giving you a sense of pride and satisfaction. Hopefully, you've enjoyed, even benefited from your art investment and now you're ready to move on to a higher quality painting, or perhaps to another kind of challenge. In order to buy another day, however, we must first learn to sell today.

Selling art should be easier, in fact, less stressful than buying art, because the buyer, not the seller, has the overwhelming burden of due diligence and financial risk. The seller, on the other hand, must know how to (1) appraise and establish a price for his painting, (2) decide when, where, and to whom to sell his painting, (3) create safeguards to protect his painting from being over shown—"shopped around"—and (4) present his painting in the best possible light: framed appropriately, cleaned, and restored if required, with provenance documentation in order.

There are many valid reasons for selling a work of art; below are some of the main ones.

FIVE REASONS WHY PEOPLE SELL ART:

- To meet an emergency
- To make a major purchase
- To upgrade or purchase a new painting
- To cash in on an investment
- To augment retirement income

MEETING EMERGENCIES

Crises happen. Meeting unexpected emergencies is part of life. Whether you need money to bail a relative out of trouble, pay a hospital bill, or put on a new roof, you don't want to borrow money in order to meet an emergency, not if you have quality art hanging on your walls.

Investment quality paintings are like money trees: you're entitled to pluck off fruit whenever you need it—or whenever you're hungry. Many an art dealer, faced with an emergency, has looked at the paintings on his wall and saying, "All right, I'll sell this one, that one, and the painting over the fireplace," in order to get out of a serious financial predicament. We have all done it.

Never be sentimental about a painting to the point that you refuse to sell it. No matter how beautiful your landscape or for how many generations it's been in your family, if your house is being foreclosed, sell the heirloom. You might be able to catch up on your back payments, possibly even pay off the entire mortgage. There are other landscape paintings you can buy when circumstances improve, and probably better quality ones too. Too often people sacrifice everything to leave a family painting to a son or daughter, only to see this painting at auction just after the estate is settled. Bottom line: enjoy it while you can, sell it when you must.

CASH FOR A MAJOR NEW PURCHASE

Opportunities often arise if you can make a purchase with cash. You'd be surprised, it might only take a few paintings to buy a retirement condominium, a new luxury car, or pay a child's tuition at an ivy-league college with cash. Whether beneficial or necessary, sell a few paintings. They're investment instruments, available for your use.

BUYING A NEW PAINTING

For the collector, investor, and dealer, buying a new painting is always a strategic option. You might want to upgrade your collection or take advantage of a rare opportunity to buy an exciting painting possibly new to the market. Usually you'll be buying a more valuable artwork. Selling two, or perhaps three paintings might enable you to move out of the ten-thousand-dollar investment range and into the fifty-thousand-dollar investment range. If a painting fits your investment strategy, and you want to feel exhilarated, sell at a rewarding profit, then re-buy.

CASHING IN ON AN INVESTMENT

Cashing in on an art investment successfully is a factor of timing. Keep a vigilant eye on the economy and monitor the art market by studying auction results. As with any investment, you want to buy low and sell high. If market conditions are perfect, sell your painting. Unlike the bond market, you don't have to wait for a certain maturity date before you can sell your investment. It's possible to achieve a higher ROI than you ever thought possible, even after only a few months of owning a painting. Regardless of the economy, a collector will pay what a collector will pay for the right painting, sometimes far exceeding logic and expectation.

AUGMENTING YOUR RETIREMENT INCOME

By investing in art you can augment your social security income when you retire. Hopefully your investment strategy and retirement date are synchronized. Now sell one painting annually for the extra $20,000 you'll need year after year. You can sell any painting in your portfolio; it need not be the one you bought seven years ago; sell the one offering the best strategic advantage.

TIMING IS EVERYTHING

The biggest obstacle to selling "right" is timing, especially if you're selling because you need money. You never want to be at the mercy of someone else, either for money or knowledge, because you'll always be disappointed. If you bought a work of art for a seven-year investment period, but now decide to sell after seven weeks, you have a serious challenge on your hands. A sudden change in investment strategy can limit your selling options and diminish your return on investment.

Opportune timing remains all important. As a rule of thumb, don't sell from after Christmas through January and from late July until some 10 days after Labor Day. These times are not good for selling quality art. Major commercial galleries and auction houses schedule their best events from the 2nd or 3rd week in September through mid-December, and from February to before graduation.

WHERE TO SELL YOUR PAINTINGS

You have to sell up, not down. If you own a major New York City gallery, you can't sell to an antique shop in rural Pennsylvania. A major dealer would not sell to someone just breaking into the trade, who was doing garage sales last week. Dealers don't sell to pickers and pickers don't sell to knockers. Below your experience level people generally don't have enough money to buy higher-end works of art, nor do they have the know-how or professional contacts to sell at a higher level. So how do you sell "up?"

First, you must develop contacts. Remember, fifty percent of success comes from your relationships (25/25/50 Rule), so selling art is really a matter of whom you know. You'll buy art from almost anyone, but sell to a much smaller inside group. Make it your business to develop high-end contacts with collectors, institutions, museums, galleries, and dealers. The best place to begin is to find out who's collecting what you're selling.

DEVELOPING CONTACTS

Developing social and professional contacts comes naturally to some people. You, however, might have to work at it. Continually develop art contacts for each category below; they will become your principal buyers:

- Private Collectors
- Corporate Collectors
- Museums
- Galleries
- Dealers
- Auctions

DEVELOPING CONTACTS THROUGH RESEARCH

Study trade papers and art magazines to build contact lists and learn who's buying what. For example, *Art & Antiques Magazine* prints its *Top 100 Collectors* every March. How easy is that? You get the names of 100 important art collectors for $3.95! (Interestingly, more and more young people are being added to this list each year.) Of course, you can't just barge into people's homes to sell your paintings. But if you have what they're collecting, figure out a way to let them know you have something they might be interested in. *Make a deal. Don't be shy.* If you don't know an important collector personally, and you can't get an introduction, find out their business address, possibly through *Who's Who in Business*, the Chamber of Commerce, or by Googling. After locating, send them a letter of introduction, including a photograph of your painting, or e-mail them a digital image. The case example below illustrates this successful method of polite intrusion.

CASE EXAMPLE: Developing a Contact

An article written in the *Antiques Trade Gazette,* one of Europe's major trade papers, reported that a wealthy businessman had donated a significant painting, valued at $1.5 million, to a major European museum. A world-class collector, this gentleman was Chairman of the Board of a major European bank. Reading this article, an astute dealer who had just bought a representative painting by one of the founders of the School of art the gentleman collected, decided to contact the bank chairman. "Why not?" the dealer reasoned. "It's worth a try." He Googled, found the bank's Web site, got its telephone number, placed an overseas phone call, and asked to speak with the secretary of the Chairman of the Board. You can't always speak with the Chairman himself, at least not at first, but speaking with his personal secretary is a wise place to start.

Within ten minutes of beginning his search, the dealer was standing as though with painting in hand, outside the Chairman's office. His secretary spoke English well; the dealer asked, "If I e-mail your chairman a message and a digital image of a painting, would you give it to him?" "Yes, of course," she said, and gave him her e-mail address.

Ten minutes later, his message of introduction and a digital image of his painting were personally given to the Chairman of the Board of a major European bank. Now how hard was that? The dealer established an important new contact. Since then, he has offered many paintings to the same gentleman.

You must be imaginative and resourceful to succeed at selling art.

SELLING ART TO PRIVATE COLLECTORS

Sometimes newspapers, magazines, and trade journals print the names of private art collectors. They can also be aired on television, spoken of in auction rooms, and talked about on the street. Make it your business to learn who they are in your city or town. These are the patrons of the arts and board members and trustees of museums and prominent nonprofit organizations; they support charities and host fundraisers. Do get to know them. They may become your most loyal customers.

Art collectors generally are experts in their field. They rely upon their own research, knowing what they're looking for. By nature, collectors are private, quiet, and conservative. Understand, you'll have to make yourself available according to their schedule and style. Don't waste a collector's time by showing him something he's not interested in. Never misrepresent a painting. Be up front with what you know about a painting's provenance and condition. Don't offend a collector; you'll not only lose a sale, you'll lose a customer. Your reputation and credibility are always on the line so never compromise them.

Your 20-Second Cold-Call Pitch

If you don't have an introduction, and don't know the collector personally, say so: "Good morning, sir. My name is John Seller, and we've never met before. I'm an art dealer, and occasionally I come across *truly exceptional* works of American (or European) art from the 19th and 20th century. My question is: Would you be interested in my letting you know when one of these *truly exceptional* paintings becomes available for sale? What are your thoughts about that, sir?" (*That's it*! 20 seconds, no more. Practice your own cold-call pitch.)

Now tell me, what collector is gong to say "No" to that kind of invitation. Of course they're going to say, "Well . . . Ah . . . Yes, of course. Please. By all means." After you've heard, "Yes. Please. By all means," follow-up with this question: "Let me ask you this, sir: *What kind of art are you looking for right now? What artist's work are you trying to collect*?" See if you can end the phone call with an invitation to find the collector a painting he can buy. Then it's up to you to contact him whenever you have something "truly exceptional." Be prepared to answer the question, "How did you get my name?" Tell the gentleman the truth: "I read about your interest in art (or your collection) in the *Wall Street Journal.*" Collectors are interested in the *art,* not the person presenting it, *providing* they perceive you as honest and trustworthy.

If you receive an invitation from a collector to find a certain kind of painting or artist's work, then follow the instructions in Chapter 9, "Buying Art," to find out who's selling that art. Perhaps you can broker a transaction without ever owning the painting. *Make a deal. Don't be shy.*

SELLING ART TO COPORATIONS

Corporations frequently make art acquisitions, which usually are media events covered by newspapers, magazines, and TV. Price is rarely a concern with a corporation; what they want is bragging rights; they truly seek a rare or exceptional painting.

Every time you read about a corporate acquisition, make a note and keep a record of what kind of art was collected, the artist's name, and how much was paid for the acquisition. Learn the curator's name for the corporate collection (call the switchboard operator), and the names of board members (study the annual report). These contacts can be enormously helpful in introducing your art to the right buyers. Find out what kind of art the CEO has in his private collection. One CEO, who collected Post-Impressionists, thought nothing of paying $125,000 for a Fauvist painting by *Maurice Vlaminck* (1876 – 1958). Don't hesitate to offer valuable art to corporations whenever it becomes available; alert them if you know of an important artwork that they collect which is coming on the market, privately or at auction. Be of service to the corporation.

SELLING ART TO MUSEUMS

Selling art to a museum may well offer the highest reward for a dealer. There's an afterglow when word gets out that you've sold an important painting to a museum. This adds to your reputation and credibility.

Selling an Old Master or a significant Impressionist painting to the Metropolitan Museum of Art is unlikely, but you well might have an opportunity to sell a suitable painting to one of the hundreds, if not thousands of other museums in the United States or around the world. For example, a primitive landscape by Charles Sullivan (1794 – 1867) with Fort Harmar in the background that's in good condition, could well be of interest to museums or historical societies in Ohio. Museums in the Marietta area might be particularly interested in this painting, as Fort Harmar was built there on the banks of the Ohio River and Muskingum River in 1785.

Charles Sullivan fails to qualify as a "well-listed" artist. He meets none of the buying criteria established in Chapter 9, yet an astute dealer can create a lucrative market for this artist. Since this painting has only limited appeal outside of Ohio, it would not do well in a New York City auction. However, a primitive Ohio landscape of historical import would appeal to a State museum and/or a regional collector, so that's where a wise dealer will find success marketing this picture.

Charles Sullivan is a barely listed artist. Based on his auction records, which are virtually non-existing, a 22" X 28" primitive landscape by him *might* fetch $5,000. However, if the same painting with Fort Harmar in the background were presented to the Cleveland Museum of Art, it would probably bring $50,000 for the same work. So before selling a painting to a dealer or consigning it to auction, consider if it might be suitable in a museum.

Because art museums have established procedures that all potential acquisitions, whether gift or proposed purchases, must be subjected to, you as possible seller or donor must be patient. Museums generally have funds available for new acquisitions. When there are insufficient funds, however, a trustee might contact a wealthy patron and request a substantial donation to acquire your painting for the museum. In fact, if a museum tells you they're interested in your work but they don't have money to purchase it, you might suggest such a proactive approach to the curator.

To find a museum near you, consider www.redozone.com, or www.museumlink.com, which plans eventually to list "*every museum on the planet.*" It already has a good start. In the United States it lists museums by State, in Canada by Province, and internationally by city.

FINDING A PATRON TO DONATE YOUR PAINTING

Visit the museums you've identified as possible buyers for your artwork. Study the plaques under the exhibited paintings, and note those that were donated as gifts. For example, one might read: "'Woman with a Parasol' by Claude Monet, 1875, Gift of Mr. and Mrs. John Nobel." Then research the names of people who gave or lent valuable paintings to the museum. You might check *Who's Who in Business,* the Chamber of Commerce, or the museum itself to find a donor's business address. Next, practice your 20-second cold-call pitch. Then call the patron and suggest that he consider buying your painting as a charitable gift to the museum (which he has done before). Of course, first check with the museum curator to confirm your painting would be a desirable addition to the museum's permanent collection. Then you can say with confidence, "I believe the museum would love to have this painting." Rarely is a proposed acquisition "certain," even if supported by the curator and director, until it's approved by the Museum Acquisition Committee and then by the Museum Board.

Take note of the kind of painting the donor previously lent to the museum—artist's name, subject, and School—because this wealthy collector is also a buyer of fine art and an excellent prospect to whom you could sell another high-end painting in the future.

SELLING ART TO GALLERIES

Galleries in Paris, London, and New York have been welcoming the Astors, Fords, and Rockefellers for generations. When a wealthy client leaves a renowned gallery empty handed, the gallery didn't show them any artworks they *had* to own, not they couldn't afford.

Major galleries have a high demand for quality artworks and thus need a continual supply of valuable paintings to satisfy their wealthy customers. Not enough exceptional artwork is available to supply the needs of major galleries. There is more money available than great works of art. Therefore if you have a painting of exceptional quality, a gallery will likely buy it, providing it's in good to excellent condition, fresh to the market, and by an artist they represent.

Private dealers such as you significantly supply worthy art to galleries. As soon as a rare or unique painting arrives in a gallery, it will confidentially offer it to a buyer from a list of stellar clients. A gallery will quickly sell an exceptional painting, but it takes a lot longer to sell a mediocre one.

By studying advertisements in fine art and antique magazines, such as those recommended in Chapter 3, you will learn which galleries represent which Schools or Periods of art. Offering the best representational work in their specialty, as examples are D. Wigmore, Hollis Taggart, Hirschl & Adler, Rehs, Spanierman, Roughton, and Questroyale, to name a few. These distinguished galleries are likely to pay cash for your painting. If your asking price is too high, and the gallery still wants to represent your work of art, it might suggest a consignment agreement.

CONSIGNING YOUR PAINTING TO A GALLERY

As a dealer your goal is to sell paintings, not to collect or hold onto them. A painting consigned to a gallery has a better chance of selling than one stored in a hall closet. Consigning a painting to a gallery does not mean you can't sell it yourself. A major gallery might insist on exclusive rights, but a smaller gallery might allow you to continue selling your own painting without penalty.

Have a digital image stored in your computer, so whenever you want to spend a few hours trying to sell your painting, you can e-mail digital images to a dealer or gallery anywhere in the world. Make sure the Consignment Agreement reflects the right to sell your own painting without penalty, and asserts your prerogative to withdraw the painting with only a few days' notice.

Never consign an important artwork to a country antique shop. Check out your city guide for galleries that sell valuable paintings. The Consignment Agreement should establish schedules and conditions, and protect your interest. For example, (1) the gallery must notify you as soon as it sells your painting, (2) it must provide full payment to you within, say, 10 days of selling your artwork, (3) it must take responsibility for your painting whether lost, damaged, or stolen, and (4) you retain "title and ownership" of your painting until you have been paid in full.

SELLING ART TO DEALERS

An art dealer is the ultimate middleman, the most costly link in the supply chain. Generally speaking, a dealer should be the last person you would approach to sell your painting, unless, of course, you need money in a hurry, or on the other hand, because you lack knowledge and experience to know where else to sell your painting. Keep in mind the purpose of this book is to offer you alternative opportunities. From information gained here, you can now consider those most advantageous to you. Nevertheless, since 80 percent of all paintings sold move from one dealer to another, you will likely sell artwork to other dealers from time to time.

However, you will make more money selling your art directly to a collector, investor, corporation, museum, or even to a gallery, as described above, than selling to a dealer. If you decide to sell your art to a dealer with more experience than you, he'll only do what you didn't know how to do or didn't take the time to do. He'll market and sell your painting to a collector, investor, corporation, museum, or gallery just as you could have done. The only difference is that he'll receive top dollar for your painting, while you might have sold too low and too soon.

A dealer will likely sell your painting to another dealer, so he'll expect a "good price" from you, meaning a low price. All this mid-level dealing robs you of a larger profit. If you can't find a collector or investor interested in buying your painting outright and you don't have enough time to put your work into auction or on consignment, at least choose a dealer higher up the art chain who will sell directly to a collector or gallery. By selling to a high-end dealer you eliminate other middlemen. By involvement in a more ambitious transaction you'll learn new techniques and strategies central to your education. Dealing at a higher level also means you'll have to find finer quality paintings to offer.

Obviously not all dealers are dishonest, but not all dealers are reputable either. Investment art can represent significant money, so you must be very careful choosing the dealer to work with. Be sure you know the dealer personally, but if you don't, get references.

CASE EXAMPLE: The Wrong Partner

Dealer A offered Dealer B an "opportunity" to buy a small landscape oil painting by Hugh Bolton Jones (1848 – 1927) for $18,000, with the view of splitting profits after the painting was resold. Cautiously, Dealer B asked for 24 hours to consider. After examining digital images of the painting and researching auction records, Dealer B graciously declined the opportunity to join with Dealer A in buying the Hugh Bolton Jones landscape for $18,000.

Several months later, Dealer B was studying auction results in the *Maine Antiques Digest* (his monthly homework routine), seeing there the exact Hugh Bolton Jones painting which had just sold at auction for $5,750. Dealer B counted his blessings upon reading how much money he would have lost had he joined Dealer A in buying the painting for $18,000.

Collaborating in buying and selling art is sometimes useful, necessary, and can even be fun. Be sure, though, you're comfortable about the integrity of the dealer you're working with. If you do partner a painting, be the partner who takes custody of it and who decides when, where, and for how much the painting will be resold.

Avoid working with an unknown dealer who is more likely to be careless, thinking little of "shopping" your painting around, thereby diminishing prospects for getting top dollar for it. Nowadays with the Internet, your painting could be shopped from Paris to Los Angeles and back again, being viewed by 12 dealers in a 24-hour period. Such over-exposure ruins a painting's chances for achieving maximum price.

Work with a dealer who can pay cash for your painting, or with someone who will likely deal directly with the ultimate customer, thereby eliminating middlemen. You can always add this caveat: "Do not shop my painting around. I'm e-mailing you a digital image, but it's only for your client who you tell me is a collector, and not another dealer. You mustn't send this digital image of my painting to anyone else. Is that understood?" Despite this warning, don't be surprised if some dealer downstream calls and offers you an "opportunity" to buy your own painting. It's happened before.

RIGHT OF REFUSAL

Almost all major art sales are sold subject to approval. No one is going to buy a $20,000 painting sight unseen; you will have to offer paintings with a "right of refusal." After a buyer has examined digital images, he has a right to inspect your painting physically before buying it.

Shipping a painting within the United States generally costs less than $200 (more by climate-controlled vehicle or escorted by an armed guard), an expense usually born by the buyer. Of course, only ship your painting when you're comfortable doing so; that is, if you've worked with the buyer before, have obtained satisfactory references, and you've received an advance deposit or some other assurance. Even then, only ship your painting after the buyer has signed an agreement. An agreement can be as informal as an e-mail message forwarded back to the sender acknowledging terms and conditions.

Shipping your painting for examination does not mean the buyer has many weeks to make up his mind. Several days are more than enough time; forty-eight hours should be sufficient. If a dealer rejects your painting, he pays freight and insurance both ways. After all, he requested to see it. If the dealer purchases your painting, you can offer to pay shipping costs. In either case, while the painting is in transit, the buyer must take responsibility for the painting whether lost, damaged, or stolen. Make sure this protection is included in your agreement.

DEPOSITS

No one ships a $20,000 picture to an unknown dealer just because he requests it. Even after references are checked, some sellers require the buyer to post a $20,000 check (whatever the price of the painting) before the painting will be shipped. The seller doesn't expect the check to be certified or even covered with cash; he just wants the payment instrument in hand should the deal go wrong, for whatever reason. Of course, the seller must promise not to cash the check without the buyer's approval. If the buyer purchases the painting, he has only to instruct the seller to deposit the check. If he rejects the painting, the seller promises to return the uncashed check when he receives his painting back in good condition.

If you're the "buyer," go ahead and send a deposit check for $20,000. Then put a "stop payment" on this check and instruct the seller not to cash it until he hears from you personally. If you decide to buy the painting, call your bank, remove the stop payment order, and instruct the seller to deposit your check.

Whether buyer or seller, create a paper trail and commit your business agreement to writing. An informal note scribbled on a piece of paper is better than nothing at all. Every time you give someone a painting, get a receipt signature for it. A sensible practice is to print a picture from the digital image stored in your computer and ask the buyer to accept responsibility for the painting by signing his name directly on the printed picture. Likewise, when FedEx drops off a painting at your door, ask the driver to wait until you open the box and examine the condition of the painting. You'll want a witness if the shipped painting was torn or damaged.

If you're dealing with a renowned gallery, its letterhead stationery requesting you to ship the painting should suffice for a security deposit. Whether a gallery or dealer, the buyer always pays shipping and insurance costs, and assumes responsibility for your painting if it's lost, stolen, or damaged at the price indicated in the agreement.

Notwithstanding the above precautions, if trust concerns intrude in processing a sale, figure out a way to solve the problem; you do want the deal to go through. If shipping your painting is an obstacle, put it in your car and drive it across country. Get the job done any professional way you can.

SELLING ART AT AUCTION

In the previous example of the primitive landscape by Charles Sullivan, this painting only has appeal to Ohio museums, historical societies, and regional collectors. The same picture would not do well in a New York City auction, which is better suited for art of a wider appeal. The people who buy at auction are generally collectors, dealers, and gallery owners—the same people you want to sell to privately, if only you knew who they were and how to contact them. Since you don't and have no other outlet for selling your artwork, you put paintings into auction and hope for the best. Upon doing that you, (1) lose control of the selling process, (2) transfer all bargaining power to the buyer, and (3) pay a high transaction cost to sell at auction. Wouldn't it be better to learn how to sell directly to the collector, dealer, or gallery, since they'll be buying your paintings at auction anyway?

SHOULD YOU SELL ARTWORK PRIVATELY, OR CONSIGN IT TO AUCTION?

When an artwork's value is known or can easily be determined, it is generally better to sell this painting directly to a collector, investor, or dealer than to consign it to auction (see Case Example below). Extremely rare, unique, or extraordinary paintings may be exceptions, however. If you have a true masterpiece, or a documented "important" painting, then better sell it at auction, such as Christie's or Sotheby's, where a wealthy audience can compete to buy such a distinguished work. Why limit your potential for achieving a record price at auction by selling a rare artwork directly to a collector, at a negotiated price. "Negotiated" prices are limited by reason and logic, generally established by previous auction results. But you have a one-of-a-kind painting. So rare, in fact, that an international audience might bid fiercely to own it. Why not put it into auction and see if it really has "legs" to rise fast in the bidding. See how far the price will run!

Consider John Whitney's Rose Period Picasso, "*Garcon a la Pipe*" ('Young Boy with a Pipe"), which recently sold at Sotheby's for $104,000,000. Do you think Mr. Whitney could have "negotiated" that price with a private collector? Hardly. How much could he have rightfully asked for his painting: $40 million? $50 million? $60,000 million? There's a limit to *chutzpa*; but at certain auctions the possibilities are practically limitless. When competitive uncertainty is mixed with a highly charged and publicized auction, in which a masterpiece is up for the taking, covetousness fires fierce bidding, usually driving up the price, at times setting a world record. Picasso's "*Garcon a la Pipe*" was the first $100 million painting (and by a 20th century artist, not an Old Master). Give the art world time—a lot of time—eventually there will be a $200 million painting. Will it be one of yours?

IF THE VALUE OF YOUR PAINTING IS KNOWN

Generally speaking, if the value of your painting is known, or knowable, sell it to an interested collector or dealer. However, for the truly rare painting, whose value is not yet fixed or limited by consensus, consider selling it at auction. The following example supports such a recommendation.

CASE EXAMPLE: Deaccessioning Art

A museum director decided to deaccession several paintings by a competent but minor artist of recorded values. With his board's approval, this director arranged a private sale with a reputable dealer specializing in the artist's work. The director negotiated top dollar for the paintings, and the transaction was about to go through when the family of the man who originally donated the paintings to the museum called and questioned, not the sale of his family's paintings, but the director's *relationship* with the dealer. Hearing of this not-so-subtle hint of impropriety, the director acted immediately: he called the dealer and canceled the transaction. He then called Christie's and consigned the artworks to auction. The paintings sold several months later for significantly less than the director had arranged privately, and probably to the same dealer.

The director, generally dealing with artworks of known value, continues to disperse museum art through private dealers, while occasionally purchasing art for the museum through auction.

The above case example is drawn from the excellent book:

Auctions: The Social Construction of Value (1989)
—Charles W. Smith

REGIONAL AUCTION ROOMS

Christie's and Sotheby's offer dealers the lowest seller's commission, around 6%. If your painting does not meet their minimum pricing requirements (usually above $20,000), try consigning your artwork to a reputable regional auction house, where commission fees can range from 12% to 19%. The auction rooms below offer excellent opportunities to buy, sell, and find an occasional "sleeper." Also consider the auction rooms listed in Appendix 6, "Regional Auction Rooms."

- Barridoff's in Maine
  www.barridoff.com
- Skinner's in Boston
  www.skinnerinc.com
- Shannon's in Connecticut
  www.shannons.com
- Freeman's in Philadelphia
  www.freemamsauction.com
- Slaon & Kenyon in Metro D.C.
  www.slaonandkenyon.com
- Charlton Hall Columbia S.C.
  www.charltonhallauctions.com
- Stair Galleries in Hudson, New York
  www.stairgalleries.com
- Ivey-Selkirk in St. Louis, Missouri
  www.iveyselkirk.com
- Coeur d' Alene Auctions in Idaho
  www.cdaartauction.com
- Leslie Hindman's in Chicago
  www.lesliehindman.com
- Butterfields in San Francisco
  www.butterfields.com
- Doyle's in New York City

www.doylenewyork.com
- Rago's in Lambertville, New Jersey
  www.ragoarts.com

ADDITIONAL AUCTION WEBSITES

For locating international auction rooms, try www.artweb.fr. This French website lists first-tier auction rooms in cities throughout Europe, South Africa, Australia, Asia, and North and South America. Additional information about auctions can be found at www.auctionguide.com, www.maineantiquedigest.com, And www.icollector.com.

AUCTION COSTS

Auction costs are higher for people not in the trade. If you plan to buy paintings at auction, obtain a resale Tax I.D. Number from your State Department of Revenue. Consigning an important artwork to auction, you can ask for, and should expect to receive certain benefits. The auction room will try to accommodate you in order to nurture future business, but you have to ask for concessions. It's not uncommon for dealers to negotiate no buy-in fees and ask for a reduced seller's commission.

Seller's Commission is the fee you pay an auction room to show and sell your painting, which generally is 10% to 20% of the hammer price, but can go as high as 25%. Seller's commissions are set relative to the selling price. For example, items sold under $5,000 may have a seller's commission of 15%; items over $10,000 could have a lower commission rate, say, 10%. Higher rates are applied to items sold under $500, which could be 20%, even 25% in some auction rooms. Christie's and Sotheby's charge only 6% to dealers with a valid Tax I.D. Number.

Seller's commissions can add up quickly. In a night of feverish bidding, an exuberant dealer can owe an additional $7,500 beyond his purchase price ($50,000 in sales at 15%). For most reputable auction rooms, such as the regional ones listed above, the seller's commissions range between 12% and 19%, depending upon the value of your painting and your relationship with the auctioneer.

Insurance Fee. The insurance fee is what the auction room charges to insure your painting while in its care, usually 1% to 2% of the mid-estimate price. You generally pay the insurance fee whether or not the painting sells.

Buy-In Fee. The buy-in fee is what the auction room charges if your painting does not sell. Some auction rooms charge between 3% and 5%; however, you should be able to negotiate out the buy-in fee altogether. In fact, insist on a no buy-in fee.

Photography/Illustration Fee. A photography fee covers the cost of illustrating your painting in an auction catalogue, and can cost up to $1,200 for a full-page color illustration. You can buy a half-page or quarter-page illustration for less; ask if you can pay actual costs.

Withdrawal Fee. Once you submit your painting for consignment, it will be costly to remove it before the auction date. You can be charged the full seller's commission, up to 15% of the low estimate for withdrawing the painting.

Additional Fees. You can be charged additional fees if the painting requires cleaning, restoration, reframing, or authentication by an outside expert.

ESTIMATES

Choosing the right estimate for your painting will improve your chances of achieving a high price at auction. The wrong estimate can contribute to your painting's demise. Many sellers wrongfully think it's an advantage to have a high estimate on their artwork. They might think it's beneficial, for example, if their painting were estimated in a catalogue at, say $20,000 to $25,000, instead of $12,000 to $18,000. If your estimate is too high, then you risk discouraging the interest of knowledgeable professionals. In most cases, allow the auction room to decide the estimate for your painting. The auctioneer knows best what will sell, and for how much. Let the auction room influence your decision.

A more successful psychology, in fact, favors pricing your painting slightly low, thereby attracting the attention of buyers who search for "bargains" (most everyone). Someone seeing a low estimate might perceive a possible "sleeper," and get involved just to see where the bidding goes. Many bidders raise their paddles to show early interest, with a plan to drop out if the bidding goes too high. But many get caught up in the excitement and competition, bidding long after they wanted to bail out. It only takes two bidders to drive up the price of your painting. However, if your high estimate scares away bidders and precludes people from entering the competition, then a single bidder might take home your painting for a song.

Consider the buyer who might have paid up to $17,500 for your painting. However, when he saw the catalogue estimate at $20,000 to $25,000, decided not to get involved at all because the low estimate already exceeded the price he was prepared to pay. Had your estimate been $12,000 to $18,000, this buyer might have participated, for example, starting at $12,000, having been long hooked by the time bidding reached $20,000, perhaps continuing to $25,000.

When he and others don't bid on your painting, it must be "bought-in"; and that's troubling, whether or not you pay a buy-in fee. If your painting passes at auction—if it doesn't sell—it's said to be "burned." A painting once burned at auction is hard to sell again, at least right away. A cloud seems to hover over the painting. Future buyers will wonder why your painting did not sell. After a painting has been burned, you might have to reduce the price drastically in order to sell it, or take it off the market for a number of years until it's considered fresh again. Try to attract bidders by letting them think they can possibly get lucky by bidding on your painting. Keep the estimate low, but not so low that it becomes suspect. You don't want it to appear as if something is wrong with a painting. You can always protect your investment with a reserve.

CASE EXAMPLE: Reasonable Reserves and Exceptional Merchandise

Record prices were achieved at the Coeur d'Alene Fine Arts Auction held in Reno, Nevada, on July 24, 2004; total sales were $18 million. Thomas Moran's "Mist of the Yellowstone," 30" X 45" sold for nearly $5 million. Its estimate was $2 to $3 million. (The previous high for Moran was $2.924 million.) 70% of all paintings sold *above the high estimate*; only one painting was bought-in.

When asked for an explanation for the brisk sales and record prices, the auctioneer replied: "Reasonable reserves and exceptional merchandise."

The Maine Antique Digest (September 2004)

RESERVE

The reserve price is the confidential minimum figure you will accept for your painting, below which you will not sell. If the bidding does not reach the reserve price, you are prepared to take the painting home (be sure to negotiate a no buy-in fee).

The reserve price helps to establish the estimate for your painting. First, determine the lowest price you will accept for your painting. Let's assume you need a minimum of $8,000; then that becomes your reserve price—$8,000. Hence, your estimate should be $10,00 to $12,000, as the reserve price is generally 80% of the low end of the estimate. An estimate of $10,000 to $15,000 would be high, and $12,000 to $18,000 would definitely scare bidders away. If your reserve is $8,000, the auctioneer will probably start off the bidding at $6,000—well below the reserve, and also well below the value of your painting. This encourages the early raising of bidders' paddles and by the time the reserve is met, there still could well be three or four bidders competing for your artwork. This painting could sell for $16,000 (twice the minimum you wanted). The reserve, however, cannot be higher than the low estimate; it must be lower or equal to the low estimate. So if your estimate is $10,000 to $12,000, the reserve cannot be $11,000. It must below $10,000.

SELLING DIFFICULT ARTWOKS

If you're having difficulty selling your painting privately, perhaps because it was bought-in at auction due to a high estimate, consider putting it into a different venue with a *lower reserve.* Check artnet.com to determine which auction house holds the highest "record price" for your artist (most likely Christie's or Sotheby's), and put it into auction there with a low estimate. For European paintings, consider consigning your artwork to London, Paris, Milan, or Munich. There, now, the dollar is weak and the Euro is strong, and the buying public has a fresh face, possibly with no knowledge of your painting's recent history.

MAGIC MINUTE

The "Magic Minute," as one California dealer explains, is the minute when the bidder decides "All right, I'll get involved with this painting *just to see* if I can buy it for a song, say $7,000," and before the minute is up his paddle is still waving in the air when the auctioneer passes $12,000. Low estimates encourage brisk bidding. Many forget when to get out.

SELLING ART THOUGH THE BACK DOOR AT ANTIQUE SHOWS

The premier American art shows, such as the *Pier Art Show* and the *Armory Antiques Show* in New York City, the *Miami Beach* and *Palm Beach Art Shows* in Florida are excellent opportunities to sell your paintings without paying for an exhibition booth!

Renowned collectors and dealers from all over the world show up at these fairs and shows, many returning home with valuable artworks. After paying the $20 entrance fee, locate the exhibition booth displaying the kind of artwork you're selling—for example, Victorian, French Realism, or American Post-Impressionism—and *wait* for an opportunity to approach the dealer very discreetly.

Carry photographs of your valuable paintings since you might be able to sell them to a dealer at the show. You want to look like a novice, so be sure the photographs are "snapshots," not professional 8" X 10" glossies. Be careful whom you approach and how you phrase your inquiry. Management will likely escort you out of the building if they see you peddling artworks. Nevertheless, most exhibitors want to see what you have to sell because they're buyers too. In fact, they might ask you to leave certain photographs, possibly selling your artwork that same day. If they're small paintings and conditions appear safe, suggest, "You can see these paintings in the parking lot after the show; they're in the trunk of my car." You might be able to take home a check that very night. From every show you attend, collect calling cards from the booths you visit; these dealers/exhibitors buy and sell high-end artworks. They're your future customers.

Consider the following Web sites for art fairs and antique shows near you, or wherever you're traveling:

- "The Red Guide" (includes list of American and European dealers, plus shows and exhibitions) at www.antiquesandfineart.com.

- Expo Central at www.expocentral.com.

- For the premier international art and antique shows, try www.artandantiuesfairguide.com.

ART IN AMERICA ANNUAL GUIDE

Art in America Annual Guide is "the" sourcebook to the U.S. art world. Published every August, it's sold in bookstores for $16. If you actively buy and sell art, this one magazine can help make possibly tens of thousands of dollars each year. I strongly recommend buying it. Call 1-800-925-8059 to inquire if last year's *Guide* is still available, or wait until August to buy next year's issue at a bookstore.

The *Guide* offers a comprehensive alphabetical listing, arranged by state and city, of U.S. museums, retail galleries, university galleries, nonprofit art organizations, corporate consultants, and private art dealers. Included are addresses, phone numbers, business hours, names of directors, and a short description of the type of artwork represented or collected.

The Guide is divided into the following eight sections:

- Private Galleries
- Private Dealers
- Print Dealers
- Museums
- University Galleries
- Corporate Consultants
- Nonprofit Art Organizations
- Directory of Auction Houses

The *Guide* provides the names and telephone numbers of hundreds of art dealers and galleries across the United States. It's particularly helpful for identifying dealers and galleries in remote regions of the country in towns and cities probably unfamiliar to you.

CASE EXAMPLE: Finding a Dealer in Ohio

In the above example, selling the primitive landscape by Charles Sullivan to the Cleveland Museum of Art, you could have just as easily sold the same painting to an Ohio art dealer.

"But how would I do that?" you might ask, living in Rhode Island and not knowing a single art dealer in

Ohio. "I wouldn't have a clue where to begin looking," you say to yourself.

Now you do. Turn to page 236 of the *2004 Guide*, where Ohio listings begin, and start counting the advertisers. There are 93 entries with names and telephone numbers of Ohio art dealers and galleries. Start calling!

Take the *Guide* with you wherever traveling in the United States. If you're passing through South Dakota, Wyoming, or Delaware, and find a valuable painting along the way, use the *Guide* to call a nearby dealer who might be interested in buying a local painting. Using the *Guide* could pay for your entire road trip.

FINDING AND SELLING CANADIAN ART AT AUCTION

The best Canadian art sells extremely well anywhere in the world, especially in Canada. Most noted are the "Canadian Group of Painters" (formerly "The Group of Seven"), who painted bold vivid landscapes in the style of the Post-Impressionist Masters. Today, works of art in very good to excellent condition by the original "Group of Seven" can easily sell for well over $1 million at auction.

Canada's long border with America is only one reason dealers and pickers should be on the lookout when searching for art in the northern United States. The following is only a partial list of Canadian artists whose valuable artworks are highly sought after.

- Franklin Carmichael (1890 – 1945)
- Lionel Fitzgerald (1890 – 1956)
- Edwin Holgate (1892 – 1977)
- Arthur Lismer (1885 – 1969)
- Frederick H. Varley (1881 – 1969)
- J. Casson (1898 – 1992)
- Lawren Harris (1910 – 1994)
- Y. Jackson (1882 – 1974)

- James E. H. MacDonald (1873 – 1932)
- Emily M. Carr (1871 – 1945)

WHERE TO SELL ART IN CANADA

Arguably, the biggest art collector in the world is Canadian billionaire Kenneth Thompson, who outbid the J. Paul Getty Museum for Peter Paul Rubens's "Massacre of the Innocent" (1612), paying $76.7 million at auction for the Masterpiece. Although you're not likely to find an Old Master painting along the border with Canada, you might well find an important landscape by one of the "Group of Seven." Try these Canadian auction rooms for expert advice and also as a possible outlet for your own Canadian artworks.

- **Toronto**: Waddingtons Auctions: www.waddingtons.ca
- (877-504-5700 or 416-504-5100)

- **Calgary**: Levis Fine Art Auctions: www.levisauctions.com.
- (403-541-9099)

- **Vancouver**: Maynards Fine Art Auctions: www.maynards.com. (604-876-6787)

- **Montreal**: Empire Auctions: www.empireauctions.com (514-737-6586)

- **All Canada:** Heffel Fine Art Auction House: www.heffel.com. (800-528-9608 or 604-732-6505)

Your art career begins on the next page.

Begin Now
Commit

Until one is committed there is hesitancy, the chance to draw back, always ineffectiveness. Concerning acts of initiative (and creation) there is one elementary truth, the ignorance of which kills countless ideas and splendid plans; that the moment one definitely commits oneself, then providence moves too. All sorts of things occur to help one that would never otherwise have occurred. A whole stream of events issues from the decision, raising in one's favor all manner of assistance, which no man could have dreamt would have come his way.

Whatever you do, or dream you can, begin it. Boldness has genius and power and magic in it.

—Goethe
1749 - 1832

WORKSHOPS

This book contains all the information you need to be successful at buying and selling art. All you need to do is study and understand what this book instructs, then apply the principles herein. Being creative and persistent, considerate and professional, diligent and hardworking, will insure success. However, even after you've done your due diligence, proceed slowly.

If you would like to attend a full-day workshop, or organize one in your area, to learn how to find, examine, research, and buy and sell valuable art, call for more information at 1-888-401-2844.

Appendix 1

Making the Art Deal

CASE EXAMPLE

One of John's pickers called him with a tip that an antique store near Palm Beach had a painting for sale by Maurice de Vlaminck (1876 – 1958). The picker shared what information he knew: a woman was trying to close a sale on the same painting, which was offered to her at $55,000, even though the retail sticker price was $150,000. The description of the painting sounded like Vlaminck's work: a night scene in a French village with snow piled in the street and on rooftops. The painting measured 25" X 30" and reportedly was in excellent condition. There was a documented provenance; the period frame bore a distinguished gallery label on the back and a nameplate on the front with a French title. The picker just wasn't sure if the work was "real" or not. His hunch was that it was authentic, and that John would be interested in it. The price was *way* out of his range. However, experience told him that John paid well for these tips.

$150,000 was a fair retail price for a representative work by Vlaminck in good condition. But John was curious why this painting sat so long in an antique store without being discovered. Vlaminck was a leader in the *Fauve* movement in France in 1905, along with Matisse and Derain, and his work was strongly influenced by Van Gogh and Cezane. It was not John's taste in art, but he knew it would be an amazing find if the painting were authentic. He would have to investigate it when he was in Palm Beach the following week.

John found the antique store, and asked the woman who greeted him if he could look around. It didn't take him long to find the Vlaminck painting hanging on a wall in an adjourning room. Approaching it slowly, he could see the workmanship was as much Vlaminck's signature as the name painted on the bottom of the canvas. John examined the fine lines of craquelure beginning to show in the night sky; the painting seemed to be in excellent condition. Alone in the room, he carefully took the painting off the wall to examine its back. A second canvas was visible at the tacking margin, signaling the painting had been lined. The label on the back bore the name of the Wally Finley Gallery in Chicago, and the overall patina corroborated the work was from the 1930s. The restoration work had been done sensitively. The impasto still had raised edges, and there was no crushing or flattening of paint from excessive heat or ironing during the lining process. Except for the liner, The picture looked in near-original condition. John was feeling a rush of excitement as he hooked the painting back on the wall.

"It's a nice picture, isn't it?" said the woman walking into the room.

"A Vlaminck," John said speculatively. "But is it real?"

"One hundred percent guaranteed" the woman replied. "It came out of a wealthy Palm Beach estate."

'What's going on with it?

"Someone is trying to buy it," said the woman. "Supposedly she's having it authenticated as we speak."

"That means it's still available. How much do you have to get for the painting?" John asked directly.

"I'm sorry, sir, the painting is spoken for."

"How long has the woman been working on the authentication process?

"About two months."

"Two months!" John exclaimed. He knew he would have to move quickly in order the get his foot in the door. "Look, I can sell this painting. I mean, like right away. I have a wealthy client asking me to find him a Modern French artwork, just like this one. He collects *Fauvists*—that's what this painting is. I know I can sell this picture, and I don't need time to raise money," said John. "Give me a chance to sell it."

The woman seemed trapped. "But the painting is already committed to someone. It's already sold, sir."

John persisted, "Look, I want to buy this painting," he said. "If you have to, *raise the price.*" He knew he needed a number—*any number,* in order to play in the game. Then he could begin his strategy, which he had already thought out. "I need a price," he said again. "*Pick a price.*"

The woman felt overwhelmed by John's determination, and she finally picked up the phone and called the storeowner, who was selling the painting on behalf of the estate of the owner.

They raised the price $20,000; when she returned she handed John a piece of paper with the price $75,000 written on it. John looked at the scrap of paper.

"Great," he said. "What time do you open the store tomorrow?"

"Eleven a.m."

"I'll be here at eleven a.m. Ask the storeowner to be here, and ask him to bring all the provenance documentation with him."

There was one more thing John had to do. Returning from his car with a digital camera, he took four JPG pictures of the painting: one full view to include the frame, one close-up to show details, one of the signature, and one of the back to show the label of the Chicago gallery.

Back at his motel, the buying strategy began to unfold. John knew he would need a 4" X 4" transparency of the painting, so he found a local photographer in the Yellow Pages and asked him to be at the antique store the next morning at eleven a.m. Then John used his laptop, searching the Internet at www.artnet.com. He checked if this Vlaminck painting was fresh to the market, and what comparable paintings by Vlaminck were selling for.

John had successful business relationships with major specialty art dealers on the East and West coasts, exactly for an opportunity such as this Vlaminck painting presented. He could not complete this transaction alone—coming up with $75,000 cash on short notice was out of the question; he also needed someone experienced in obtaining a *catalogue raisonné* approval. So he chose a New York City dealer as partner, with whom he had worked before selling to high-end clients.

After spending thirty minutes on the phone with his anticipated partner, they agreed that if they could get the Wildenstein Institute in Paris to authenticate the painting based on a 4" X 4" transparency, the partner in New York felt he could sell the painting for $125,000 to a major collector of Modern French paintings.

It was a race because the woman working the authentication process in Paris would be close to obtaining approval. They had to do in *one week* what she was trying to do in two months. But there was no better week to do it in than the coming one, because every major art dealer in the western hemisphere would be in New York City for the spring sales at Christie's and Sotheby's. Perhaps Monsieur Petrides himself, the recognized expert on Maurice de Vlaminck, would be in New York City next week. If Monsieur Petrides gave a verbal approval in New York City based on the transparency, and also assured that the painting would be included in the next *catalogue raisonné*, they could proceed by offering their client the painting with a guarantee.

John agreed to send the transparency and the provenance documentation to his partner in New York City the next day by four p.m., by overnight Federal Express. *The hunt was on.*

At eleven a.m. the next morning John walked into the antique store. He met the photographer and the storeowner, who were waiting for him with fresh coffee. After instructing the photographer on how he wanted the transparencies taken, John sat down and studied the provenance documents.

He was surprised to see such complete documents, which indicated the painting was executed in 1938, going from the artist to two prominent Parisian families, whose names were on the documents. The painting was later shipped to New York in October 1966, where it sold in November at auction by Parke-Bernet Galleries. Then the painting was sent to Chicago and exhibited at Wally Finley Gallery, its buyer. Subsequently there were even Internal Tracking Reports, showing the painting had been checked in and out of the gallery several times, presumably for customer approval. Finally, there was documented proof that the painting was sold to its present owner, a prominent Palm Beach family.

"These are extremely detailed," said John looking up at Ben the storeowner.

"Believe me, the painting is authentic. It's *really* by Vlaminck. A lot of people have looked at the painting, but no one has felt comfortable buying it, because no one knew how to have it authenticated. Someone is now trying to do that, but it's taken her two months so far. If you want to buy the painting, I'll sell it to you."

"I want to buy the painting," John said. "I'll need one week, and you'll have your $75,000. Guaranteed. Will you give me one week's time?"

"OK. One week, but that's all."

"Great," John said taking out a piece of paper. "I've typed up an agreement that says you will give me one week to buy the painting at $75,000. I need this signed by you. I can't ask my client to wire $75,000 without assurance that I can buy the painting."

Ben signed the agreement. "One week," he said, and they shook hands.

John followed the photographer back to his studio, paying twice the going rate to have the transparencies developed while John waited. Then at the Federal Express Office by two p.m., he sent the provenance documents and transparencies to his partner in New York City by overnight delivery.

John now had three or four days to wait. He decided to drive to Atlanta to attend the Scott Show, where there would be over 1,500 art dealers selling thousands of paintings by well-listed artists. The Scott Show was the biggest exhibition of art on a regular basis on the East Coast. It was open only four days a month, Thursday through Sunday, always on the second weekend of every month (www.scottantiquemarket.com).

This exhibition was a must-see for John, if at all possible. From there he could monitor the Vlaminck deal by cell phone and be back in Palm Beach within eight hours if necessary. Now his partner in New York City had to complete the job. John knew from experience that no one else could conclude as effectively an art transaction as could his partner.

Monday morning, John spent an hour on the phone with his partner. Foremost Vlaminck expert, Monsieur Petrides, unfortunately, had not come to New York for the spring auctions; this was a setback. Their client, the CEO of a public New York company, had seen the transparencies and agreed to buy the painting for $125,000 as originally discussed, and this was subject to physical inspection and assurance that the painting would be included in the next *catalogue raisonné*. John's partner was now sending everything to Paris by overnight Federal Express. Even so, a successful conclusion to the transaction seemed unlikely to occur by Wednesday, the end of the time period agreed upon with Ben.

On Wednesday John received a call from his partner with bad news on two fronts. First, M. Petrides was out of town for a long weekend, not returning to Paris until Monday. Secondly, the Institute had received their documents and transparencies, but reported that an American woman had submitted the *same documents* for approval of the same painting. The Institute officially examined Vlaminck paintings only four times a year, and the woman's documentation would not be reviewed for another month. Now the ball was back in John's court, he had to buy more time in Palm Beach, at least until next Monday, in order for M. Petrides to have a chance to look at the transparencies.

"Ben," John said over the phone, "Paris is closing down for a long weekend, and our contact there won't be back until Monday. I need a few more days, and this is what I would like to do. I'm sending you a certified check for $2,500 to buy another ten days. If I don't close the deal by next Friday, you keep the $2,500." They agreed.

John was now $2,500 into his own money. But his partner assured him that their client would wire $125,000 to John's bank account as soon as Monsieur Petrides gave verbal approval that the painting would indeed be included in the *catalogue raisonné*. It was a tense weekend waiting for word from Paris.

On Tuesday morning John received the phone call that the deal was done! Monsieur Petrides had given his approval: the painting would be included in the next *catalogue raisonné*. The client was wiring the money.

With one day to spare, John walked into the Palm Beach store with a certified check for $72,500; the balance owed, and picked up the painting.

The new owner was sailing his yacht off the coast of New England, and asked for the painting to be sent to a conservator's studio in Maine, where he would pick it up after pulling into port. John typed up the invoice and bill of sale, shipped the painting to Maine by Federal Express; then sent his partner a check for $22,500, and $2,500 to his picker.

$22,500 was a sweet reward for two weeks of intense work. But for John it was the *discovery* and *hunt* that most excited him.

In the above case example, John did everything he knew how to do in order to keep the doors of opportunity open, and the art transaction alive. Such perseverance you also will need.

Creating opportunities where none previously existed is the challenge in life.

The Third Certainty

Through the Dark Ages, the great famines, the plague, world wars, and the Great Depression, art has been shown, sold, stolen, collected, criticized, condemned, and cherished. In 2003, worldwide art sales were estimated at $5 billion. Nothing is certain but death, taxes, and art—the third certainty.

—**Louis M. Salerno**, Owner, Questroyal Fine Art

Appendix 2

Where to Find Art

The possible locations of where to find worthy art might seem endless, but I've reduced your search to six sources. The below table lists art valued from $500 to $500,000, and shows where you are most likely to find that art, and also where to sell it when you find it.

The dealer's advantage in buying art is in knowing more than the seller. When the seller knows more about art than you, be very careful. The best place to buy art is out of a private home where the owner does not know the value of his painting; and that is often the case. Many paintings are handed down generation to generation; and in some families there's always someone who can't stand Grandma's old painting, and is willing to sell it. -

Painting Location & Value	Museums Institutions Corporation	Galleries Private Dealers	Private Collections (Known)	Private Homes (Unknown)	Antique Shops/ Malls	Unknown Lost Forgotten
$ Value	% Found	% Found	% Found	% Found	% Found	% Found
$500,000	70	15	10	4	0	1
$100,000	55	20	15	7	0	3
$25,000	10	50	20	13	2	5
$5,000	5	45	15	13	15	7
$1,000	0	5	10	40	25	20
$500	0	0	5	40	30	25
What they Buy/Pay	Highest Price	Fair Price	High Price	Least Price	Fair Price	Least Price
What you Receive	Excellent	Good	Excellent	N/A	Fair	N/A
Your Profit	Excellent	Fair	Good	Excellent	Fair	Excellent
Trust Factor	High	low	High	High	Low	High

When your lucky day comes along and you find a painting worth $25,000, where will you sell it? You'll waste time offering it to an antique shop, and possibly "burn it" by over showing it. Antique shops are generally buying art less than $500. A well established gallery might be interested in buying it, and should be able to raise the money quite easily. However, beware of the trust factor when working with high-end galleries and dealers. It's hard to outsmart a world class art dealer. They're *that* good.

If you find a $25,000 painting, try selling it to a private art collector, who generally will pay top price for your painting. These are people who have money and like art. Here your trust factor should be moderate to high. Don't hesitate to offer your painting to a museum which could have reason to collect the artist. There you'll get the best price, the safest transaction, and the most prestige and reward from selling your painting.

Try cultivating a list of private art collectors in your city or community, and learn what they collect. They should be your first choice when offering your painting. Except, if you believe a museum might be interested in your art. Reread Chapter 9, Buying Art; and continually develop your skills and sources for buying art.

Recently I went to a new Flea Market in town; something I rarely do, and never at 6 AM. I was talking with a lady setting up her booth with old 78 records and 8-track tapes. That's all she had. Before leaving, I asked "Do you have any old paintings you want to sell"? She said, "No, but my sister does. She described the painting, and added, "I told my sister I could probably get $100 for her painting here at the Flea market." I said, "I'd like to see the painting. I might be interested in it." She invited me to her house, but her sister was not ready to sell her painting. It was indeed a painting I'd like to own. I won't give up trying to buy this painting. Politely, I call every month of so and ask if she is interested in selling her painting. One day she might need money and say "Yes, as a matter of fact, I am ready to sell my painting."

Appendix 3

What is a Print?

Understanding "prints" will add money to your annual revenues. But the subject has few teachers willing to share their expertise. Most serious art dealers search for original works of art, such as this book teaches; they know very little about prints. You'll do well to study prints. It will give you an advantage over most art dealers. Check your local universities and art appraisal societies for opportunities to learn about prints. Below is a useful guide for understanding prints offered by The Cummer Museum.

WHAT IS A PRINT?

"Simply stated, a print is ink on paper, often existing in an edition or multiples. It is created through the transfer of an image directly from a plate, stone, screen, or block. The majority of the printmaker's effort is spent developing the creative image on one of these materials to produce many original works of art. Among the advantages of creating prints is that numerous "impressions" of the same image can be made, because new pieces of paper can be sent through the same print process. The artists decides how many to make, and that total number of impressions is called an "edition." In contrast, a mass-produced commercial reproduction is based on an original work of art, but is not itself original.

Various printing methods have evolved over the long history of the process. The four best-known are relief, intaglio, lithography, and screenprint. Depending on what an artist wants to express, one or another technique is chosen for its very distinct visual effects. For example, a woodcut yields a rough-hewn appearance filled with gouged shapes and textures, while an etching is often characterized by delicate lines and exacting details. Since some of these techniques are complicated to perform, many artists employ the expertise of a master printer or assistant.

RELIEF

Woodcut, the earliest print technique, first appeared in China in the ninth century. The technique was originally used to make functional items such as stamped textiles and playing cards. Western artists have used relief printing to produce works of art for hundreds of years. The making of a relief print is a straightforward process. After sketching a composition onto a piece of wood or linoleum, the artist cuts away areas from the block using gouges, chisels, and knives. Areas remain which are raised. Ink is then rolled onto the surface of the block. Since only the raised surfaces hold the layer of ink, the recessed areas do not print. Next, both block and paper are run through a press or printed by hand to the transfer the image.

LITHOGRAPHY

Lithography literally mans "stone writing." The technique was invented in 1798 by Aloys Senefelder. Lithography as an artistic process experienced its golden age during the nineteenth century in the hands of artists Francisco Goya, Honoré Daumier, Pierre Bonnard, Henri Toulse-Latrec and others. The printing of lithography is based on the resistance between grease and water. An image is achieved by first drawing on the surface of a stone or plate with a greasy substance. The artist may choose to use either a lithographic crayon or tusche, which is a liquid applied with a brush to the plate or stone. When a lithography is ready to be printed, the stone is chemically treated to securely bond the drawn image to the surface. The stone is dampened, and those areas where the image was drawn repel the water. With a roller, oily printer's ink is applied to the stone. The ink sticks only to the drawn sections, with the blank areas protected by the film of water. Paper is then aid on the stone and run through a press to transfer the image.

SCREENPRINT

Silkscreen printing is a form of stenciling, a common procedure used to apply words or images to paper and other materials, including signs. During the 1930s, a group of American artists creating works using silkscreen devised the term "serigraph" to distinguish fine art screenprinting from commercial applications. In making a serigraph, finely woven mesh screen is stretched tautly over a frame. Parts of the screen are blocked out, laving some areas exposed for the printing of the image. Paper is placed beneath the screen, and a tool with a flat rubber edge, called a squeegee, is used to push ink through the exposed screen onto the paper. Separate screens are used for each color.

INTAGLIO

Intaglio comes from the Italian word *intagliare*, meaning "to incise." Lines or tones are incised into a metal plate, usually copper or zinc, so that the resulting series of lines or pits will hold ink. The method of incising lines into the plate determines the specific name of the resulting original print. If a sharp tool is used to gouge lines into the plate, the resulting print is called an engraving. If a sharpened point is used to scratch the surface of the metal, the print is called a drypoint. If acid is used to "bite" or etch an image into the plate, the resulting print is an etching. This is the print technique that has been favored by artists since the Renaissance. Rembrandt and Goya, among others, created some of their most important works using the etching process.

To make an etching, the artist starts with a metal plate that has been coated with a waxy ground. The image is drawn trough the ground with a pointed metal tool called an etching needle. Next, the plate is immersed in a bath of acid. Since the ground covering the plate serves as a protective barrier, the acid goes only into the drawn lines and eats into the exposed metal. Once the ground is removed, ink is then rubbed into the resulting incised lines. The surface of the plate is then wiped clean. Dampened paper is placed over the plate, and the paper and plate are run through a printing press. The pressure of the press forces the soft paper into the etched lines to "pick up" the ink. Other intaglio methods include techniques such as monoprints, embossments, mezzotints, and collographs.

Appendix 4
Timeline for 600 Years of Art

Millennia and centuries have specific timelines, but periods of art, culture, and human expression are not so clearly defined. A new School of art emerging out of political or cultural upheaval makes its epochal statement while the waning School continues to produce examples for another fifty years. There is significant overlapping between periods of art. Often, artistic influences can be seen in previous and successive Schools. Even scholars are not always in agreement on timelines for the history of art. Your road map for measuring 600 years of art is outlined below. To deal in art successfully, you must familiarize yourself with timelines for all periods and expressions of art, specializing in one or two Schools you intend to collect or invest in. Other important art movements occurred between the ones shown below. *The Story of Painting* by Sister Wendy Beckett is an excellent source for exploring art timelines, and was a major source for this appendix.

- Gothic (1100 – 1300)
- Renaissance (1350 – 1600)
- Baroque (1600 – 1700)
- Rococo (1700 –1800)
- British Art (1750 – 1850)
- Pre-Raphaelite (1850 – 1880)
- French Realism (1850 – 1900)
- Impressionism (1860 – 1900)
- American Impressionism (1870 – 1900)
- Post Impressionism (1885 – 1910)
- Modern Art (1900 – 1960)
    - Expressionism
    - Cubism
    - Abstract Art
    - Surrealism
    - Abstract Expressionism

Gothic Art

(1100 - 1300)

The Dark Ages really were the early part of the Middle Ages, coinciding with the Byzantine Empire (300 – 1450), then culminating in the period of Gothic Art (1100 – 1300). The word *Gothic* was coined by Renaissance classicists to describe the period of art that preceded them, referring to the barbaric Northern Goths who destroyed Rome. Eventually the word "Gothic" came to describe the architecture and art that followed the Romanesque period that ended in 1075, and lasted 200 years.

The Gothic period was known mostly for architecture and the building of cathedrals, especially around Paris, the 100-mile radius called the Ile-de-France. This period became known as the "Age of the Great Cathedrals" (1150 – 1250). While stone, sculpture, and stained glass dominated the Paris skyline, paintings began to emerge with greater relevance. Beginning first with religious pictures, icons and illuminated manuscripts were displayed in cathedrals to help instruct an uneducated population to understand spiritual Christianity. Later, fresco murals and panel paintings became prominent.

Early Gothic Florentine artist, Cimabue (1240 – 1302), thought to be Giotto's teacher, broke from the traditional flatness found in Byzantine icon painting. He created a more realistic style, helping to shape the future of Western Art. Sienese painter Duccio di Bouninsegna (1278 – 1319) advanced the style of realism initiated by Cimabue, and further distanced himself from Byzantine art by adding volume and depth to his characters, both in dress and figure, and introducing perspective and narrative. His Florentine contemporary, Giotto di Bondone (1276 – 1337), is considered by many to be the father of Renaissance Art, introducing scale, spatial dimensions, perspective, fluidity, and a greater emphasis to narrative and story.

By the latter half of the 14th century, Italian and Northern European art merged into what became known as the "International Gothic Style." It displayed courtly and aristocratic grace, influenced greatly by Sienese painter Simone Martini (1285 - 1344). In the 15th century, International Gothic Art branched in two directions, both revolutionary. In the South, Florence gave birth to the Renaissance, and in the North, Flemish painters Hubert and Jan van Eyck, Robert Campin, and Rogier van der Weyden mastered the new realism with light and emotion.

Renaissance

(1350 - 1550)

First used by French historian Jules Michelet in 1855, the word Renaissance came to symbolize a "cultural rebirth" in Europe—coming out of the Dark Ages. The word Renaissance applies both to an artistic style and a technological epoch. Between 1350 and 1600 Western Europe changed dramatically from a feudal ecclesiastical society to an urbanized population with people living in major cities. It was a time of new discovery in science and art, including oil paint, said to be invented in the Netherlands by the van Eyck brothers, Jan and Hubert in the first quarter of the 15th century. While tempera paint was still being used, most Renaissance works of art were executed in oils after 1475.

The Great Renaissance movement was divided into two Periods: Early Renaissance which is understood to apply to Tuscan Art, from 1400 to 1500; High Renaissance to art in Florence, Rome, and Venice, roughly from 1500 to 1600; and Northern Renaissance to art from 1400 to 1550 (in regions north of the Alps).

Renaissance art focused on (1) a "return to nature" and (2) a "revival of classical antiquity."

Early Renaissance art can be traced back to Giotto di Bondone (1267 - 1337) who first realistically depicted naturalist figures in "architectural space," and his followers, Masaccio, Ghiberti, and Danatello who advanced the techniques of linear perspective. These early Renaissance Masters were greatly influenced by the sculpture of the day, particularly the works of Nicola Pisano (d. 1278) and his son Giovanni (1250 - 1314). Many historians place the magnificent works of Botticelli (1444 – 1510), Cosimo (1462 – 1521), and Mantegna (1431 – 1506) in the last part of the Early Renaissance.

High Renaissance art begins with the new century. The great Leonardo da Vinci (1452 - 1519) stands at the pinnacle of High Renaissance art, painting the Mona Lisa in 1503. Following him was the monumental work of Michelangelo Buonarroti (1475 - 1564), painting the "Last Judgment" in the Sistine Chapel (1536 – 1541, 44 X 48 ft). Raphael (Raffaello Sanzio (1483 - 1520) was also a genius, and an absorber of many influences, painting masterpieces that rivaled his Florentine contemporaries, da Vinci and Michelangelo. Considered by many to be Raphael's crowning achievement, "The School of Athens," immortalized the Greek philosophers. The Venetian greats were just as illustrious as the Florentine masters. Titan (Tiziano Vecellio (1488 - 1567), referred to as "The Modern" Painter, lived long enough that he matured through periods of his own art, growing at each stage of his development, until old age. Tintoretto (Jacopo Robusti) and Paolo Veronese were also Venetian greats, but no match for Titan.

Northern Renaissance art has its earliest beginnings in Flemish art, particularly that of, Hubert and Jan van Eyck (1385 – 1441), Robert Campin (active 1406 – 1444), and Petrus Christus (1410 – 1473). Albrecht Durer (1471 – 1528) was the German visionary Northern Renaissance artist. Like Leonardo da Vinci in the south, Durer also was multifaceted; he created many woodcut prints. Other remarkable Northern Renaissance artists were Hans Holbein (1497 - 1543) and Pieter Brueghel (1525 - 1569), called the "peasant painter." Just before this book went to print, Pieter Brueghel's "The Kermesse of St. George," a painting of raucous excess, sold for $7.6 million at auction in London.

Baroque
(1600 - 1700)

At the turn of the 17th century, the contrived, elegant style of Mannerist art gave way to emotions and human drama in Baroque art, which emphasized vivid colors and dramatic gestures. The word "Baroque" initially was used to describe bad taste or degenerate art. Oddly enough, when "baroque art" was first coined in the 19th century, the establishment then had little respect for the works of 17th century masters like Caravaggio and brothers Carracci.

Known for contrasting, even stark vivid colors, Caravaggio (Michelangelo Meris da, 1573 – 1610) painted genre pictures with a sweet, sensuous, even lascivious nuance, inviting the viewer's utter indulgence. His early work, "The Lute Player" (1596), for example, makes the pretty lute player (a boy) look seductively girlish. Caravaggio greatly influenced Italian Baroque masters that followed him, such as Orazio Gentilschi (1563 – 1639) and his daughter, Artemisia (1593 – 1653).

Baroque art, spurred on by a prosperous culture, spread through Europe during the early part of the 17th century. Antwerp became the center for Flemish Baroque art, and the greatest painter from Flanders was Peter Paul Rubens (1577 – 1640). In 1600 Rubens went to Italy to study the Renaissance masters, especially Titian; and then to Spain, where he became friends with Diego Velazquez (1599 – 1660). While Flanders remained loyal to both Catholicism and Spain, the Northern Netherlands claimed independence in 1579, and a protestant vision for simplicity and everyday things began to dominate Dutch art. The Master Dutch painter of the day in Amsterdam was Rembrandt (van Rijn, 1606 – 1669), who produced realistic paintings of everyday life and periodic self-portraits. Flemish, Dutch, French, and Italian Baroque art flourished until the turn of the 18th century.

Rococo

(1700 - 1800)

The word Rococo describes the style of interior decorating in 18th century France. It emphasized ornamental schemes and bright colors—even fun and frivolity. Artists gave attention to furnishings, drapes, clothing, ribbons, and excessive curlicues. Jean Antoine Watteau (1684 – 1721) was the first Rococo master, followed by Francois Boucher, Jacques-Louis David, and Jean Auguste Ingrres. Science and democracy dominated 18th century French culture and politics, which gave rise to the Rococo art movement that spread throughout Europe.

British Art

(1750 - 1850)

British art was a combination of Neoclassicism and Romanticism. Thomas Gainsborough (1727 – 1788) incorporated the natural environment into his artwork, becoming England's first great portrait artist. His paintings were as much landscapes as they were portraits. Gainsborough greatly influenced both British landscape and portrait painting. Fifty years after Gainsborough's death, John Constable would write about his own works: "I see Gainsborough in every hedge and hollow tree I paint."

A line of great portrait artists followed Gainsborough, notably, and perhaps the greatest of them all, Allan Ramsay (1713 – 1784); Sir Henry Raeburn, who painted the famous "The Rev. Robert Walker Skating" in the mid 1790s; and Sir Joshua Reynolds. These luminaries greatly influenced American Portraiture artists, most notably, Gilbert Stuart (1755 – 1828), who painted George Washington, and who was a student of Benjamin West (1738 – 1820).

John Constable (1776 – 1837), arguably became England's greatest landscape artist. He painted nature as it really is, without artificial stylization. His paintings mark the beginning of British "romantic landscapes";

even Eugéne Delacroix, who visited England in 1825, was impressed by Constable's brushwork in his six-foot canvases.

The other great, early 19th century British landscape artist was J.M.W. Turner (1775 - 1851), who painted romantic landscapes with brilliant light and color; his Venice pictures dazzled the viewer with shimmering light.

Other British masters of the time were George Stubbs, who painted horses set in landscapes, and watercolorists William Blake and Samuel Palmer.

Pre-Raphaelite

(1850 - 1880)

Realism actually begins in England in 1849 with the Pre-Raphaelite Brotherhood (PRB) of painters. These artists rebelled against academic traditions of pomp and hypocrisy. They admired 15th century Renaissance painting prior to Raphael, hence their School became known as "Pre-Raphaelites." They found wide acceptance, though short lived, exhibiting in the Royal Academy. Their early pioneers were John Everett Millais, William Holman Hunt, and Dante Gabriel Rossetti. Many of their works simply were monogrammed "PRB."

French Realism

(1850 - 1900)

It was Jean-Baptiste-Camille Corot (1796 - 1875) who gave realism its start in France, where truth and simplicity were exemplified in all of Corot's works. Corot enormously affected his followers, particularly Jean-Francois Millet (1814 - 1875), who painted peasant workers in fields at evening time, like "The Gleaners" (1857). Said to be the greatest realists, Gustave Courbet (1819 - 1898), was resolute in his commitment to reality painting, influencing many who followed him. In 1836 Theodore Rousseau settled in the hamlet of **Barbizon** on the edge of the Forest Fontainebleau. Starting with the new train service in 1840, artists flocked to Barbizon, one hour south of Paris, to paint *plein air* landscapes. Among the first were Camille Corot, influencing all who followed, such as Charles Daubigny, Diaz de la Pena, Francois Millet, Theodore Rousseau, and American artist William Morris Hunt. Even Renoir painted on Daubigny's houseboat, and was influenced by the Barbizon School.

Impressionism
(1860 - 1900)

Impressionism begins at the Paris *Salon des Refuses* in 1874, when a group of young artists exhibited what appeared to be "unfinished" works of art, showing new naturalism and greater luminosity than before seen. Impressionism, however, really begins with Edouard Manet (1832 - 1883), referred to as "The Father of Modern Art," who broke from Courbet's realism to express, not in subtle nuances, but in bold colors and sharp contrasts, what the eye could see. Manet greatly influenced his contemporaries, Berthe Morisot, Mary Cassatt, and Edgar Degas, including the Great Impressionists who followed: Claude Monet, Auguste Renoir, Camille Pissaro, Alfred Sisley, and Paul Cezanne.

American Impressionism
(1870 - 1900)

Impressionism became an international movement, influencing American artists starting in the 1870s. Those first applying the new style of "naturalism" were James Whistler, Winslow Homer, and Thomas Eakins, all of whom traveled to Europe to study with the great French Impressionists, taking the new painting techniques back to America. (Many other Schools of American art preceded and followed the Impressionist movement that began in America in the 1870s.)

Post-Impressionism

(1885 - 1910)

Post-Impressionism was more about painting emotions than objects, and bright colors and loose borders expressed this new freedom in art, which eventually gave rise to abstract painting. Vincent van Gogh (1853 - 1890) painted the loneliness of life as he saw it, as did his Nordic contemporary Edvard Munch (1863 - 1944). The Period was rife with genius, with the likes of Paul Gauguin, Toulouse-Lautrec, and Paul Cezanne (his later years). These luminaries often employed the off-centered focus and flat surfaces found in Japanese woodcuts. The late Post-Impressionists, particularly the **Nabis** group with Pierre Bonnard and Edouard Vuillard, and later Gustav Klimt, relied on imagination as much as painterly skills, adding symbolism to their artworks.

Modern Art

(1900 - 1960)

20th Century Modern Art begins with radical ideas and a bold new freedom. The **Fauvist** movement emerged in Europe in 1900 with Henri Matisse (1860 - 1954) experimenting with bright colors and emotional themes. Matisse greatly influenced his followers, Maurice de Vlaminck, André Derain, and Raoul Dufy.

EXPRESSIONISM, especially in Germany starting in 1905, used overstated color themes to explore the darker side of the human psyche. Notable among German/Austrian Expressionists were Ernst Kirchner, Erich Heckel, Karl Schmidt-Rottluff, Egon Schiele, and Max Beckmann. In the 1930s, art which did not conform with Aryan ideology was declared "**Degenerate Art**" by the Nazi Party, forcing the best **German Expressionists** into exile or concentration camps.

JEWISH ÉMIGRÉS fleeing Germany and Eastern Europe found freedom for artistic expression in Pairs. The most notable émigrés were Marc Chagall (Russian, 1887 - 1985), Chaim Soutine (Russian 1893 - 1943), and Amedeo Modigliani (Italian, 1884 - 1920).

CUBISM, in fact, "Modern Art," is said to begin with Picasso's "*Les Demoiselles d'Avignon*" (1907). Pablo Picasso (1881 – 1973), like Modigliani, was fascinated by African sculpture, and "*Les Demoiselles*" expresses native women with a raw emotional force. Cubism is somewhat omnipresent, showing art from all sides at once, creating a new cognitive reality. Georges Braque worked with Picasso; both influencing all cubists who followed, such as Juan Gris, Umberto Boccioni, Fernand Leger, and Robert Delaunay.

ABSTRACT ART starts in Germany in 1910, following the Expressionist movement, with Wassily Kandinsky painting the first abstract picture. His followers were Fanz Marc, August Macke, Paul Klee, and Kasimir Malevich.

SURREALISM started in 1924. It stemmed from **Dada** art, which rebelled against the atrocities of World War I. Dreams, distorted reality, and ideas from Sigmund Freud influenced the most noted surrealists, Salvador Dali, Joan Miro, and Max Ernst.

ABSTRACT EXPRESSIONISM marks America's influence on the world of art. Following World War II, in the 1940s several artists emerged as leaders of what became known as "The New York School" of artists. Most notable were Jackson Pollock, Willem de Kooning, Franz Kline, Barnet Newman, Robert Motherwell, and the "colorist" Helen Frankenthaler, to name only a few Abstract Expressionists, who painted into the 1960s.

MINIMALISM and **POP ART** emerged in the 1960s, bringing notoriety to innovative artists such as Ad Reinhardt, Frank Stella, Agnes Martin, Andy Warhol, and Roy Lichtenstein.

Appendix 5

Shipping Paintings

Dealers and galleries ship paintings every day across the country and around the world to collectors, auction houses, conservation studios, and other dealers. Trusting the process, dealers ship fine art on commercial carriers, generally choosing one of the following:

- **FedEx**
  www.fedex.com, 1-800-GOFEDEX (800-463-3339)
- **UPS**
  www.ups.com, 1-800-742-5877
- **DHL**
  www.dhl-usa.com, 1-800-225-5345

STRONGBOX

Serious dealers ship framed paintings in a Strongbox: a humidity-resistant 350-lb. single-wall corrugated cardboard box, providing the strength of plywood without the weight. The framed painting is protected in three layers of convoluted and Perf-Pack foam. A Strongbox for a framed painting, for example, measuring 28" X 33" X 2" costs $55.95. The box weighs 10 lbs., and is shipped from Tupelo, MS, by Air Float Systems, Inc., 1-800-445-2580 (www.airfloatsys.com). Many dealers own several Strongboxes to fit various frame sizes. **Instructing the buyer to return the Strongbox** (costs less than $20), dealers use the same Strongboxes over and over again. Otherwise, crease, fold, and wrap cardboard around your framed painting, then put it into another painting box, which you can buy at any FedEx, UPS, or packing store. For transporting valuable artworks, consider using a professional mover.

"You can learn more in painting one street scene than in six months' work in an atelier.

—**George Bellows** (1882 – 1925)

Appendix 6

REGIONAL AUCTION ROOMS

New York City auction houses vet most artworks, and a "sleeper" rarely goes unnoticed. However, regional auction houses still offer opportunities for the vigilant collector, investor, and dealer to find a real winner. The "sleeper" you buy might be an unsigned piece or one with an indistinguishable signature. Perhaps you'll discover that an inexperienced researcher made a wrong attribution, and your knowledge of art gave you clear advantage over the competition, taking home this night a valuable painting that you bought for a song.

Art & Antiques magazine, October 2004, lists regional auction houses: "Auction Houses Based Outside of Manhattan are Making a Big Play for Collector Dollars." Consider calling these auction houses and request that your name be placed on their mailing list. You'll soon be receiving catalogues and notices of upcoming auctions. Search their Web sites to view artworks that appeal to you, fit your collection, or strike your imagination. (Also, ask smaller auction rooms and country auctions to notify you when interesting artworks come up for sale. Check *Maine Antique Digest's* "Antique Trade Directory" for auction room locations near you, available on its Web site at www.maineantiquedigest.com.) The following regional auction rooms offer excellent opportunities to buy and sell art:

Northeast

David Rago Auctions, Inc., Lambertville, N.J. (609) 397-9374
Eldred's, East Dennis, Mass. (508) 385-3116
Kamelot Auctions, Manayunk, Pa. (215) 482-0411
Northeast Auctions, Portsmouth, N.H. (603) 433-8400

Pook & Pook, Inc., Downington, Pa. (610) 269-4040
Skinner Inc., Boston: (617) 350-5400; Bolton, Mass (978) 779-6241
Weschler's, Washington, D.C. (800) 331-1430.
Sloan's & Kenyon, Bethesda, Md. (301) 634-2330
Stair Galleries, Hudson, New York (518) 851-2544

Midwest

Bunte Auction Services, Elgin, Ill. (847) 214-8423
Dallas Auction Gallery, Dallas, (866) 653-3900
DuMouchelles, Detroit, (313) 963-6255
Frank H. Boos Gallery, Troy, Michigan (248) 643-1900
Garth's Art and Antiques, Delaware, Ohio (740) 362-4771
Hart Galleries, Houston, Texas (800) 284-2783
Ivey-Selkirk, St. Louis, (314) 726-5515
Leslie Hindman Auctioneers & Appraisers, Chicago, Illinois (312) 280-1212
M. Klein Auctions, Chicago, Illinois (312) 948-0080
Susanin's Chicago Auctions, (312) 832-9800
Treadway/Tooney Galleries, Cincinnati (513) 321-6742 & Oak Park, Ill. (708) 383-5234
Wright, Chicago, Illinois (312) 563-0020

South

Brunk Auctions, Ashville, N.C. (828) 254-6846.
Great Gatsby's, Atlanta, Georgia (770) 457-1903.
Neal Auctions Co., New Orleans, (800) 467-5329.
Red Baron Antiques, Atlanta, Georgia (404) 252-3770.

West

Bonhams & Butterfields, San Francisco, (415) 861-7500.
John Moran Auctioneers Inc., Altadena, Calif. (626) 793-1833
I. M. Chait Auctions & Gallery, Beverly Hills, Calif. (800) 775-5020.
San Rafael Auction Gallery, San Rafael, Calif. (415) 457-4488.
Auctions by the Bay, Alameda, Calif. (510) 740-0220.
A. N. Abell Auction Co., Los Angeles, (800) 404-2235.
Clars Auction Gallery, Oakland, Calif. (888) 339-7600

Index

Quick Order Form

- **Fax/Phone orders**: 904-381-1258.
- **Telephone orders**: call 888-401-2844 toll free.
- **E-mail orders**: Rondavis77@aol.com
- **Postal orders**: Ron Davis, Capital Letters Press 4276 Verona Avenue, Jacksonville, Florida 32210

Please send ____________copies of *Art Price Indicator* (1,752 pages containing over 50,000 artists' auction records) $19.95 each; or ___________ copies of the *Art Dealer's Field Guide* at $19.95 each;

Please send more Free information on:

❑ workshops ❑ keynote speaker ❑ consulting

Name:____

Address: ____

City:________________________________State:______Zip:______

Telephone:____

E-mailaddress:_____________________________________

Sales tax: please add 7% for products shipped to Florida addresses.

All shipping by air:

U.S. $4.80 for Priority Mail two day shipping

Payment : ❑ Cheque ❑ Credit Card ❑ Visa ❑ Master Card

Card Number:______________________________________

Name on card: _______________________ exp date:____________